Pro Jakarta Velocity: From Professional to Expert

ROB HARROP

D1396734

Apress®

Pro Jakarta Velocity: From Professional to Expert
Copyright © 2004 by Rob Harrop

ISBN (pbk): 1-59059- 410-x

Printed and bound in the United States of America 9 8 7 6 5 4 3 2 1

Lead Editor: Steve Anglin

Technical Reviewer: Jan Machacek

Editorial Board: Steve Anglin, Dan Appleman, Ewan Buckingham, Gary Cornell, Tony Davis, Jason Gilmore, Chris Mills, Steve Rycroft, Dominic Shakeshaft, Jim Sumser, Gavin Wray

Project Manager: Tracy Brown Collins

Copy Edit Manager: Nicole LeClerc

Copy Editor: Kim Wimpsett

Production Manager: Kari Brooks

Production Editor: Laura Cheu

Compositor: Linda Weidemann, Wolf Creek Press

Proofreader: Linda Seifert

Indexer: Valerie Perry

Artist: Kinetic Publishing Services, LLC

Cover Designer: Kurt Krames

Manufacturing Manager: Tom Debolski

Distributed to the book trade in the United States by Springer-Verlag New York, LLC, 233 Spring Street, 6th Floor, New York, NY 10013 and outside the United States by Springer-Verlag GmbH & Co. KG, Tiergartenstr. 17, 69112 Heidelberg, Germany.

In the United States: phone 1-800-SPRINGER, e-mail orders@springer-ny.com, or visit http://www.springer-ny.com. Outside the United States: fax +49 6221 345229, e-mail orders@springer.de, or visit http://www.springer.de.

For information on translations, please contact Apress directly at 2560 Ninth Street, Suite 219, Berkeley, CA 94710. Phone 510-549-5930, fax 510-549-5939, e-mail info@apress.com, or visit http://www.apress.com.

The source code for this book is available to readers at http://www.apress.com in the Downloads section.

*To my Dad, Ken, who bought me my first computer
and supplied me with endless programming manuals
when I was just a wee boy. And, of course, to my girlfriend Sally,
who put up with the late nights and lack of weekends
while the book was underway.*

Contents at a Glance

Contents

About the Author

Rob Harrop is the lead software architect of the UK-based development house, Cake Solutions Limited (http://www.cakesolutions.net). At Cake, Rob leads a team of six developers working on enterprise solutions for a variety of clients, including the Department of Trade and Industry, the Metropolitan Police, and NUS Services Limited. Rob (and Cake) specializes in both .NET- and J2EE-based development, with Rob having been involved with .NET since the alpha stages.

Rob is also the coauthor of *Pro Jakarta Struts*, Second Edition (Apress, 2004), *Pro Visual Studio .NET* (Apress, 2004), and *Oracle Application Server 10g: J2EE Deployment and Administration* (Apress, 2004).

In his limited spare time, Rob enjoys playing with different technologies; his current favorites are Groovy and AOP. Rob is a committer on the open-source Spring project (http://www.springframework.org), a Java and .NET application framework built around the principle of dependency injection. When not sitting in front of the computer, Rob usually has his head buried in a book and prefers the fantasy parodies of Terry Pratchett's Discworld.

About the
Technical Reviewer

Jan Machacek is the lead programmer at the UK-based software company Cake
Solutions Limited (http://www.cakesolutions.net), where he has helped design
and implement enterprise-level applications for a variety of UK- and US-based
clients. In his spare time he enjoys discovering new software and hardware
technologies. Apart from Java, Jan is interested in the .NET Framework and non-
procedural and AI programming. As a proper computer geek, Jan loves *Star Wars*
and *The Lord of the Rings*. Jan lives in Manchester, UK, and can be reached at
jan@cakesolutions.net.

Acknowledgments

MORE WORK THAN most people can appreciate goes into making a book ready for the shelves. This book is no exception, and thankfully I had a fantastic team backing me up. First, thanks go to my technical reviewer and co-worker Jan Machacek for his excellent reviewing and insightful comments. Second, my thanks go to my editor, Steve Anglin, for his support and input throughout the project and to Tracy Brown Collins for ensuring that everything during the course of this project ran smoothly. My final thanks go to the production team, to Kim Wimpsett for correcting my atrocious grammar, and to Laura Cheu for getting the book through production.

Introduction

As Java programmers, we should consider ourselves lucky. We have a vast range of open-source tools available to us. For almost any problem you can conceive, you have numerous open-source tools that can solve that problem. This is especially evident in the glut of MVC frameworks available for building Java-based Web applications. It was while I was working on *Pro Jakarta Struts*, Second Edition (Apress, 2004) that I realized that although the ability for Struts to use different technologies for the view layer of the MVC triad was much lauded, these view technologies suffered from a lack of exposure and documentation. During the course of writing the Struts book, I worked on a single chapter to demonstrate Velocity integration, but it quickly became apparent that much more could, and should, be written about Velocity.

I'm a great fan of Velocity mainly because of its simplicity and fantastic performance. Wherever possible I prefer to use Velocity in preference to JSP as the view technology in my Web applications. More than that, I find Velocity is the ideal tool for a myriad of tasks that go well beyond the Web and well beyond the capabilities of JSP.

What shocks me most is that Velocity doesn't have the same level of exposure and widespread acceptance as Struts. In my eyes, you get a much clearer benefit, namely in performance, using Velocity rather than JSP; therefore, Velocity should be the natural choice for developers in many cases. Add to this the ability to use Velocity in applications that run outside of the Web context, and you have a powerful tool ready to exploit. I was surprised during a conversation with several developers at a conference how many were unaware of Velocity and how many were aware of Velocity but had never used it. For this reason, I decided the time was right for a book on Velocity that covers all aspects of the technology and acts as an instructive guide for using all things Velocity related.

My overriding aim with this book is to help other developers enjoy the same success with Velocity that my team and I enjoy. I believe I've achieved this aim, and I hope that in this book you'll find all the information necessary to use Velocity in your projects.

CHAPTER 1

Introducing
Velocity

I'M GUESSING that since you've picked up this book, you already have more than a passing familiarity with Java. You may have noticed over the past few years that text-based output formats have been at the forefront of the Java world. Certainly XML is perhaps the most talked about output format, and HTML is definitely the most widely used. Whilst these formats are fantastic in terms of ease of creation when dealing with simple, static content, creating complex output from dynamic data can prove to be much trickier, and maintaining that content is even harder. Some of you may be thinking that the problem is solved, in part, by JSP.

Sure, JSP makes creating text-based output to send to Web clients easier, but it's by no means the simplest solution, and it doesn't solve the problem of creating text-based output for use in other areas, such as e-mail messaging or desktop applications. The common solution in those areas is to assemble the text content manually, intermixing static content with dynamic data in a mish-mash of hideous Java code. Creating code in this way is error-prone and difficult to maintain, especially if it has to be maintained by someone other than the original developer. This is where Velocity comes in. Simply put, Velocity takes the pain out of creating complex text output and makes creating simple text output even simpler. Velocity isn't perfect, however; it lacks in one important area—documentation. Whilst the documentation is not particularly bad for an open-source project, it leaves a lot of things uncovered and doesn't cover other features in enough detail. That's where this book can help. During the course of the book, I'll take you through all aspects of Velocity, from downloading and getting started to dissecting the code that goes into making Velocity work.

What Is Velocity?

The Jakarta Velocity project is a Java implementation of a template engine. The term *template engine* is quite broad, but in the context of Velocity and the like, it means a piece of software that takes as input a template or templates and couples this with variable data to produce some form of output. In the case of Velocity, your template is simply plain text containing Velocity Template Language (VTL) directives, coupled with static content. The VTL directives tell Velocity how to combine the static content in the template file with the variable data from your Java application to provide the desired output. The variable data can come from anywhere within your Java applications; as you'll see in Chapter 2, the mechanism for transferring data between your application and Velocity is flexible, allowing you to work with all kinds of Java Objects, including Collections and Arrays. Output from Velocity is always text-based, but the format of the text you generate isn't constrained. This means you can use Velocity to create HTML or XML output as well as plain-text output.

Although what Velocity does is simple and using it is easy, the Velocity engine is sophisticated and offers a quick, robust parser, template caching, and pluggable introspection. Many other tools have been built on top of Velocity, and some of these, such as Anakia, which is covered in Chapter 8, come in the standard Velocity distribution. For the most part, these tools make it simpler to use Velocity in a specific context. Chapters 7 and 8 cover a choice selection of these add-on tools.

Introducing Java Template Engines

Of course, Velocity isn't the only template engine available for you to use. In keeping with most open-source projects, you have plenty of alternatives to Velocity. Since this book focuses on Velocity, I won't cover these other tools in too much detail; I'll leave the exploration of these topics to you, but the following list describes them briefly:

WebMacro: The WebMacro template engine is kind of the precursor to Velocity. In fact, the reason Velocity was originally created was because of the then-restrictive licensing of WebMacro. Velocity and WebMacro share similar syntax, making it quite simple to move templates between the two systems. You can find more details at http://www.webmacro.org.

StringTemplate: This is one system to look at if you require inheritance in your templates. StringTemplate was created by Terrence Parr of ANTLR fame. You can find more details on StringTemplate at http://www.antlr .org/stringtemplate/index.html.

Jamon: Jamon is quite a complex and involved template engine. It differs greatly from Velocity in that it compiles your template files into Java classes, which you can then use within your application just like normal classes. Jamon resides at http://www.jamon.org.

JBYTE: The JavaBY Template Engine (JBYTE) is a simplistic, lightweight template engine that can generate any kind of text-based output. You can find more information on JBYTE at http://javaby.sourceforge.net/.

Enhydra XMLC: Like Jamon, XMLC creates compiled templates that can then be accessed directly from your code. XMLC is quite tightly coupled to produce output for Web applications, so it may not be ideal if you want to produce a desktop application. You can find the XMLC Web site at http://xmlc.objectweb.org/.

So, Why Use Velocity?

With so many choices, you may be wondering why you should use Velocity and not one of the other solutions. Well, obviously the choice is yours; however, I recommend Velocity for the following four main reasons:

Simplicity: A template engine should be lightweight and unobtrusive. In other words, you don't want a template engine that reduces your application to a crawl, and you certainly don't want to have your application constrained by a restrictive API. In addition, you don't want a template engine that's bogged down by unnecessary features that deter from the main aim of generating content. Velocity satisfies the need for a simple, capable template engine. The Velocity API places no specific requirements on the architecture of your application, allowing you total control, and Velocity does nothing other than templating.

Integration: As part of the Apache Jakarta project, Velocity is in the company of many other excellent projects. Wherever possible, you'll find that Velocity is well integrated with other Jakarta projects such as Struts, Torque, and Tapestry. Chapter 6 covers integration with Struts in more detail.

Proven success: As you'll see in the "Seeing Velocity in Action" section, Velocity is already in use in many different areas, including some commercial desktop applications. Many developers, myself included, have successfully used Velocity in a wide range of applications. Velocity has been through many revisions and is now a highly robust, mature technology.

Supporting documentation: None of the other projects has such a fantastic book to accompany them! On a serious note, Velocity has at least one other book written about it, but the other engines have none. Velocity is established enough as a technology to warrant books being written about it, which means you have access to useful documentation.

The Benefits of Templating with Velocity

Depending on the type of applications you create, using a template engine has many benefits. For applications where you have to produce the output manually, such as a desktop application or an e-mail newsletter service, the following core benefits make using Velocity a sensible decision:

Code separate from content: By using a template engine, you can factor all the static content into template files so that it isn't intermixed with your Java code. By using this approach, you'll find that obtaining correct output is far easier and also that you can make most modifications without having to touch your Java code.

Simple syntax: Nondevelopers can understand the simple syntax employed by Velocity. In the case of the e-mail newsletter service, this means that the marketing people could change the content of the newsletter without having to get the development team involved.

Performance: For the most part, generating output using Velocity will be quicker than manually constructing the text. Also bear in mind that Velocity is in constant development, so the performance will continue to improve.

In the case of Web-based applications, you get all the same benefits, but you get the most important benefit of all: complete separation of the logic of your application from the presentation. With JSP, you can quite easily perform a bunch of business logic using JSP scriptlets, but with Velocity, the language constructs are limited to allowing you to perform the simple decisions and looping necessary to produce your output—you can't, for instance, modify a database from a Velocity template.

CAUTION   *What I've said here is only partially true. Velocity itself doesn't provide support for any kind of business logic or data access. However, as you'll come to see, you can make any object accessible to a template, and you can access any of the methods on that object from within that template. So, if you really go out of your way to do so, you can perform data access from a template; it's just not as simple as with JSP scriptlets where you can directly instantiate an instance of any object.*

Understanding the Uses of Velocity

I've included this section in the hope of debunking a common misconception about Velocity. Velocity isn't just a tool for building Web applications. Velocity is an excellent tool for this purpose, but that's just a small part of what it's all about. If you were expecting to see me jump straight into MVC-based Web applications and how Velocity can help you to build this kind of application, then don't worry—that's all covered; it's just later in the book than you may have expected.

 NOTE *If you aren't familiar with the term* MVC, *don't worry too much; it's explained in much more detail in later chapters.*

The focus of this book isn't on building Web applications but on improving all kinds of applications using Velocity. Web applications are just a one part of this. Velocity has many uses, and during the course of this book I'll explore the most common types of applications, including Web applications, e-mail applications, console applications, and desktop GUI applications.

Seeing Velocity in Detail

Now that you're familiar with the concept of what Velocity and template engines are in general, the following provides a more detailed look at the features of Velocity:

Flexible template mechanism: Whilst the easiest method of generating output is to use templates that are stored as files, Velocity is just as comfortable working with templates that are dynamically generated or that are loaded from a database. If you find that you can't load templates from your desired source, then you can easily extend Velocity to provide this functionality, as detailed in Chapter 10.

Servlet integration: As part of the standard distribution, Velocity includes the VelocityServlet, which eases the use of Velocity in a servlet environment. You need to create your own servlet derived from this class to process the Velocity content.

Simple syntax: The template language used by Velocity, VTL, is simple enough to be understood by nonprogrammers, making Velocity an ideal solution for use in Web development where designers need to modify page layout.

Texen: Texen is a text-generation tool, built on top of Velocity and integrated with Ant. You can use Texen to generate any kind of text-based output, and it's used to great effect in the Jakarta Torque project for generating SQL scripts. Texen is included as part of the standard Velocity download and is covered in much more detail in Chapter 8.

Anakia: Using Anakia, you can transform XML documents into any other text-based format. Anakia uses Velocity and JDOM internally and, like Texen, is integrated with Ant. Also like Texen, you'll find Anakia in the standard Velocity distribution. I cover Anakia in more detail in Chapter 7.

VelocityTools: This is a subproject of the main Velocity project and as such has to be downloaded separately. The VelocityTools project is a collection of plug-ins for Velocity that overcomes some of the shortcomings of the standard engine. Specifically, the VelocityTools project makes it much easier to get desirable output from your templates by providing a range of math and formatting functions. You'll also find that building Web applications with Velocity is much easier using VelocityTools because of the extra support for servlets and for Struts. VelocityTools is covered in more detail throughout the book.

Seeing Velocity in Action

As I mentioned earlier, Velocity is in use in a wide range of applications, both on the Web and on the desktop. It's worthwhile to take a few minutes to check out a couple of these projects to see how other people are putting Velocity to use— who knows, you may be inspired.

Velocity on the Web

The most common use for Velocity is in Web applications, and because of this, many Web-based tools run on Velocity. I've included two I think are quite cool. Download them and give them a go, and then you can dissect the code to see how Velocity is employed.

Scarab

Scarab is an open-source issue and project artifact–tracking application, which has been built using Velocity and Apache Turbine. You should download this application anyway—it's really quite handy for use in your projects, and it has some good Velocity code to explore. You can obtain the latest version of Scarab from http://scarab.tigris.org/.

Roller Weblogger

Weblogging is the current craze, and a whole host of open-source Weblogging tools have popped up, built not just in Java but also in PHP, Python, and Perl.

Roller is one of the better Webloggers and is a great example of how to use Struts and Velocity to put together a robust Web application. Velocity is used as an alternative to JSP to allow end users to customize their own pages on a Roller-based Weblog. The Roller project is hosted at `http://www.rollerweblogger.org/`. If you're going to download this application, you should definitely refer to the article at `http://www.onjava.com/pub/a/onjava/2002/04/17/wblogosj2ee.html`, which includes one of the developers of Roller talking about the development of Roller using various open-source technologies, including Velocity.

Velocity on the Desktop

As I mentioned before (and no doubt will mention again), Velocity is much more than just a tool for building Web applications. Many quality desktop applications use Velocity to produce their text-based output.

IntelliJ IDEA

A very well-known project, IDEA is one of the best Java IDEs on the market. IDEA uses Velocity for code generation, reducing the amount of repetitive code that you as a developer need to write. If you want to see this generation process in action, you can download a 30-day trial of IDEA from the IntelliJ Web site at `http://www.intellij.com/`. Unfortunately, the source code for IntelliJ isn't available, so you can't see how it was done, but by the end of the book you'll be able to reproduce the behavior anyway.

Gentleware Poseidon

Gentleware Poseidon is one of my favorite UML tools, which will transform my UML model directly into Java code. Can you guess which tool they use to do this? That's right, Velocity! You can try out the Java code generation capability by downloading the free community edition at `http://www.gentleware.com/products/descriptions/ce.php4`.

Generic Velocity Tools

Of course, Velocity isn't limited to use in a desktop or Web application. Many of the best applications are cool little utilities or plug-ins that make life that little bit easier. Here again, Velocity makes creating text-based output simple and fast.

Middlegen

Middlegen is a nifty little tool for anyone who has to write data access code. Using Middlegen, you can automatically generate the code required to access a database using EJB 2.0, JDO, Hibernate, or JSP/Struts. Velocity is used as a means to generate the code necessary to access the database. Middlegen is all open source, so you can delve into the code to see how Velocity is used. The code is available for download along with a binary at `http://boss.bekk.no/boss/middlegen/index.html`.

Luxor

Luxor is a Java XML User Interface Language (XUL) toolkit. Using Luxor, you can build cross-platform rich-client applications without having to get your hands dirty with Swing. As part of the toolkit, Luxor includes a templating engine, which is, of course, Velocity. Luxor is an interesting project even without the Velocity connection, so you should download the code and have look around—you'll find it useful for a variety of reasons. Just visit `http://luxor-xul.sourceforge.net/`.

 NOTE *I found all these projects when looking for Velocity samples on the Velocity Web site. You can find a much more comprehensive list of projects on the Powered by Velocity page at* `http://jakarta.apache.org/velocity/powered.html`.

Summary

By now you should be more than familiar with the concept of a template engine and also with the specific uses of a template engine. I've given you a whirlwind rundown on the basics of Velocity's feature set. No doubt you can see from the simple descriptions that Velocity is quite a simple, lightweight technology, but you may not yet appreciate the flexibility it offers. In next chapter, I'll take you through the basics of getting Velocity installed, writing some templates, and creating some output. After that, I'll move on and give you a fuller look at VTL and some advanced features of the Velocity engine, and then it's onto the good stuff when I start to show you how to put Velocity to good use. If you're already familiar with how to install Velocity and VTL, you can skip the next two chapters and move straight onto the specific discussions of how to use Velocity. For those of you who are completely unfamiliar with Velocity, I recommend you look at some of the applications mentioned previously to get some idea of what Velocity can do and how it works and then move onto the next chapter.

### CHAPTER 2

Getting Started with Velocity

Now that you're familiar with what Velocity is all about, it's time to get on with the show. In this chapter, I'll discuss how to obtain both Velocity and VelocityTools and how to configure the tools within your environment. Once you have Velocity up and running, I'll show some simple examples to demonstrate how to use Velocity.

Installing Velocity

Before you can start with any of the examples, you'll need to install Velocity on your machine. You can download the latest version of Velocity from the Web site at http://jakarta.apache.org/velocity. The download comes in two versions: the precompiled binary version and the source code version. I prefer to get the source code version and build from there, as it means that I have the source code if I need to do any debugging. You'll need the source code for some of the discussions in later chapters, but if you choose to download the binary version instead, you can skip to the "Creating Hello World" section. The version of Velocity I've used in this book is 1.4.

Building from Source Code

The first thing to do is obtain the correct source package for your platform. Since Velocity is 100 percent Java, there are no actual differences in the contents of the package; they're just compressed differently to suit both Windows and Unix users. Once you've downloaded the source archive, extract it to somewhere on your machine. I recommend you don't include any spaces in the path, since some machines may experience problems.

Before you proceed, make sure that the JAVA_HOME environment variable on your machine is pointing to the directory containing your Java SDK.

Installing Ant

The next step is to install Apache Ant. If you already have Apache Ant on your machine, make sure it's at least version 1.3; otherwise, you'll need to download a later version. You can obtain the current version of Ant from `http://ant.apache` `.org`; for this example, I used version 1.5.4. For this part, I recommend you download the binary package unless you're familiar with Ant, since building Ant from the source is a little more complicated than building Velocity.

Once you've downloaded Ant, you need to extract the archive to a directory on your machine, again avoiding spaces in the path. Next, you need to set the ANT_HOME environment variable on your machine to point to the directory to which you extracted the Ant files. You should also add the Ant bin directory to your PATH environment variable so that you can run Ant easily from other directories. If you're unsure on how to set environment variables, you can find a sample in the Ant user manual at `http://ant.apache.org/manual/index.html`.

Verifying Ant

Once you've done that, you can verify that Ant is installed by typing `ant -help` at the command prompt. If Ant is installed correctly, you'll receive a message from Ant informing you of the command-line options available. If you don't get this message, then you should verify that you've completed the previous steps correctly. Failing that, check the Ant Web site for troubleshooting tips.

Building the Velocity Source Code

Once Ant is installed, building Velocity is a simple job. At the command prompt, switch to the directory where you extracted the Velocity source package, and from there switch into the build directory. Now simply type the following command:

```
ant
```

You should see a mass of Ant build messages scroll by until you get the BUILD SUCCESSFUL message. If you don't see any messages, make sure the ant command is accessible from your path. If you get a BUILD FAILED message, check that you're using an Ant version greater than 1.3. This will build the standard Velocity JAR file without any of the dependencies; you can build a JAR file with the dependencies included using the command `ant jar-dep`.

Once the build is complete, you'll find the Velocity JAR file in the Velocity home directory. You'll also find that all the JavaDoc documentation has been generated for the code as well, which you'll no doubt find useful as you use Velocity.

Building with J2EE Support

Velocity includes one class, DataSourceResourceLoader, which provides additional support in a J2EE environment. Chapter 10 covers using DataSourceResourceLoader in more detail. However, if you want to take advantage of this feature, you must build Velocity with this class included. To do this, you need to copy the JAR file from your J2EE application server that contains the `javax.sql.DataSource` class into the `build/lib` directory inside your Velocity directory. Then you can build with Velocity with the `DataSourceResourceLocator` class using either `ant jar-J2EE` or `ant jar-J2EE-dep` to build without dependencies and with dependencies, respectively.

Testing the Velocity Build

Before moving on, it'd be wise to check that Velocity did indeed build correctly and that the build is functioning as the developers intended. Fortunately, the developers took the time to package the JUnit unit tests with the Velocity download. To run these tests, simply run the following command from the Velocity build directory:

```
ant test
```

Ant will now run your Velocity through a series of tests, which should result in a nice BUILD SUCCESSFUL message. If you get BUILD FAILED, this means one of your tests failed. You should try building the source again and running the tests again. If the problem still exists, try to build and test against the latest nightly build of Velocity available from the Web site. If still you have problems, it's most likely a configuration issue on your machine. Check the Velocity Web site for assistance.

Which JAR File?

As I mentioned previously, you can build two types of JAR files containing Velocity. One of the JAR files contains just the Velocity classes and nothing else; if you want to use Velocity, you'll have to add all the appropriate dependencies to your classpath as appropriate. The second JAR file, which has the word *dep* in the filename, contains all the dependencies that are needed by Velocity, so you can avoid having to find and download the correct versions yourself. For the most part, it's easier to use the JAR file containing all the dependencies, but if you want to use the version without the dependencies, then you'll need to download Jakarta Commons Collections and Jakarta ORO from `http://jakarta.apache.org`. You'll also need to have a logging tool; the "Configuring Velocity Logging" section covers this in more detail.

Building VelocityTools from Source Code

For many of the examples in this book that you'll build with Velocity, and indeed for most if not all of the applications, you'll need VelocityTools. As I mentioned previously, the VelocityTools project overcomes some of the shortcomings in the Velocity runtime and makes your life that little bit easier. Rather than address all the features of VelocityTools here, I'll cover them as they become required by the examples.

Building VelocityTools isn't much different from building Velocity, given that it uses Ant to control the build. The main differences lie in the way the project is structured. To start with, you need to download the source code from the VelocityTools site at `http://jakarta.apache.org/velocity/tools/index.html`. The examples in this book are written from VelocityTools version 1.2.

Once you've downloaded the source code, extract it from the archive and put the resulting folder in an accessible location on your machine. From the command line, change to the directory where you placed the VelocityTools files. Unlike Velocity, there's no build directory, and the Ant build file resides in the main VelocityTools directory. To build the VelocityTools JAR files, simply run this command:

```
ant
```

Note that you don't need to specify a build target, since the default target will build the appropriate JAR files. By default, the build produces two JAR files: one containing all the tools and another containing everything but the Struts integration tools. You can also build a smaller JAR containing none of the Struts or servlet tools. To do this, simply run the following command from the command line:

```
ant jar.generic
```

Now you're ready to get started with Velocity.

About the Examples

Before I start with the examples, I'll add this a quick note about compiling and running the examples. As you're aware, compiling even a simple application with javac can be a nightmare, with many issues related to classpaths and JAR locations. I wrote all the examples using Eclipse, but I used Ant to build them all because it's so simple. If you're experiencing problems building any of the examples, you can download all the code and the Ant build script from the Downloads section of the Apress Web site (`http://www.apress.com`).

When you're running the examples, you need to make sure you have all the correct libraries on your classpath. If you're having problems running the examples, then it's most likely because of issues with the classpath.

Creating Hello World

It would be almost sacrilegious if I neglected the traditional Hello World example with Velocity. Getting Velocity to say "hello" to the world is quite simple. First, you need a template. A template is just a plain-text file containing VTL markup and static content. In this case, you have no dynamic content, so you just want to include static content, like so:

```
Hello World!
```

Save this file to a location that will be accessible from your code. I suggest you follow a directory structure similar to the sample code so the examples are easier to follow. With the template in place, you can move onto the Java code (see Listing 2-1).

Listing 2-1. The Hello World App

```java
package com.apress.pjv.ch2;

import java.io.StringWriter;
import java.io.Writer;

import org.apache.velocity.Template;
import org.apache.velocity.VelocityContext;
import org.apache.velocity.app.Velocity;

public class HelloWorld {

    public static void main(String[] args) throws Exception {
        // initialize Velocity
        Velocity.init();

        // get the template
        Template template =
            Velocity.getTemplate("src/templates/ch2/HelloWorld.vm");

        // create a context for Velocity
        VelocityContext context = new VelocityContext();

        // create the output
        Writer writer = new StringWriter();
        template.merge(context, writer);

        // write out
        System.out.println(writer.toString());
    }
}
```

Once you've completed the code, compile it and then run it. You'll see the following familiar message:

```
Hello World!
```

Now, you're probably thinking that Listing 2-1 contained an awful lot of code just to write "Hello World" to the console, and you'd be right. However, this is just a simplified example; as you move onto some more examples, you'll see how this code doesn't change much, but the amount of output can greatly increase.

Dissecting Hello World

So now that you've seen Velocity in action, you'll look at what you just wrote. First, you created the template. The Hello World template was basic and contained absolutely no VTL content whatsoever; it was simply the content you wanted to display on the screen. Next came the Java class, which was a little more complicated; you'll now look at it bit by bit:

```
// initialize Velocity
Velocity.init();
```

The first line of code initializes the Velocity runtime with the default set of parameters. The init() method can be passed as either a Properties argument containing configuration properties for the Velocity runtime or a String argument that indicates the path to a file containing the configuration properties. The "Configuring the Velocity Runtime" section discusses the available configuration properties in more detail.

The next step is to obtain a reference to the actual template. Velocity has the following Template class to refer to templates:

```
// get the template
Template template =
    Velocity.getTemplate("src/templates/ch2/HelloWorld.vm");
```

In this case, the template is loaded from the file system using Velocity.getTemplate(). With the template now loaded, the code now creates the following instance of the VelocityContext class:

```
// create a context for Velocity
VelocityContext context = new VelocityContext();
```

The VelocityContext class is pivotal to making your Velocity-based applications do anything useful. Using VelocityContext, you can pass data from your

Java program into the Velocity runtime when rendering output from your templates. You can see this in action in the next example:

```
// create the output
Writer writer = new StringWriter();
template.merge(context, writer);

// write out
System.out.println(writer.toString());
```

In the last step of this example, the code creates the output and writes it to the console. The `mergeTemplate` method will merge the data in the `VelocityContext` object, with the static content and VTL markup in the template, and write the result to the `Writer` instance provided by the code. In this case, the template contains no VTL markup, and the `VelocityContext` contains no data, so the output is simply the static content from the template file.

Improving Hello World

In the previous example, the code really did nothing spectacular. In other words, there was nothing dynamic about the output at all; all the code in the `main()` method could have been replaced with a single line, and the output wouldn't have been different.

The real power of Velocity comes when combining the static content in a template with some VTL constructs and some dynamic data from your Java application. Quite surprisingly, it takes hardly any extra code to give the Hello World application some dynamic behavior. First, you need to modify the template, adding some VTL markup, like so:

```
Hello $who!
```

Don't worry too much about the syntax just yet; Chapter 3 explains VTL in full, so the behavior of this particular piece of code will become apparent soon. Although I've created a separate class, the changes to the code are minimal (see Listing 2-2).

Listing 2-2. The Improved Hello World App

```
package com.apress.pjv.ch2;

import java.io.StringWriter;
import java.io.Writer;
```

```
import org.apache.velocity.Template;
import org.apache.velocity.VelocityContext;
import org.apache.velocity.app.Velocity;

public class HelloWorldImproved {

    public static void main(String[] args) throws Exception{
        //initialize Velocity
        Velocity.init();

        // get the template
        Template template =
            Velocity.getTemplate("src/templates/ch2/HelloWorldImproved.vm");

        // create a context for Velocity
        VelocityContext context = new VelocityContext();

        // set the who variable
        context.put("who", "Gandalf");

        // create the output
        Writer writer = new StringWriter();
        template.merge(context, writer);

        // write out
        System.out.println(writer.toString());
    }
}
```

Notice that the only differences are the name of the template file and the addition of this extra line:

```
// set the who variable
context.put("who", "Gandalf");
```

The VelocityContext class allows you to pass data from your application into the Velocity runtime. VelocityContext works on a name/value basis, with the name you provide when adding data to the VelocityContext class being used to refer to that data from within your template. If you recall the change I made to the template, I replaced the word *World* with the VTL variable $who. Then in the code I set the value of the $who variable to Gandalf. When you run the example now, you'll get the following output:

```
Hello Gandalf!
```

Try changing the value of the $who variable from within your Java code, and verify that the output changes appropriately.

Using Context Chaining

With Velocity it's possible for multiple contexts to be merged and passed to the runtime as a single context. This can help when many components are interacting to produce the context; rather than pass a single context from component to component, which will have performance implications if the context is particularly large and it's being passed across the network and back, each component can create its own context, and then the main application can chain the contexts together. To see this in action, you'll now build a simple example. First, create a new template with the following code:

```
This is my first name $firstName
This is my last name $lastName
```

Second, create a Java class to create some output from this template. Listing 2-3 shows the code in full; the lines of interest are explained afterward.

Listing 2-3. Context Chaining

```java
package com.apress.pjv.ch2;

import java.io.StringWriter;
import java.io.Writer;

import org.apache.velocity.Template;
import org.apache.velocity.VelocityContext;
import org.apache.velocity.app.Velocity;

public class ContextChaining {

    public static void main(String[] args) throws Exception {
        // initialize Velocity
        Velocity.init();

        // get the template
        Template template =
            Velocity.getTemplate("src/templates/ch2/ContextChaining.vm");

        // create two separate contexts
        VelocityContext context1 = new VelocityContext();
        VelocityContext context2 = new VelocityContext(context1);

        // set the firstName variable
        context1.put("firstName", "Rob");
        context2.put("lastName", "Harrop");
```

```
        // create the output
        Writer writer = new StringWriter();
        template.merge(context2, writer);

        // write out
        System.out.println(writer.toString());
    }
}
```

Notice that when you're creating the `context2` object, you pass the `context1` object as an argument as the constructor, like so:

```
// create two separate contexts
VelocityContext context1 = new VelocityContext();
VelocityContext context2 = new VelocityContext(context1);
```

This will place the data in `context1` inside `context2`. Note, however, that the data isn't simply copied from one context to the other; the second context, `context2`, maintains a reference to `context1` and will check this context when trying to resolve references within a template. For this reason, you're able to add data to `context1` after the constructor on `context2` has finished executing and still have the data accessible via `context1`. Running this code will yield the following output:

```
This is my first name Rob
This is my last name Harrop
```

As you can see, both variables are resolved correctly, and the correct data is rendered, even though only the `context2` object was passed to the Velocity runtime directly. When trying to resolve the `$firstName` reference, the `context2` object has delegated to the chained `context1`, once it determined that it didn't contain the data. For the most part, you won't use this feature in your day-to-day programming—you'll simply create a context, populate it, and then generate content from it. However, it can be useful if you're building complex applications with many different components because it helps decouple the components from each other. Context chaining also becomes useful when you build framework services for your own application—perhaps you want to guarantee that a certain piece of data always exists in the context—and then use context chaining to allow your application to provide its own context and have the framework chain the extra data on top.

Configuring the Velocity Runtime

The Velocity runtime is highly configurable and has a large selection of configuration properties that you can use to customize the behavior of the runtime.

Understanding how to configure the Velocity runtime correctly will help when building more complex applications.

Setting Configuration Parameters

You have two ways to set the Velocity configuration parameters when first initializing the Velocity runtime. The first way is simply to create a `Properties` instance from within your code and then pass this instance to the `Velocity.init()` method (see Listing 2-4).

Listing 2-4. Configuration Using the `Properties` *Class*

```java
public class HelloWorldProperties {

    public static void main(String[] args) throws Exception {
        // set some properties
        Properties props = new Properties();
        props.put("input.encoding", "utf-8");

        // initialize Velocity
        Velocity.init(props);

        // get the template
        Template template =
            Velocity.getTemplate("src/templates/ch2/HelloWorld.vm");

        // create a context for Velocity
        VelocityContext context = new VelocityContext();

        // create the output
        Writer writer = new StringWriter();
        template.merge(context, writer);

        // write out
        System.out.println(writer.toString());
    }
}
```

The main drawback of this method is obvious; any changes to the configuration require a change to your Java code, which in a large application means a recompile and no doubt a bunch of testing to make sure something didn't go wrong in the process. A better solution to this is to use an external properties file and pass the name of the properties file to the Velocity runtime when you call `init()`. I'm sure most of you are familiar with the format of Java property files, but just in case, you can achieve the same behavior as the previous example with this property file:

```
# set the input encoding
input.encoding=utf-8
```

Then, to use this property file to configure the Velocity runtime, you just pass the filename to the Velocity.init() method (see Listing 2-5).

Listing 2-5. Configuration Using a Properties File

```java
public class HelloWorldExternalProperties {

    public static void main(String[] args) throws Exception{
        // initialize Velocity
        Velocity.init("src/velocity.properties");

        // get the template
        Template template =
            Velocity.getTemplate("src/templates/ch2/HelloWorld.vm");

        // create a context for Velocity
        VelocityContext context = new VelocityContext();

        // create the output
        Writer writer = new StringWriter();
        template.merge(context, writer);

        // write out
        System.out.println(writer.toString());
    }
}
```

Unless you plan to have some kind of dynamic configuration for the Velocity runtime that can be modified through some user interface in your application, I recommend you use an external properties file for configuration. That way, you can make any changes to the configuration quickly and without touching your application code.

Introducing General Configuration Parameters

You can use some general configuration parameters to configure the behavior of the Velocity runtime (see Table 2-1).

Table 2-1. General Velocity Configuration Parameters

Parameter Name	Description
`input.encoding`	This allows you to specify the encoding of your input data. By default, this is set to ISO-8859-1. Change this only if you have templates that aren't ISO-8859-1 encoded.
`output.encoding`	This property is used by the `VelocityServlet` to set the response encoding, and by Anakia when writing output files. The default is ISO-8859-1.
`parser.pool.size`	The Velocity runtime maintains a pool of parsers that parse your templates. If you have enough memory available on your machine and your application is parsing a lot of templates concurrently, you should consider increasing the size of the pool. By default, the pool size is set to 20.
`runtime.interpolate.literals`	The value of this property determines whether the Velocity runtime will interpolate string literals that are contained within a template. Chapter 3 includes a more detailed discussion of the effect of this parameter.
`runtime.introspector.uberspect`	Velocity heavily uses introspection, mainly to provide a simple, JavaBeans-based syntax for accessing properties on your Java objects. The actual introspection is pluggable, so you can replace the default implementation with one of your own. Bear in mind that Velocity already has an excellent implementation that has been improved even more in version 1.4. You should use this only in special cases. The value of this property should be set to the fully qualified class name of the introspector; the default is `org.apache.velocity.util.introspection.UberspectImpl`.

Configuring Velocity Logging

As you start to build more complex applications using Velocity, you're bound to come across the need to debug your templates. Often you'll find that the output isn't as you expected or that output isn't generated at all and you get an exception. The logging mechanism is useful when you're experiencing problems with Velocity locating templates, which becomes even more complicated when you start to use multiple resource loaders. Thankfully, Velocity has quite a good logging system, which outputs some detailed information about the parsing and execution of your template. The information in the logs is often sufficient for you to find out what's wrong with your templates and fix it.

If you've been running the examples up to this point, you may have noticed the log. By default, Velocity will look for the Avalon LogKit on your classpath and use this if it's found. If Avalon LogKit isn't found, then Velocity will look for log4j and use that. You'll find that Avalon LogKit is included in the dependencies JAR file that's created when you build Velocity, so if, like me, you've used this dependency JAR to build the examples, your logs will have been written using Avalon LogKit. The default output path for the log is from the root of your execution path to a file named `velocity.log`.

Introducing Velocity LogSystem

At the core of the Velocity logging system is the `LogSystem` interface. All log messages from the Velocity runtime are written to an object that implements this interface. The standard distribution of Velocity contains implementations of `LogSystem` for Avalon LogKit and Apache log4j, along with an implementation to ignore all log messages. As well as these implementations, you'll also find an implementation of `LogSystem` that will write log messages using the Jakarta Common Logging system included in the VelocityTools project. If you don't see your favorite logging tool listed here, don't worry; it's a trivial job to create a custom implementation of `LogSystem` and have Velocity use that as its logger. Chapter 10 covers this topic in more detail.

Configuring Velocity to Use log4j

As I mentioned earlier, the Velocity runtime will, by default, use Avalon LogKit as the logging implementation when writing any log messages. If Avalon LogKit isn't found on the classpath, Velocity will then look for log4j and use that, if found. This is all well and good when you're using the simple Velocity JAR file without all the dependencies, as you can choose to have just log4j on classpath. However, when using the JAR file containing the dependencies, Avalon LogKit is included in that JAR so Velocity will always pick it up before log4j. Fortunately, you can tell Velocity to ignore that Avalon LogKit is available and use the log4j logger by setting the `runtime.log.logsystem.class` configuration parameter to the class name of the log4j `LogSystem` implementation (in this case, `org.apache.velocity.runtime.log.SimpleLog4JLogSystem`). You can set this parameter either by passing it to `Velocity.init()` method as described earlier or by placing it in an external properties file as described in the previous example.

NOTE *Another implementation of* LogSystem *for log4j is included with the Velocity distribution:* Log4JLogSystem. *This class has been deprecated since version 1.3 of Velocity and shouldn't be used. You should also be aware that the current log4j support in Velocity uses the older concept of a* Category, *which has been replaced in log4j by the* Logger *class. The* Category *class still works in log4j, however version 1.5 of Velocity will introduce a* LogSystem *implementation that uses* Logger *instead of* Category.

So, you'll now try it out. Using the previous example, when you first run it without any special configuration parameters, the first line of the log file reads as follows:

```
Fri Feb 13 10:43:10 GMT 2004  [debug] AvalonLogSystem initialized using logfile
'velocity.log'
```

As you can see, Velocity is clearly using Avalon LogKit as the logging implementation. Now to switch to log4j, you simply add the following line of code to the configuration file and run this:

```
runtime.log.logsystem.class=org.apache.velocity.runtime.log.SimpleLog4JLogSystem
```

Now when you look into the log file, you'll see that the first line of log messages written is this:

```
2004-02-13 10:45:21,125 - SimpleLog4JLogSystem initialized using logfile ➡
'velocity.log'
```

Now you can see that log4j log system is being used to write the log messages. By default the SimpleLog4JLogSystem will use its own class name as the name of the log4j Category. However, you can change this by setting the runtime.log.logsystem .log4j.category property to the name of the category you want to use. Once you're using log4j to log the Velocity messages, you can configure the output of the messages just as you would with any log4j application. For instance, to output all the Velocity messages to the console, create a simple log4j.properties file with the following code and place it in the root of your classpath:

```
log4j.rootLogger=DEBUG, stdout

log4j.appender.stdout=org.apache.log4j.ConsoleAppender
log4j.appender.stdout.layout=org.apache.log4j.PatternLayout

# Pattern to output the caller's filename and line number.
log4j.appender.stdout.layout.ConversionPattern=%p [%t] [%c] %C{1}.%M(%L) | %m%n
```

Be aware that it seems that the configuration file will be picked up by log4j and Velocity only if you set your own Category name as described. I found that when I had this configuration file in the classpath and I passed Velocity a specific Category name to use, the log message went to the console as desired. However, when I didn't pass Velocity the Category name, no log messages were written to the console. For more information on log4j configuration, read *Logging in Java with the JDK 1.4 Logging API and Apache log4j* (Apress, 2003).

Using Commons Logging with Velocity

As part of the VelocityTools project, a LogSystem implementation will allow you to write all log output via the Commons Logging tool. If you intend to use log4j as the actual logging implementation, I advise that you use the SimpleLog4JLogSystem and resist the temptation to pass log messages from Velocity to Commons Logging and then onto log4j. However, if you want to use a logging provider that has no LogSystem implementation and you don't fancy writing your own, then Commons Logging may well have an adapter. A good example of this would be if you wanted to use Java 1.4 Logging as the mechanism for writing your log messages.

For this example, I used the code from the HelloWorldExternalProperties example. No modifications to the Java code were needed; only the configuration file was changed. To use Commons Logging, first you need to download it from the Jakarta Commons Web site at http://jakarta.apache.org/commons. Once you've downloaded it, include the JAR file in the classpath of your application. You'll also need to include the VelocityTools JAR file, as this contains the LogSystem implementation for Commons Logging. Once that's done, you need to set the runtime.log.logsystem.class property to org.apache.velocity.tools.generic.log.CommonsLogLogSystem. If you still have log4j in your classpath and configured correctly, then you can run the example now, but you'll still be using log4j as the underlying logging provider. To switch to the JDK 1.4 Logging API as the logging mechanism, simply remove log4j from the classpath and, of course, make sure you're running on a 1.4 JVM. Now run the example. You'll see that the Velocity log file shows that CommonsLogLogSystem is being used to write the log messages, and you should also see that the log messages are written to the console. This is the default JDK 1.4 logging setup provided to Velocity via Commons Logging. Phew! So many different adapters—it can get quite complicated. For the most part, I recommend you stick with log4j as your logger and that you use SimpleLog4JLogSystem to interface it with Velocity. Log4j is a powerful logging tool, and using SimpleLog4JLogSystem provides the simplest and best-performing mechanism to link it with Velocity. For most applications, I recommend you use Commons Logging at code level but use log4j as the actual logging tool. This way, you can easily replace log4j with another logging tool for both your application and Velocity log messages without having to rework your code. For a more in-depth discussion of using Commons Logging, you should check out the Jakarta Web site and also read my discussion of Commons Logging in *Pro Jakarta Struts, Second Edition* (Apress, 2004).

Additional Logging Configuration

Besides just configuring which tool is going to perform the actual logging, you can use a few additional configuration parameters to customize the logging behavior (see Table 2-2).

Table 2-2. Additional Logging Configuration Parameters

Parameter	Description
runtime.log	Using this parameter, you can specify the name of the log file created by Velocity. By default, this parameter is set to velocity.log, and the file is created in the root of the execution path.
runtime.log.logsystem	You can use this parameter only from code; you can't use it from the configuration file. Using this parameter, you can pass an instance of a class that implements LogSystem to Velocity and have it use that class to write the log messages. This can be quite useful if you want to be able to build the logging configuration dynamically in your code.
runtime.log.xxx.stacktrace	Using this parameter, you can specify whether Velocity should output stack traces in the log files for the error, warn, and info message levels. By default, this option is set to false for each level. To turn stack traces on, set this parameter to true, replacing xxx with the level name.
runtime.log.invalid.references	By default, Velocity will write a log message each time it finds a reference in one of your templates that isn't valid. This is one of my main uses of the log file when I'm debugging my applications, but it's useful to turn this off in a production. Set this option to false to disable invalid reference logging.

Understanding Resource Loaders

In each of the previous examples, the templates have been loaded from a file, and you'd be forgiven for thinking this is the only way to load a template for Velocity. This is, however, not the case. Velocity has a flexible resource management system that allows for resources to be retrieved from a wide variety of sources. Templates are the most common resource loaded by Velocity, but as you'll see when you look at the #include directive in Chapter 3, they aren't the only resources loaded by Velocity.

Central to the resource management system in Velocity are *resource loaders.* Resource loaders are responsible for retrieving the resource from a specific location and passing the contents to the Velocity runtime. Consider the examples you've seen. All of them include a call to Velocity.getTemplate(), which loads a template resource into the Velocity runtime. At first glance, you'd think that the String argument the getTemplate() method takes is actually the path to the template, but in fact it's just an identifier that's used by the resource loader to retrieve a particular resource. In some cases, this resource can be a filename; in others, it may just be a designated identifier for your templates. The Velocity distribution comes complete with four resource loaders for loading resources: from the file system directly, from a JAR file, from the classpath, and from a J2EE DataSource. In the next section, I'll demonstrate how to use the first three and also show configuration options available for the fourth.

Using Multiple Resource Loaders

For this section, I've built an example to test three of the four supplied resource loaders. Rather than talk you through entering the code bit by bit, I'll include it all here and then show the relevant bits for each resource loader.

The Java code for this example should seem quite familiar; I've just refactored it a little to make it simpler (see Listing 2-6).

Listing 2-6. Using Resource Loaders

```
package com.apress.pjv.ch2;

import java.io.StringWriter;
import java.io.Writer;

import org.apache.velocity.Template;
import org.apache.velocity.VelocityContext;
import org.apache.velocity.app.Velocity;

public class ResourceLoaders {

    private static final String FILE_RESOURCE_LOADER_TEMPLATE =
        "ResourceLoader1.vm";
    private static final String JAR_RESOURCE_LOADER_TEMPLATE =
        "ResourceLoader2.vm";
    private static final String CLASSPATH_RESOURCE_LOADER_TEMPLATE =
        "ResourceLoader3.vm";
```

```java
public static void main(String[] args) throws Exception {
    processTemplate(FILE_RESOURCE_LOADER_TEMPLATE);
    processTemplate(JAR_RESOURCE_LOADER_TEMPLATE);
    processTemplate(CLASSPATH_RESOURCE_LOADER_TEMPLATE);
}

private static void processTemplate(String templateName) throws Exception {
    // initialize Velocity
    Velocity.init("src/velocity.properties");

    // get the template
    Template template = Velocity.getTemplate(templateName);

    // create a context for Velocity
    VelocityContext context = new VelocityContext();

    // create the output
    Writer writer = new StringWriter();
    template.merge(context, writer);

    // write out
    System.out.println(writer.toString());
}

}
```

I've created three templates: ResourceLoader1.vm, ResourceLoader2.vm, and ResouceLoader3.vm, each with a single line of static text. I've placed the first template, ResourceLoader1.vm, in the same directory as all the templates from the previous examples. I've packaged the second template, ResourceLoader2.vm, inside a JAR file and then placed it in the same directory as ResourceLoader1.vm. I've stored the third template, ResourceLoader3.vm, in the root of the classpath. The placement of these files is important; if you place all the templates in the same directory as ResourceLoader1.vm, they will be picked up by the same resource loader, and you won't be able to see the others in action.

Testing FileResourceLoader

The first resource loader to test is the file resource loader, which is implemented by the FileResourceLoader class in the org.apache.velocity.runtime.resource .loader package. By default, Velocity will use an instance of FileResourceLoader configured to look in the current directory when searching for resources. So, in all the previous examples, the `FileResourceLoader` has been used to load the templates based on the path specified in the call to `Velocity.getTemplate()`. If you look closely at the current example, you'll notice that I've specified just the filename for `ResourceLoader1.vm`, not the whole path. If you ran the example without any further configuration, Velocity would be unable to find this template because it doesn't reside in the current directory. However, you can configure a different resource loader than the default and have Velocity look for my resources there. To do this, first you need to tell Velocity the name of my resource loader and then, using this name, configure the options for it. You can do this with a few lines in the `velocity.properties` file:

```
resource.loader=file

# File Resource Loader
file.resource.loader.class= ➥
org.apache.velocity.runtime.resource.loader.FileResourceLoader
file.resource.loader.path=./src/templates/ch2
file.resource.loader.cache=true
file.resource.loader.modificationCheckInterval=2
```

Note that you can also pass these options to Velocity inside an instance of the `Properties` class. The `resource.loader` option specifies the name of the resource loader that Velocity should find. By default, Velocity will look for a resource loader named `file`, but I prefer to define the name explicitly—if only because it makes my intentions clearer. To configure a particular resource loader, you need to include the configuration options prefixed by the name given to the `resource.loader` option. As you can see from the previous code, the four configuration parameters after the `resource.loader` parameter are prefixed with the name `file`. This means that these parameters are being set for just the resource loader named `file`. This is useful when you have more than one resource loader working in your application.

If you run the example now, you'll see output for the first template, but you should get an error for the second template, as Velocity won't be able to find the appropriate resource until you configure the JAR resource loader. It's useful to check the Velocity log file, as it will tell what resource loaders it's using and which one was used when a particular resource was loaded.

Table 2-3 describes the configuration options for the `FileResourceLoader`.

Table 2-3. `FileResourceLoader` Configuration Parameters

Parameter	Description
`<name>.resource.loader.class`	This specifies the name of the implementation class of the resource loader. For the `FileResourceLoader`, this will be `org.apache.velocity.runtime.resource.loader` `.FileResourceLoader`. This parameter is always required.

Table 2-3. `FileResourceLoader` *Configuration Parameters (continued)*

Parameter	Description
`<name>.resource.loader.path`	Use this parameter to specify the path in which the `FileResourceLoader` should look for resources. You can specify more than one path, each one separated by a comma.
`<name>.resource.loader.cache`	By default, this parameter is set to `false`, which means each time you want a resource from this resource loader, it will be reloaded from the filesystem. This is quite useful when debugging, since you're likely to change your templates quite a bit. However, in a production environment, you can really improve performance by setting this parameter to `true`, in which case the resource loader will place resources in a cache once they've been loaded and then retrieve them from the cache for subsequent requests.
`<name>.resource.loader` `.modificationCheckInterval`	This parameter is used only if you turn on caching. Use this parameter to specify the interval, in seconds, between checks to see if a cache resource has been modified. If you're in a production environment and want the performance benefit of caching but don't want the hassle of having to restart your application every time you change a resource, then set this parameter to the highest interval you can manage.

Testing JarResourceLoader

If you ran the example after the previous step, you'll no doubt have received an error message telling you that Velocity couldn't find `ResourceLoader2.vm`. This is no wonder, really, when you consider that this resource is actually packaged inside a JAR file. For this you need to use the `JarResourceLoader`, which will load resources that are packaged within a JAR file.

Configuring the `JarResourceLoader` isn't much different from configuring the `FileResourceLoader`. First, you have to add another resource loader name to the `resource.loader` parameter; second, you declare the configuration parameters for this resource loader, like so:

```
resource.loader=  file, jar

# File Resource Loader
...

# JAR Resource Loader
jar.resource.loader.class = ➥
org.apache.velocity.runtime.resource.loader.JarResourceLoader
jar.resource.loader.path = jar:file:/tmp/ResourceLoader2.jar
```

Notice that I've specified only two parameters for this resource loader; Table 2-4 describes the full list of parameters recognized by the JarResourceLoader. Run the example again, and this time you should get output from both the first and second templates, with only the third throwing up an error.

Table 2-4. JarResourceLoader *Configuration Parameters*

Parameter	Description
<name>.resource.loader.class	This parameter has the same meaning as for the FileResourceLoader and is always required. For the JarResourceLoader, this will be org.apache.velocity .runtime.resource.loader.JarResourceLoader.
<name>.resource.loader.path	Use this parameter to specify the paths to the JAR files that the JarResourceLoader will look in for resources. As with FileResourceLoader, you can specify more than one path using commas to separate each path. The syntax of the paths should correspond with that defined by the java.net .JarURLConnection class. See the JavaDoc for that class for more details.
<name>.resource.loader.cache	Although you can turn on caching for the JarResourceLoader, support for caching in this loader isn't yet fully implemented. The JarResourceLoader will always inform the runtime that a particular resource has changed, regardless of whether this is the case. You should note, however, that the resource loader will have the opportunity only to notify the runtime that the resource has been modified after the amount of seconds set in modificationCheckInterval has elapsed. For instance, consider an application where you've set modificationCheckInterval to 20 seconds. You run the application and the template is processed once, being loaded from the JAR file. Then, 19 seconds later the template is processed again, being retrieved from the cache since the modificationCheckInterval hasn't yet elapsed. Then the template is processed again in 30 seconds. This time, the runtime will check to see whether the resource has been modified since the amount of time specified by modificationCheckInterval has elapsed. Now, regardless of whether the resource has been modified, it will be reloaded.
<name>.resource.loader .modificationCheckInterval	As with FileResourceLoader, this is the amount of time, in seconds, that the runtime will wait before checking to see whether the resource has changed. See the previous discussion of the cache parameter for more details.

Testing ClasspathResourceLoader

All that's left is to configure Velocity to find the third template. As you may have noticed, I got you to place this template in the root of the classpath. The reason for this is so that I can highlight the use of the ClasspathResourceLoader. This resource loader is the easiest to configure and is perhaps the most useful in a Web-based environment, as you have no issues with paths; all the resources are simply included in the classpath. You should note that you don't have to place your resources loose at the root of your classpath; you can put them in a JAR file and place the JAR file in your classpath. This is useful in a servlet environment since you can place all your resources in a JAR file and pop that in the /WEB-INF/ lib directory, and your resources are all available through the classpath.

I mentioned that the ClasspathResourceLoader was easy to configure, and it is. You don't have any paths to worry about, just the following class name:

```
resource.loader=  file, jar, class

# File Resource Loader
...

# JAR Resource Loader
...

# Classpath Resource Loader
class.resource.loader.class =
org.apache.velocity.runtime.resource.loader.ClasspathResourceLoader
```

Now, run the example again, and you should get output from all three templates, with no errors at all. Table 2-5 describes the configuration parameters for this resource loader.

Table 2-5. ClasspathResourceLoader *Configuration Parameters*

Parameter	Description
<name>.resource.loader.class	This parameter has the same meaning as for the FileResourceLoader and is always required. For the ClasspathResourceLoader, this will be org.apache.velocity .runtime.resource.loader.ClasspathResourceLoader.
<name>.resource.loader.cache	As with FileResourceLoader, you can enable caching for resources loaded by the ClasspathResourceLoader by setting this parameter to true. You should note that this resource loader doesn't support modification detection; it will always inform the runtime that the resource hasn't been changed, even if you change it. This can be quite infuriating during debugging, since you need to restart your application just to check for changes in your template.

Table 2-5. ClasspathResourceLoader *Configuration Parameters (continued)*

Parameter	Description
<name>.resource.loader .modificationCheckInterval	This parameter, although supported for this resource loader, is kind of pointless, since if you have caching enabled, the resource will never be reloaded despite any modifications you may make to it.

Configuring DataSourceResourceLoader

Before proceeding with this section, you should refer to the earlier "Building with J2EE Support" section, which discusses building Velocity with support for the DataSourceResourceLoader class.

Using DataSourceResourceLoader, you can store your Velocity resources in any data store that can be accessed via a javax.sql.DataSource instance. Using this resource loader is restricted to J2EE environment. I've purposely avoided going over the details of configuring a DataSource in your application server, since I think that if you want to use this feature, then you're already more than familiar with that process. I will, however, show you how to set up Velocity so that you can use the DataSourceResourceLoader in your J2EE applications.

The first step is to create a table in your data store that will store the Velocity resources. This table must include at least three columns: one to store the resource name, one to store the resource content, and one to act as a time stamp. You'll find a sample SQL script included in the JavaDoc for the DataSourceResourceLoader class.

Next, you need to configure the resource loader in Velocity. You do this just like any other resource loader; however, you have to specify many more parameters. This is a sample configuration for the DataSourceResourceLoader:

```
ds.resource.loader.class
org.apache.velocity.runtime.resource.loader.DataSourceResourceLoader
ds.resource.loader.resource.datasource = java:comp/env/jdbc/Velocity
ds.resource.loader.resource.table = velocityResources
ds.resource.loader.resource.keycolumn =  resourceKey
ds.resource.loader.resource.templatecolumn = resourceDef
ds.resource.loader.resource.timestampcolumn = resourceTimestamp
ds.resource.loader.cache=true
ds.resource.loader.modificationCheckInterval = 60
```

Table 2-6 gives a full description of each parameter.

Table 2-6. `DataSourceResourceLoader` *Configuration Parameters*

Parameter	Description
`<name>.resource.loader.class`	As with all the previous resource loaders, you should set this to the name of the resource loader class (in this case, `DataSourceResourceLoader`).
`<name>.resource.loader` `.resource.datasource`	This is the full JNDI name of the data source. You must configure the data source separately within your application server.
`<name>.resource.loader` `.resource.table`	This is the name of the table in the data store that contains your resources.
`<name>.resource.loader` `.resource.keycolumn`	This is the name of the column in your table that contains the resource name. This is the argument you pass to `Velocity` `.getTemplate()` when you want to load a template.
`<name>.resource.loader` `.resource.templatecolumn`	This is the name of the column that contains the actual resource contents.
`<name>.resource.loader` `.resource.timestampcolumn`	This is the name of the column containing a time stamp. This is used for caching purposes.
`<name>.resource.loader.cache`	This resource loader fully supports caching, using a time stamp stored alongside a resource in the data store. Set this parameter to `true` to enable caching.
`<name>.resource.loader` `.modificationCheckInterval`	This one should be familiar—it's the amount of time the Velocity runtime will wait before checking to see whether a resource has been modified. Bear in mind that this will involve queries being run against the data store.

Configuring the Resource Manager

You can use three parameters to control the overall behavior of the Velocity resource manager (see Table 2-7).

Table 2-7. Resource Manager Configuration Parameters

Parameter	Description
`resource.manager.logwhenfound`	By default, this parameter is set to `true`, which causes the resource manager to write a log message the first time it finds a resource. You can set this to `false` in a production environment, but it's useful in a debugging environment.

Table 2-7. Resource Manager Configuration Parameters (continued)

Parameter	Description
resource.manager.cache.class	Using this parameter, you can specify the name of class that will be used to cache resources once they're loaded. Chapter 10 covers how to create a custom cache implementation. The default for this parameter is org.apache.velocity.runtime .resource.ResourceCacheImpl. This class uses a least recently used caching algorithm to remove old items from memory, keeping memory consumption at a sensible level.
resource.manager.cache.size	Use this parameter to set the default cache size. When using the default cache, this parameter is set to 89.

Choosing a Resource Loader

You have quite a few choices available for resource loaders; as you'll see in Chapter 10, you can even implement your own resource loaders. However, for the most part you should stick with either FileResourceLoader or ClasspathResourceLoader because that way you can easily modify the template contents; when you have your templates packaged away in a JAR file or stored in a database, editing the template isn't as easy as just modifying a file in the file system. This is especially true if the templates are used for output created by nonprogrammers. Nonprogrammers already have to learn the Velocity syntax; you don't really want to start having to show them how to create and extract JAR files or interact with your RDBMS.

The lack of caching on the JarResourceLoader makes it a bad choice for production environments, as you can get quite a performance boost from the effective use of caching. I imagine that caching will eventually be added to the JarResourceLoader, but my guess is that it will detect only when the entire JAR file has changed, which means that changing one template in the file will invalidate the cached versions of any other templates in the JAR file, whether or not they've changed.

In a Web environment, I almost certainly recommend you use the ClasspathResourceLoader; it'll remove the need to worry about paths and will ensure that your application will still function when deployed as a WAR file in containers such as JBoss, which run the application directly from the WAR without extracting the files. One thing to be aware of in ClasspathResourceLoader is that if you have caching enabled, once a template has been loaded and placed in the cache, it'll always be retrieved from the cache, irrespective of whether the resource has changed. This is different from JarResourceLoader, which will always tell the runtime that the resource has been modified; ClasspathResourceLoader always tells the runtime that the resource has *not* been modified.

Configuring VTL

Using configuration, it's possible to modify the way in which certain VTL constructs work. I've saved the discussion of these configuration options until Chapter 3 where they're discussed in the context of the corresponding VTL constructs.

Configuring Velocimacro Libraries

Velocimacros are an advanced feature of VTL that are discussed in full in Chapter 3. Essentially, Velocimacros allow you to build reusable snippets of VTL code that you can use multiple times throughout a template. Velocity allows Velocimacros to be grouped together and stored globally in a library—Chapter 4 covers this topic in more detail.

Using VelocityEngine

In the previous examples, all interaction with the Velocity runtime has been through the Velocity helper class. Using this class, you're accessing a single instance of the Velocity runtime, which in most cases is perfectly adequate. However, as the needs of your applications increase, you may find that you need to use two instances of the Velocity runtime that are configured differently, within the same JVM. Fortunately, this capability has been present in Velocity since version 1.2, in the VelocityEngine class.

Using the VelocityEngine class is very much like using the Velocity class, except you're dealing with methods on a specific instance rather than static methods on a class. You still initialize the runtime with a call to the init() method, still get an instance of a template using the getTemplate() method, and still generate the final output with a call to mergeTemplate(). So, what's the point? Well, as I mentioned previously, you may want to have multiple instances of the runtime within your application, each with its own configuration. You may not have many uses for this in a generic Web application, but what if you're building a framework or a tool that may be embedded inside an application that's using Velocity? If your tool uses the Velocity helper class, it'll be sharing its configuration with the containing application, and nothing is stopping that application from modifying the configuration to such an extent that your tool will stop functioning. By using the VelocityEngine class, your tool can have its own isolated instance of the Velocity runtime that will not be affected by the configuration of any other Velocity runtimes in the containing application.

So, that's the theory; you'll now see this in action. In this example, I have two instances of the Velocity runtime that generate output from a template. Both instances use the same template name when obtaining an instance of the Template class, but they both have differently configured resource loaders, which will load the templates from different locations.

The first thing to do is to create two templates with the same name, but in different directories. Give each template different content so you'll be able identify the output from each template. My first template looks like this:

```
# template 1
This is template number 1
```

And the second one looks like this:

```
# template 2
This is template number 2
```

Next is the Java code to create the output from these templates. I want to create two instances of the Velocity runtime, each with a different resource loader configured. In this way, I can point each resource loader at one of the directories containing the templates, so even though the two instances will be looking for a template with same name, they'll be looking in different directories and thus retrieve different templates. Listing 2-7 shows the code in full; I'll explain each part in detail afterward.

Listing 2-7. Using VelocityEngine

```java
package com.apress.pjv.ch2;

import java.io.StringWriter;
import java.io.Writer;
import java.util.Properties;

import org.apache.velocity.Template;
import org.apache.velocity.VelocityContext;
import org.apache.velocity.app.VelocityEngine;

public class VelocityEngineTest {

    private static final String TEMPLATE_NAME = "VelocityEngineTest.vm";

    public static void main(String[] args) throws Exception {

        // create the properties for each engine
        Properties p1 = new Properties();
        p1.put("resource.loader", "file");
        p1.put(
            "file.resource.loader.class",
            "org.apache.velocity.runtime.resource.loader.FileResourceLoader");
        p1.put("file.resource.loader.path", "src/templates/ch2/ve1");
```

```
    Properties p2 = new Properties();
    p2.put("resource.loader", "file");
    p2.put(
        "file.resource.loader.class",
        "org.apache.velocity.runtime.resource.loader.FileResourceLoader");
    p2.put("file.resource.loader.path", "src/templates/ch2/ve2");

    //now create the engines
    VelocityEngine ve1 = new VelocityEngine();
    ve1.init(p1);

    VelocityEngine ve2 = new VelocityEngine();
    ve2.init(p2);

    // now get the output for each engine
    writeTemplateOutput(ve1);
    writeTemplateOutput(ve2);

}

public static void writeTemplateOutput(VelocityEngine ve) throws Exception {
    Template t = ve.getTemplate(TEMPLATE_NAME);

    Writer writer = new StringWriter();
    t.merge(new VelocityContext(), writer);

    System.out.println(writer.toString());
}
}
```

The first part of the code is building the different configurations for the two runtime instances. Here, I've created the configuration in code rather than using property files so that the example is a bit simpler:

```
// create the properties for each engine
Properties p1 = new Properties();
p1.put("resource.loader", "file");
p1.put(
    "file.resource.loader.class",
    "org.apache.velocity.runtime.resource.loader.FileResourceLoader");
p1.put("file.resource.loader.path", "src/templates/ch2/ve1");

Properties p2 = new Properties();
p2.put("resource.loader", "file");
p2.put(
    "file.resource.loader.class",
    "org.apache.velocity.runtime.resource.loader.FileResourceLoader");
p2.put("file.resource.loader.path", "src/templates/ch2/ve2");
```

Notice that the only difference is the path in which the resource loader will search for resources. The names of the resource loaders are the same, since these two resource loaders won't exist in the same runtime instance. Next, I create the two runtime instances using the VelocityEngine class, like so:

```
//now create the engines
VelocityEngine ve1 = new VelocityEngine();
ve1.init(p1);

VelocityEngine ve2 = new VelocityEngine();
ve2.init(p2);
```

Notice that the configuration is applied using the init() method, just as with the Velocity class. Finally, the output for the templates is generated and written to the console, like so:

```
// now get the output for each engine
writeTemplateOutput(ve1);
writeTemplateOutput(ve2);
```

The writeTemplateOutput() method should look quite familiar; the mergeTemplate() and getTemplate() methods of the Velocity class have been used in all the previous examples. In the following code, they're used on the VelocityEngine instances but to the same effect:

```
public static void writeTemplateOutput(VelocityEngine ve) throws Exception {
        Template t = ve.getTemplate(TEMPLATE_NAME);

        Writer writer = new StringWriter();
        t.merge(new VelocityContext(), writer);

        System.out.println(writer.toString());
    }
```

Running this example gives the following output:

```
This is template number 1
This is template number 2
```

Even though each runtime instance is looking for a template with the same name, their resource loaders are configured differently, so they're looking in different directories and will therefore find the different templates.

Use VelocityEngine wherever you want an isolated runtime with its own configuration. You should consider creating your own singleton wrapper around the VelocityEngine if you need to use it so you can take advantage of the caching functionality. Consider a Web application where you create a new instance of `VelocityEngine` for each request. Doing this will prevent resources from being cached between the different requests, as each request will have its own short-lived instance of the Velocity runtime.

Summary

This chapter introduced many new concepts that are core to the way the Velocity runtime works. It started by showing how to build the different Velocity JAR files and what differences these JAR files have. You'll now be able to decide which JAR file is suitable for you and build it from the source code. You've seen both the `Velocity` and `VelocityEngine` classes in action and taken an in-depth look at the similarities and differences between the two. A big part of this chapter focused on configuring the Velocity runtime to your liking. You looked at logging and the various different logging implementations Velocity can use, and you took a detailed look at the concept of resource loaders, how to configure them, and which ones are most suited to normal application development.

In the next chapter, you'll look at the templating language used by Velocity, VTL. The chapter will take you through every VTL construct included in the standard Velocity download and will also introduce some of the extra constructs in the VelocityTools project.

CHAPTER 3

Using the Velocity Template Language

IN THE PREVIOUS two chapters, I showed you many different examples that generate some form of output using Velocity. However, they have been trivial at best and have served more to highlight the Java API than to demonstrate how to use the Velocity Template Language (VTL). In this chapter, I'll explain all VTL constructs that are available out of the box with the standard Velocity distribution. I'll also demonstrate some of the more pervasive extensions included in the VelocityTools project.

Introducing VTL

Whenever you create a template in Velocity, you create it using VTL markup. Whether you store your templates on the file system, in a JAR file, or in a database, you'll create them using VTL markup. VTL is the biggest plus for anyone who is getting started with Velocity; forget about the nifty caching support or the high-performance parser—for anyone wanting results, VTL is where it's at. For this reason, I've decided to include this full chapter on VTL *before* showing some real examples of how Velocity works. VTL provides a simple syntax for template creation that nonprogrammers can easily understand. Many different tools purport to be able to separate layout from data, and then they go and include a language for layout that only a programmer can understand. Of course, in many cases you'll edit templates yourself, but if, like me, you have no graphic design skills, then you'll relish the opportunity of handing that responsibility to someone with an eye for design. A real boon of VTL is the ease with which you can mix static content and dynamic content. You'll have no more `StringBuffer.append()` statements chained together containing all your static content before you can even begin to think about the dynamic content—with VTL and Velocity, just enter the static content as you want it to appear, right alongside the VTL markup for dynamic content, and Velocity takes care of the rest.

One important point to remember is that Velocity is capable of generating any kind of text-based output. If you want it to generate HTML, it will do that, but VTL has no built-in HTML support. VTL is all about manipulating text-based output, regardless of what that output represents.

Introducing VTL Constructs

All VTL constructs follow the same basic syntax rules, and the core set of VTL directives provides all the functionality you'll require to build most of your templates. Most of the examples in this section use variations of the same Java code to load the template and merge it with the data. Listing 3-1 shows the code to use.

Listing 3-1. The Driver Application

```
package com.apress.pjv.ch3;

import java.io.StringWriter;
import java.io.Writer;

import org.apache.velocity.Template;
import org.apache.velocity.VelocityContext;
import org.apache.velocity.app.Velocity;

public class Driver {
    public static void main(String[] args) throws Exception{

        // init
        Velocity.init("src/velocity.properties");

        // get the template
        Template t = Velocity.getTemplate("src/templates/ch3/templateName.vm");

        // create context
        VelocityContext ctx = new VelocityContext();

        // create the output
        Writer writer = new StringWriter();
        t.merge(ctx, writer);

        // output
        System.out.println(writer);

    }
}
```

In the code download on the Apress Web site, you'll find a template file for each example, but I used the same driver program to produce all the output. Wherever the Java code is distinctly different, I'll highlight it alongside the template code.

Annotating Templates

As your applications grow and your templates get more complex, you'll need a mechanism for annotating what you did and why you did it. Like just about every other programming-related language under the sun, VTL supports comments.

As with Java, VTL supports both single-line and multiline comments. A single-line comment is denoted by two # characters at the beginning of a line; any text on that line is then considered part of the comment and is ignored by Velocity. For example:

```
## This is a comment
Hello World!
```

This template yields this output:

```
Hello World!
```

One area where single-line comments differ from Java is that you can't use them at the end of a line. Consider the following Java code:

```
int x = 0; // this is an integer
```

This would be perfectly legal in Java, but the equivalent VTL isn't legal.

```
Hello World! ## end of line comment
```

Using this template in a Velocity application would cause a ParseErrorException to be thrown. As well as single-line comments, you can use multiline comments when you need to provide more detailed annotation of your templates. Multiline comments are useful for creating a header for your template file where you can put some kind of documentation for your template. A multiline comment starts with #* and ends with *#. For example:

```
#* This is the start of my multiline comment
and it finishes on this line *#
Hello World!
```

This produces the following output:

```
Hello World!
```

The blank line before "Hello, World!" isn't a printing error; it's part of the output. Although Velocity ignores the comment text, it doesn't ignore the line break after the end comment marks, which results in the blank line. This doesn't cause too much of a problem for HTML or XML output, but for plain-text e-mail you may find yourself with stray lines if you use multiline comments.

Although you can't use single-line comments at the end of a line, you can use multiline comments to add a comment to the end of a line. For instance, the following VTL is valid:

```
Hello World! #* this is a comment *#
```

This produces the following (predictable) output:

```
Hello World!
```

Using Variables

Without variables, Velocity would be pretty useless. Without variables, you'd be able to produce only static content using Velocity, as there would be no mechanism for passing dynamic data to the Velocity runtime and for accessing that data within your templates. You can assign pretty much any Java object to a Velocity variable, and you can access object properties and methods from within your templates.

Accessing Data Within a Template

To access some dynamic data from within a template, first you need to add the data to the context and give it a name. The name you give to the data when adding it to the context is the name of variable that you can access within your template. Consider the following Java snippet that adds some data to the context:

```
// create context
VelocityContext ctx = new VelocityContext();
ctx.put("myName", "Rob Harrop");
```

This creates a variable called myName and assigns the String value Rob Harrop to it. To access a variable from within a template, you prepend the name with $, so to access the myName variable, you'd use $myName. For example:

```
My name is $myName
```

This generates the following output:

```
My name is Rob Harrop
```

Since you put a String object into the context, this output isn't surprising, but what happens when you put a non-String object in the context? In this situation, the Velocity runtime will call toString() on the object to generate the output.

Now see what happens when you replace the value of the $myName variable with an instance of Date, like so:

```
ctx.put("myName", new Date());
```

When you run the example, now you get the following output:

```
My name is Fri Feb 20 10:12:44 GMT 2004
```

As you can see, the value generated by the Date.toString() method is now included in the output.

Using Methods

In all the previous examples, the output generated for each variable has been based on the toString() method of the corresponding object. However, in some cases you may want to access the values of some of the methods on an object. Of course, you could add the result of each method to the context as separate variables, but that isn't really ideal. Thankfully, VTL supports using methods directly from within your templates, so you can add an object to the context and then access the methods from within your template. Consider the previous example where you added a Date object to the context. If you want to output the values for the current day, month, and year on each line, then you can access each method separately within the template, like so:

```
Day: $aDate.getDate()
Month: $aDate.getMonth()
Year: $aDate.getYear()
```

Running this gives the following output:

```
Day: 17
Month: 1
Year: 104
```

Don't be alarmed by the strange-looking result for the year. The Date object represents the year as 1900 subtracted from the current year, which results in 104.

Using JavaBean Properties

Whilst using methods to create output makes creating complex output much easier, the syntax is quite intimidating for nonprogrammers. Thankfully, Velocity can use JavaBeans' naming conventions to provide a much simpler syntax for getXXX() and setXXX() methods. You can modify the template from the previous example to use this simpler syntax:

```
Day: $aDate.Date
Month: $aDate.Month
Year: $aDate.Year
```

> **NOTE**   *You can replace* $aDate.Date *with* aDate.date; *the casing of the first letter is unimportant. You should note, however, that the casing of the rest of the name is important; therefore, you can't use, for instance,* $aDate.dATE.

The output from this template is the same as from the previous example, but the syntax in the template is much simpler. If your object model is quite complex, you can access nested properties such as $contact.Address.PostCode, which would translate to contact.getAddress().getPostCode() in Java.

Storing Properties in a Map

An interesting feature of Velocity is the ability to use a Map to store properties and then access these properties using just the name of the property. In fact, you aren't limited just to using Map; you can use this method for any of your classes. Essentially, it's just another shortcut implemented by Velocity, so when you have $obj.property in your template, it'll translate this in Java to obj.getProperty(). If this method isn't found, then Velocity will try to get the value by calling obj.get("property"). To see this in action, create a Map instance, add some data to it, and then add the Map to the context, like so:

```
// add a Map to the context
Map map = new HashMap();
map.put("firstName", "Rob");
map.put("lastName", "Harrop");
ctx.put("map", map);
```

Now create a simple template with the following code:

```
My first name is $map.firstName
My last name is $map.lastName
```

When you run this code, you get the following output:

```
My first name is Rob
My last name is Harrop
```

Notice that in the template you can refer to each value using just the property name; you have no need to call Map.get() explicitly. If your classes have a get(Object) method as well, then you can use the same syntax in your templates as you can with Map.

Introducing Quiet References

If you try to access a variable from within a template that doesn't exist within the context, then the Velocity runtime will leave the variable name in the output. For example, consider this template:

```
Hello $undefinedVariable
```

If you run the Java driver program without adding a value for $unspecifiedVariable to the context, the output is the same as the template. For the most part, this is desirable behavior, as it enables you to spot spelling mistakes in your template quickly. However, sometimes a variable is optional, and it's valid for that variable not to exist in the context. In this case, you don't want the name of the variable appearing in your output. For this purpose, Velocity supports quiet reference notation, which will output the variable value if the variable exists in the context but nothing if it doesn't. To make a variable reference quiet, simply add ! after the $ symbol, like so:

```
Hello $!undefinedVariable
```

When you now run the example, the output is simply Hello; the variable name isn't included at all in the output.

Creating Variables in a Template

Up to this point, you've created all the variables in Java code and passed them to the runtime using the VelocityContext. Whilst this is the most common mechanism for passing data to the Velocity runtime, it isn't the only way. You can also add variables to the context from within your templates. I tend to use this functionality as a means of factoring out common content in my templates to a single place. That way, I make a change in one place and have it reflected throughout the output. You should use this only when that particular piece of information won't be supplied by your Java application.

You create variables in a template like this:

```
#set($msg = "Hello World!")
I have a message for you: $msg
```

The first line of this template uses the #set directive (you'll learn more about directives in the "Using Directives" section) to assign the value "Hello World" to the variable $msg. As you can see from the second line in this template, variables created in this way are accessed in the same way as variables passed from your Java application. The output of this template is as follows:

```
I have a message for you: Hello World!
```

When assigning a variable from within a template, you use String literals like in the previous example, numeric literals such as 12345, and Boolean literals (true or false). You should note that Velocity can only handle numeric literals that are integers; it has no support for declaring floating-point literals within a template (although you can put Float and Double instances in the VelocityContext from your Java application). This template is an example of these different variable types in action:

```
#set($str = "A String")
#set($num = 12345)
#set($bool = true)
Output
------

$str
$num
$bool
```

Running this example gives the following output:

```
Output
------

A String
12345
true
```

You've probably noticed that you could have declared the $num and $bool variables as String literals, and the output would have been the same. This is true, but you should be aware that the type of variable will become important when you start to look at arithmetic and logic within Velocity templates.

Introducing Variable Concatenation

You'll often find it necessary to concatenate the values of two variables to produce the output you require. The simplest way to do this is to place the variable names next to each other in your template; that way, Velocity will render the values of the variables next to each other. For example:

```
#set($uname = "robh")
#set($suffix = "@cakesolutions.net")

My e-mail address is: $uname$suffix
```

When I run this template, I get the desired output, which is my full e-mail address:

```
My e-mail address is: robh@cakesolutions.net
```

Now, this is fine when I just want to output the value once, but what if I want to output the value multiple times? Repeating this same procedure multiple times throughout the template increases the chance that I will mess up and also makes modifications a nightmare. To solve this problem, in Java I'd simply create another variable that held the result of the concatenation and use that variable whenever I wanted to access the full e-mail address. Fortunately, I can do the same thing from within my Velocity template, like so:

```
#set($uname = "robh")
#set($suffix = "@cakesolutions.net")
#set($address = "$uname$suffix")

Mail me at: <a href="mailto:$address">$address</a>
```

Take a careful look at the syntax for concatenating the values and assigning the result to a new variable. The important part is that the two variable names are enclosed in double quotes. This behavior is known as *string interpolation*, and you can disable it by setting the `runtime.interpolate.string.literals` configuration property to `false`. You can also prevent individual `String` literals from being interpolated by enclosing them in single quotes instead of double quotes. By default, Velocity will look at all `String` literals and will attempt to replace any variable names with the corresponding value. The output generated by this template is as follows:

```
Mail me at: <a href="mailto:robh@cakesolutions.net">robh@cakesolutions.net</a>
```

The previous example of string interpolation is quite trivial, but it's powerful when used in the right places. What would happen if I wanted to output the e-mail link multiple times? I could cut and paste the appropriate template code for that fragment, which would give me the desired output, but when the time came to format the link, perhaps using CSS, I'd be forced to format each link individually. A better solution would be to create a variable to hold the link code and use that variable to output the link when needed. This does, however, throw up an interesting problem if I want the resultant output to be XHTML compliant and that is how I embed double quotes within the string. My first thought was to use single quotes to wrap the entire literal, and then I remembered that the string wouldn't get interpolated if I did, and I'd end up with the variable names in my output. My next thought was to use the escape character, a backslash like in Java, to escape the quotes and have them display. With the backslashes in the template, the code runs without any errors, but the slashes get included in the output, which isn't the desired effect. Finally, I came up with this solution:

```
#set($uname = "robh")
#set($suffix = "@cakesolutions.net")
#set($address = "$uname$suffix")
#set($quote = '"')
#set($link = "<a href=${quote}mailto:$address${quote}>$address</a>")

Mail me at: $link
```

The interesting lines in this example are the fourth and fifth lines. On the fourth line I created a variable named $quote and assigned it the value of one double quote. To assign this value I had to wrap it in single quotes, which meant I couldn't use string interpolation when assigning the value, but I didn't need to anyway, so that was unimportant. On the fifth line I created the $link variable using string interpolation to add the e-mail address and quotes at the correct places. The syntax used to access the $quote variable is the interesting part. Instead of just $quote, I used ${quote}; this is known as a *formal reference* and is used when you want to concatenate the value of a variable with some static content in the template. If I used a normal reference, the Velocity engine would think that $quotemailto: was the name of the variable I was trying to access. Using a formal reference, I can tell Velocity exactly which part of the string is the variable name and which part isn't. The output of this template is as follows, as desired:

```
Mail me at: <a href="mailto:robh@cakesolutions.net">robh@cakesolutions.net</a>
```

String interpolation is a powerful feature of Velocity, but it can prove tricky to get the output exactly as you want when using characters reserved for use by Velocity. If you follow the practices from the previous example, you shouldn't have any problems in this area.

Outputting Variable Names and the Dollar Symbol

In the previous example, I showed you how to output double quotes when using string interpolation. Although Velocity has no formal syntax for that kind of escaping, it does have support for outputting the names of variables and the dollar symbol.

Consider the following template example:

```
#set ($widgetCost = "12.99")
#set ($wotsitCost = "13.99")
Price List
----------

$widgetCost = $widgetCost
$wotsitCost = $wotsitCost
```

Whilst it's clear I want to display the variable name and the value, it's also clear that the actual output will be as follows:

```
Price List
----------

12.99 = 12.99
13.99 = 13.99
```

To display the name of variable that has a value, you need to prefix the variable name with the escape character, which, in keeping with Java, is \. So, to correct the previous template, you'd simply need to prefix each variable name with \ when you want the name to be displayed, like so:

```
#set ($widgetCost = "12.99")
#set ($wotsitCost = "13.99")
Price List
----------

\$widgetCost = $widgetCost
\$wotsitCost = $wotsitCost
```

Now that the template is corrected, the following output is as desired:

```
Price List
----------

$widgetCost = 12.99
$wotsitCost = 13.99
```

To display the \ character itself, you can just include it the template, but displaying $ isn't as simple. In the case where you want to display the $ character immediately before a variable value, you can simply include the $ character before the variable in your template, like so:

```
#set ($widgetCost = "12.99")
#set ($wotsitCost = "13.99")
Price List
----------

\$widgetCost = $$widgetCost
\$wotsitCost = $$wotsitCost
```

Notice that where I'm getting the values of the $widgetCost and $wotsitCost variables, I've added an additional $ character before the variable. When I run the example now, I get this output:

```
Price List
----------

$widgetCost = $12.99
$wotsitCost = $13.99
```

In fact, you can place the $ character on its own almost anywhere in the template, and it'll display just fine. The only place you can't have a $ character is as the last character in your template. So this template will work fine:

```
#set ($widgetCost = "12.99")
#set ($wotsitCost = "13.99")
Price List
----------

\$widgetCost = $$widgetCost
\$wotsitCost = $$wotsitCost

All prices in USD ($).
```

But if I remove the trailing) and . characters, I'll get a ParseException. The only way around this is to declare a variable with $ as its value and use that as the last value in your template, like so:

```
#set ($widgetCost = "12.99")
#set ($wotsitCost = "13.99")
#set ($dollar = "$")
Price List
----------

\$widgetCost = $$widgetCost
\$wotsitCost = $$wotsitCost

All prices in USD $dollar
```

Variables are an important part of how Velocity works, and understanding them correctly will enable you to get the most of the Velocity engine. This section has pretty much exhausted the topic of variable creation and manipulation; in the next section you'll look at the support for arithmetic in the Velocity runtime.

Performing Arithmetic

Along with support for integer primitives inside your templates, Velocity provides support for simple integer arithmetic. The arithmetic support is basic, supporting only five operators: +, -, *, /, and %. You're no doubt more than familiar with the first four operators, but you may not be as familiar with the fifth. The modulo (%) operator returns the remainder of a division. As an example, 20 / 3 equals 6 with 2 remaining, so 20 % 3 equals 2. All arithmetic works on integers, and the results will only ever be an integer, so 20 / 3 would return 6 as the answer when executed inside a Velocity template.

In the following example, I've used the arithmetic support of Velocity to add the shipping costs to my list of products:

```
#set ($widgetCost = 13)
#set ($wotsitCost = 14)
#set ($shipCost = 2)
#set ($widgetTotal = $widgetCost + $shipCost)
#set ($wotsitTotal = $wotsitCost + $shipCost)
Price List
----------

\$widgetCost = $$widgetCost $$widgetTotal
\$wotsitCost = $$wotsitCost $$wotsitTotal

All prices in USD ($).
```

Notice that the $widgetCost and $wotsitCost variables have been changed to integer literals as opposed to String literals. The arithmetic functions will work only on integer literals and not numbers contained within a String. You should also note that I had to change the item costs to integers, as Velocity doesn't support floating-point literals inside its templates. This template gives this output:

```
Price List
----------

$widgetCost = $13 $15
$wotsitCost = $14 $16

All prices in USD ($).
```

Using Directives

Up to now, the templates I've built have been quite small and basic; other than a few bits of simple arithmetic, they've done nothing particularly dynamic, and you may be thinking that you could have produced much of the output more easily using just Java—and for the most part you'd be right. This is where directives come into the picture. Using directives, you can start to make the output from your templates much more dynamic, as well as increase the reusability and modularity of the output. You've already seen one directive, #set, in action; the following sections cover the remaining directives that are included in the standard Velocity distribution.

Including Static Content with #include

If you're planning on building a Web site with Velocity, you'll no doubt have a large amount of content that's going to be common across your templates, such as page headers and footers. Thankfully, you aren't forced to include this content in every template. Instead, you can place the common content in a separate file and use the #include directive to have Velocity include it in another template. For example, consider a template to produce an HTML page, like this:

```
<html>
    <head>
        <title>Legolas Industries Homepage</title>
    </head>
    <body>
        <h1>Welcome!!</h1>
        #include("pageFooter.vm")
    </body>
</html>
```

Notice the #include directive near the bottom. This instructs the Velocity runtime to find the resource called pageFooter.vm, using the currently loaded resource loaders, and include it as-is into the output stream. If you couple this with the following pageFooter.vm template:

```
<h3>Copyright &copy; Legolas Industries 2004</h3>
```

and then run the driver program using only the path to the main template in the call to getTemplate(), you'll get the following output:

```
<html>
    <head>
        <title>Legolas Industries Homepage</title>
```

```
    </head>
    <body>
        <h1>Welcome!!</h1>
        <h3>Copyright &copy; Legolas Industries 2004</h3>    </body>
</html>
```

Notice that the #include directive has been replaced by the content of the resource that was provided as an argument to the #include directive. With #include, the contents of the include file are substituted for the directive itself. You can also pass multiple arguments to the #include directive to import multiple files in one go:

```
#include("HTMLFooter.vm", "HTMLLinkBar.vm")
```

If an error occurs when trying to include the content, then Velocity will write an entry in the log file, but you'll receive no error in your output, other than that the #include directive will render. You can tell Velocity to write error messages for the #include directive to the output stream by setting the directive.include.output.errormsg.start and directive.include.output.errormsg.end properties to the characters you want to be rendered at the start and end of the error message. An error message will be outputted only if both of these properties are set. So, what do you set them to be? Well, that all depends on the environment. If you're using Velocity in a production Web application but you want the error messages to be displayed in the output stream, then you can use <!-- for start and --> for end so that the message gets rendered inside an HTML comment. Of course, if you're in a development environment, you can make the error messages display in big, red text.

It's important to remember that resources included in the output using either #parse or #include are loaded using the resource loaders in the same way as your templates resources are. Be sure that the resource name you specify when calling #include or #parse is accessible using the current resource loader configuration.

The drawback of the #include directive is that any VTL content in the include files is ignored by Velocity and treated as static content, so you can't change the content of the included files based on any of the variables in the current context. However, this leads me quite nicely into a discussion of the #parse directive.

Embedding Other Templates with #parse

The #parse directive is designed to overcome the drawbacks with the #include directive by first running include files through the Velocity engine before including the fully parsed contents into the parent template. To highlight this, I've made a few small changes to the previous templates. In the main template, I've replaced the company name with a variable that's defined in the first line of the template.

You'll also notice that I've replaced the #include directive with a #parse directive and changed the resource name argument to pageFooter2.vm.

```
#set ($companyName = "Legolas Industries")
<html>
    <head>
        <title>$companyName Homepage</title>
    </head>
    <body>
        <h1>Welcome!!</h1>
        #parse("pageFooter2.vm")
    </body>
</html>
```

In the pageFooter2.vm template I replaced the company name with a reference to $companyName variable as I did in the main template, but you'll notice that this template doesn't define a value for the variable, as I want to use the value that's defined by the parent template.

```
<h3>Copyright &copy; $companyName 2004</h3>
```

When I run this through the same Java code as before, I get the following output:

```
<html>
    <head>
        <title>Legolas Industries Homepage</title>
    </head>
    <body>
        <h1>Welcome!!</h1>
        <h3>Copyright &copy; Legolas Industries 2004</h3>    </body>
</html>
```

As you can see, not only have the contents of the pageFooter2.vm template been included in place of the #parse directive, but the value of the $companyName variable has been replaced in both templates by the variable defined in the main template.

When using the #parse directive, the template containing the directive is considered the parent, and the template being parsed is considered the child. In this case, the child has access to all the variables in the parent template's context. When you define a variable in the child template, it's actually added to the parent template's context—essentially, all the templates in the tree share the same context. This may trip you up a little if you try to access a variable that's defined in the child template from the parent template *before* the child template has been parsed. In this case, the variable has no value and the name will be outputted, but if the child template has already been parsed, the variable value will be outputted. I know this is quite a complex topic to understand, so being the generous, kind-hearted person that I am, I have made another example. In this code, I have created another footer template, pageFooter3.vm, and have added a single variable declaration to it:

```
#set ($innerVar = "This is an inner variable")
<h3>Copyright &copy; $companyName 2004</h3>
```

I've also modified the main template and added two references to the $innerVar variable—one before the #parse directive and one after it.

```
#set ($companyName = "Legolas Industries")
<html>
    <head>
        <title>$companyName Homepage</title>
    </head>
    <body>
        <h1>Welcome!!</h1>
        $innerVar
        #parse("pageFooter3.vm")
        $innerVar
    </body>
</html>
```

If you run this example, you'll be presented with the following output:

```
<html>
    <head>
        <title>Legolas Industries Homepage</title>
    </head>
    <body>
        <h1>Welcome!!</h1>
        $innerVar
        <h3>Copyright &copy; Legolas Industries 2004</h3>
        This is an inner variable
    </body>
</html>
```

Notice that before the #parse directive the variable has no value, so the name is outputted, but after the #parse statement, when the child template has been parsed, $innerVar has a value, which is included in the output.

When Velocity parses a template that's embedded inside another template, the embedded template may also include #parse directives that Velocity will also process. Because of this behavior, it's possible you may eventually end up with circular references where one template includes another using #parse and that template in turn includes other templates through various nested #parse statements. The trouble occurs when one of these templates includes a #parse statement that refers to the root template and the parsing process continues on in an infinite loop. Well, not exactly. To prevent this kind of problem, Velocity has a built-in threshold—it'll support only ten nested #parse statements. If you have a real need for more nested #parse statements than this, then you can set the directive.parse.maxdepth property appropriately.

You may be wondering what the point of #include directive is when you have the #parse directive at your fingertips. Well, the answer is simple: performance. When you use the #parse directive, the Velocity engine will treat the file as another Velocity template and will parse it for variables and directives, but with the #include directive, Velocity will just read in the file contents and insert them into the output stream. When all you need to do is include the contents of a static resource, use #include, avoiding the overhead introduced by the Velocity engine.

Making Decisions with #if, #else, and #elseif

So far, all the templates I've written have been quite static. Aside from the occasional variable substitution or template import, nothing much has changed within the templates I've written—certainly, I haven't changed the structure of the output dramatically.

Velocity has quite sophisticated support for conditional blocks within your templates, and without them it wouldn't prove to be such a useful tool. The idea of the conditional statements in Velocity isn't to allow for complex business logic but more to support the logic needed to produce the kind of complex views that are required by today's Web applications. Can you imagine trying to build a Web application without being able to change the interface that's displayed to your users? How well would the login/logout functionality of any standard Web application work if you were unable to hide the logout button when a user is logged out and show it when they're logged in?

You'll be glad to hear that using the conditional directives in Velocity is no more complex than using any of the other VTL directives described previously.

At the most basic level, you have the #if directive, which is synonymous with the Java if statement. The #if directive is complemented by the #else directive, which allows you to provide some alternative output if the condition in the #if directive evaluates to false. To demonstrate this functionality, I've created the following variation on the previous example:

```
#set ($companyName = "Legolas Industries")
<html>
    <head>
        <title>$companyName Homepage</title>
    </head>
```

```
    <body>
        <h1>Welcome!!</h1>
        #if ($userType == "elf")
            <h2>You are an elf!</h2>
        #else
            <h2>I don't know what you are!</h2>
        #end
        #parse("pageFooter.vm")
    </body>
</html>
```

I've also changed the Java driver code slightly to add the $userType variable to VelocityContext. When you run this example, you get the following output:

```
<html>
    <head>
        <title>Legolas Industries Homepage</title>
    </head>
    <body>
        <h1>Welcome!!</h1>
                    <h2>You are an elf!</h2>
                <h3>Copyright &copy; Legolas Industries 2004</h3>
    </body>
</html>
```

You should also try running this example with a different value set for $userType. Of course, you're not just limited to simple conditional statements such as this one. Velocity also supports the #elseif directive, allowing you to make more complex decisions within your templates. For example:

```
#set ($companyName = "Legolas Industries")
<html>
    <head>
        <title>$companyName Homepage</title>
    </head>
    <body>
        <h1>Welcome!!</h1>
        #if ($userType == "human")
            <h2>You are a human!</h2>
        #elseif ($userType == "orc")
            <h2>You are an orc. Damn you're ugly!</h2>
        #elseif ($userType == "elf")
            <h2>You are an elf! How goes the pointy ears?</h2>
        #else
            <h2>I don't know what you are!</h2>
```

```
        #end
        #parse("pageFooter.vm")
    </body>
</html>
```

Try running this one with different values set for the $userType variable. You've seen the examples; now comes the science. The arguments within a conditional statement (the bit between the brackets) must evaluate to either true or false. You can obtain a true or false value from the result of a comparison, such as in the previous examples, and Velocity supports the following comparison operators: ==, !=, <, >, <=, and >=. You can also use the value of a Boolean variable as the value for your comparison. For example:

```
#set($myBool = true)
#if($myBool)
It is true
#else
It is false
#end
```

In this scenario, Velocity supports the use of the Boolean NOT operator (!), like so:

```
#set($myBool = false)
#if(!$myBool)
It is true
#else
It is false
#end
```

You should also be aware that although you can't pass in primitive boolean values from Java, you can pass in instances of the Boolean class, and they'll be treated appropriately in conditional statements.

Working with Collections Using #foreach

Building a Web application usually means working with a database, and this, in turn, usually means one thing: lists. The main reason you'd use a database is to store data, and since you're using a database to store the data, you're probably storing large lists of data rather than individual items. No view technology would be complete without the ability to output lists in a quick and efficient manner, and in Velocity this is executed with typical simplicity.

Using the #foreach directive you can repeat a block of your template for each item in a list of data, changing the output based on the current item in the list. When it comes to the actual lists, you have the following three options:

- Velocity arrays

- Velocity ranges

- Java collections (including Maps and Sets)

Velocity provides a simple syntax to build arrays internally, which can then be used with the #foreach directive to output a list of data. To declare an array variable, you use the #set directive with a different syntax for the variable value, like so:

```
#set (myArray = ["one", "two", "three"])
```

Notice that for the value I've added three separate values, delimited by commas, and I've wrapped the whole thing in square brackets. Once you have an array available in the active context, you can use the #foreach directive to loop through the elements and output them, like so:

```
#set ($myArray = ["one", "two", "three"])
#foreach($item in $myArray)
    List Item: $item
#end
```

When you run this through Velocity, you get the following output:

```
List Item: one
List Item: two
List Item: three
```

You should note that you don't have to declare the array as a variable; instead, you can use the array syntax in place of the array variable in the #foreach directive. The range operator in Velocity provides a simple way to declare an array of integers without having to specify every single integer; you just specify the beginning and end of the range, like so:

```
#foreach($number in [1..5])
        Current Index: $number
#end
```

In this example, the range is declared using [1..5], with 1 being the start of the range and 5 being the end. You can, of course, specify any integer for the start and end of the range. This example will create this output:

```
Current Index: 1
Current Index: 2
```

```
Current Index: 3
Current Index: 4
Current Index: 5
```

Note that in the previous example, I could have assigned the range to a variable instead of creating it directly inside of the #foreach directive. If you need to use a range of numbers or an array more than once in the same template, you should consider creating a variable to hold it, rather than re-creating it each time you use the #foreach directive.

Of course, both of these features are quite useful, but the real power comes from being able to pass in a Collection from your Java code and access the objects contained in it. Once you have a Collection of Objects, you can pass them into Velocity and have the template render the data as appropriate.

This next example is slightly more involved than the previous ones and returns to the previous example of a price list. What I want to achieve is a list of products and their prices. The products are described in Java as the Product class and are loaded from some data store and passed to the presentation tier in a Collection. I want to use Velocity to take this Collection of objects and build an HTML price list.

So first, I need the Product class in Java to hold the product details (see Listing 3-2).

Listing 3-2. The Product *Class*

```java
public class Product {

    private String name;
    private double price;

    public Product(String aName, double aPrice) {
        name = aName;
        price = aPrice;
    }

    public String getName() {
        return name;
    }

    public double getPrice() {
        return price;
    }

    public void setName(String val) {
        name = val;
    }
```

```
    public void setPrice(double val) {
        price = val;
    }
}
```

This is a basic class to hold the data for one product. It has two properties: Name and Price, with the corresponding get() and set() methods. The next thing I need to do is to create a Collection of Product objects and store the Collection in the VelocityContext; here is the code I added to the main() method of the driver program to do this:

```
// add products collection to the context
Collection products = new ArrayList();
products.add(new Product("Widget", 12.99));
products.add(new Product("Wotsit", 13.99));
products.add(new Product("Thingy", 11.99));
ctx.put("products", products);
```

As you can see, constructing the Collection and storing it in the VelocityContext is pretty basic stuff, but in real life you'd probably load the Product objects from a database, rather than having them hard-coded into your application. The final piece for this example is the template (see Listing 3-3).

Listing 3-3. Product List Template

```
<html>
    <head>
        <title>Gimli's Widgetarium</title>
    </head>
    <body>
        <table>
            #set ($rowCount = 1)
            #foreach($product in $products)
                #if ($rowCount % 2 == 0)
                    #set ($bgcolor = "#FFFFFF")
                #else
                    #set ($bgcolor = "#CCCCCC")
                #end
                <tr>
                    <td bgcolor="$bgcolor">$product.Name</td>
                    <td bgcolor="$bgcolor">$product.Price</td>
                </tr>
                #set ($rowCount = $rowCount + 1)
            #end
        </table>
    </body>
</html>
```

This template is quite complex and requires a little bit of explanation. Ignoring the static content, the bulk of the content in this template is created in the #foreach loop. The #foreach loop looks at each Product object stored in the $products Collection and outputs a table row for each one. If you look at the table cells, you'll notice that the actual properties of the Product objects are accessed using the shortcuts discussed earlier. The other interesting part of this template is the use of the modulo operator, coupled with the #if and #else directives. Using these constructs, I've differentiated between odd and even numbered rows in the table and colored them accordingly.

In the previous examples, I created a variable specifically to hold the row count. However, this was unnecessary, as the #foreach directive adds its own variable to the context, which maintains the current row count. By default, the name of this variable is $velocityCount, but you can override this by setting the directive.foreach.counter.name property to the name you'd like to use (don't include the dollar symbol). By default, Velocity starts this counter variable at 1; if you'd like to start at some other value, then you can set the directive.foreach.counter.initial.value property accordingly.

As you can see, using the #foreach directive is actually easy; you're limited only by your creativity. As with all of the directives in Velocity, #foreach has a simple syntax that provides enough power to support the creation of your view, but it's of little use for performing any kind of business logic. Most people, myself included, would find this to be a godsend, as it prevents any lax developers on your team from breaking your strict architecture.

Summarizing Directives

As you can see from the last few examples, the directives included with Velocity give you most of the features you need to create complex output quickly and easily. A trend you may have noticed from the examples is that whilst the templates themselves stay quite simple, the output they produce can be quite complex. This is especially true when you combine the decision-making functionality of the #if, #else, and #elseif directives with the Collection-handling capabilities of the #foreach directive. If you haven't fully understood the usage of these directives, I suggest you look over the previous section again and try out the examples for yourself before proceeding with the rest of the book.

Improving Reusability with Macros

In the previous section, I showed Velocity directives, but those of you familiar with Velocity will probably have noticed that I missed one. Velocity provides excellent support for macros, sometime called *Velocimacros*, using another directive: #macro. I've decided to separate the #macro directives from all of the other directives since you'll rarely use #macro directive within the body of your template; it tends to be something you use once or twice near the top of your template or in a separate include file, instead of referring to your defined macros in the body of your template.

For those of you who aren't familiar with the concept of macros, they're a way of packaging bits of functionality into a reusable unit. Macros in Velocity are simply a way of reducing the amount of code you need to type and maintain. When your template is parsed, any calls to a macro are expanded into the full code of that macro at the point in the template where the macro call exists. It's sort of like an automatic find and replace!

Using Macros

To declare a macro within your code, you use the #macro directive. Rather than give you a trivial example, I've rewritten the product list example to use a macro to output the table of products. The Java code for this example is the same; all that changes is the template, as shown in Listing 3-4.

Listing 3-4. The writeTable Macro

```
#macro (writeTable $productList)
    #set ($rowCount = 1)
    #foreach($product in $productList)
    #if ($rowCount % 2 == 0)
        #set ($bgcolor = "#FFFFFF")
    #else
        #set ($bgcolor = "#CCCCCC")
    #end
        <tr>
            <td bgcolor="$bgcolor">$product.Name</td>
            <td bgcolor="$bgcolor">$product.Price</td>
        </tr>
        #set ($rowCount = $rowCount + 1)
    #end
#end
<html>
    <head>
        <title>Gimli's Widgetarium</title>
    </head>
    <body>
        <table>
            #writeTable($products)
        </table>
    </body>
</html>
```

Notice that I've created a macro with the #macro directive. Inside the parentheses, the first argument for the #macro directive is the name of the macro you want to create; in this case, it's writeTable. All the remaining arguments are the names of arguments that you can pass to the macro; in this case, I have just one argument, $productList, but you can have as many arguments as you like. Inside the macro body, I use the #foreach directive to output the list of Product objects contained in the $productList argument. As you can see, the code inside the macro body is identical to the code used in the body of the previous example. Whereas before I had the code to render the table, I now call the macro using the #writeTable directive that's created by the macro declaration instead. In this particular case, using macro has no particular benefit; it would've been simpler to render the table directly. However, if I wanted to render the table again, I could reuse the macro. In the next section, I'll show you how to build a library of macros that can be used throughout your application.

Building a Macro Library

Macros provide a great way to reuse code within a template, but face it: The chances of you wanting to produce the same kind of table twice in an HTML page are slim. However, the chances of you wanting to create the same kind of table twice across an entire Web site aren't that slim. In fact, I'd wager you'll probably end up using the table more than twice. Consider a simple e-commerce site—on this type of site, a customer can view a list of all products ordered alphabetically, a list of products in a certain category, and a list of products that match certain search criteria. One thing is common across each of these three pages: They all display a list of products. Sure, the data in the lists will be different, but the structure and formatting of the list won't be—only the data changes. This is an ideal example of where a macro would be useful—if only you could share it across more than one template...well, thankfully, you can.

Creating a macro library for your Velocity application is simple. The first step is to create a file and put your macros into it. For example, I've taken the following macro from the previous section, renamed it, and put it into a file called macroLibrary.vm:

```
#macro (writeProductList $productList)
    #set ($rowCount = 1)
    #foreach($product in $productList)
    #if ($rowCount % 2 == 0)
        #set ($bgcolor = "#FFFFFF")
    #else
        #set ($bgcolor = "#CCCCCC")
    #end
        <tr>
```

```
            <td bgcolor="$bgcolor">$product.Name</td>
            <td bgcolor="$bgcolor">$product.Price</td>
        </tr>
        #set ($rowCount = $rowCount + 1)
    #end
#end
```

The next step is to let the Velocity runtime know where your macro library is. To do this, add the following line to your `velocity.properties` file:

```
velocimacro.library=macroLibrary.vm
```

Macro library resources are loaded in the same way as template resources, via a resource loader, so make sure that the `macroLibrary.vm` file is in a directory accessible by a currently configured resource loader. You don't actually need to set this property, since the Velocity runtime will automatically attempt to load a macro library from a resource named `VM_global_library.vm`. However, I prefer to override this and specify my own location because there's no guarantee that the default value won't change in some future release. You should also note that you can provide a comma-separated list of resource names, and Velocity will load macros from all the resources. This allows you to split macros into logical groups, making them much easier to manage in larger projects. Once you've done this, you can start with your templates. I've created two templates, which are identical apart from the value of the HTML `<title>` tag, based on my e-commerce site example. The first one is as follows:

```
<html>
    <head>
        <title>Gimli's Widgetarium | All Products</title>
    </head>
    <body>
        <table>
            #writeProductList($products)
        </table>
    </body>
</html>
```

And the second one is as follows:

```
<html>
    <head>
        <title>Gimli's Widgetarium | Search Results</title>
    </head>
    <body>
        <table>
```

```
                #writeProductList($products)
        </table>
    </body>
</html>
```

You can run this example without any changes to the Java code as the Collection of Product objects should already exist in the context from the previous macro example. Running the example for both templates gives you the output shown in Listing 3-5.

Listing 3-5. Product List Output

```
<html>
    <head>
        <title>Gimli's Widgetarium | All Products</title>
    </head>
    <body>
        <table>
        <tr>
            <td bgcolor="#CCCCCC">Widget</td>
            <td bgcolor="#CCCCCC">12.99</td>
        </tr>
        <tr>
            <td bgcolor="#FFFFFF">Wotsit</td>
            <td bgcolor="#FFFFFF">13.99</td>
        </tr>
        <tr>
            <td bgcolor="#CCCCCC">Thingy</td>
            <td bgcolor="#CCCCCC">11.99</td>
        </tr>
        </table>
    </body>
</html>
```

And it gives you the output shown in Listing 3-6.

Listing 3-6. Search Results Output

```
<html>
    <head>
        <title>Gimli's Widgetarium | Search Results</title>
    </head>
    <body>
        <table>
        <tr>
```

```
            <td bgcolor="#CCCCCC">Widget</td>
            <td bgcolor="#CCCCCC">12.99</td>
        </tr>
        <tr>
            <td bgcolor="#FFFFFF">Wotsit</td>
            <td bgcolor="#FFFFFF">13.99</td>
        </tr>
        <tr>
            <td bgcolor="#CCCCCC">Thingy</td>
            <td bgcolor="#CCCCCC">11.99</td>
        </tr>
        </table>
    </body>
</html>
```

All in all, that took about three minutes to get up and running, and if you
want to add another product list page to the site, then you can do so easily by
using the macro from the macro library.

Configuring Velocimacro

In the previous section, I showed you how to set up a library of macros for use
throughout an application. You can use a few more configuration parameters to
configure the behavior of macros within your application (see Table 3-1).

Table 3-1. Velocimacro Configuration Parameters

Parameter Name	Description
velocimacro.permissions.allow.inline	By default, this property is set to true, allowing for macros to be defined in templates as well as globally. Setting this to false means that macros can't be defined inside a template, and you must define them globally. You should note that if you set this parameter to false and then define a macro in a template, no error will occur. Instead, any attempt to reference the macro will result in the VTL markup being included in the output instead of the results of the macro.

Table 3-1. Velocimacro Configuration Parameters (continued)

Parameter Name	Description
`velocimacro.permissions.allow.inline.to.replace.global`	Setting this parameter to `true` allows for macros defined within a template to replace those defined globally. For instance, consider the previous example. By setting this parameter to `true`, you could define a macro called `#writeProductList` in each template. When the template then called the macro, the locally defined version would be used instead. You should remember two important points about this parameter. First, if inline macros are disabled, the value of this parameter is ignored and the global macro will be used; second, if this parameter is set to `false` and you do define an inline macro with the same name as a global macro, the inline macro is ignored and no error occurs.
`velocimacro.context.localscope`	By default, this parameter is set to `false`, which means that any modifications to variables using the #set directive are visible outside the macro. By setting this parameter to `true`, modifications to variables are visible only inside the macro.
`velocimacro.library.autoreload`	Setting this to `true` tells the Velocity runtime to check each macro library resource for modifications before parsing the macro. This works only if the caching is disabled on the resource loader that loaded the macro library resource. This feature isn't intended for a production environment. The default value is `false`.

You have one more configuration parameter; the effect of it is a little more complex than the rest, so it calls for an example to demonstrate it. This parameter is `velocimacro.permissions.allow.inline.local.scope`, and it defines whether an inline macro is visible outside of the defining template. By default, this value is set to `false`, meaning that inline macros are accessible only from within the template in which they're defined and can't be accessed from global macros. By setting this property to `true`, you can give global access to your local macros, allowing for some nifty little tricks. To see this in action, add the following two macros to your global macro library:

```
#macro (macro1)
Some output: #macro2()
#end
```

```
#macro (macro2)
I am a global macro!
#end
```

Now create a template with the following code and run the driver program:

```
Macro Output: #macro1()
```

The output should be as you expect:

```
Macro Output: Some output: I am a global macro!
```

You're probably thinking that nothing special has happened here, and it hasn't. The template calls #macro1, which is defined in the global macro library, which in turn calls #macro2, also defined in the macro library, and the output is created. However, the clever bit is yet to come. Create another template similar to the last, but this time add an inline macro declaration for #macro2, like so:

```
#macro (macro2)
I am a local macro!
#end
Macro Output: #macro1()
```

Before you run the driver program again, set the velocimacro.permissions .allow.inline.local.scope property to true in the velocity.properties file. Now run the driver program and marvel at the output:

```
Macro Output: Some output: I am a local macro!
```

That's correct; the global macro definition for #macro2 has been overridden by the local definition; not only that, but the global macro #macro1 was able to access it. Whilst the example was quite trivial, this mechanism provides a perfect way for you to provide hook points into your global macros that can be overridden in each template. For instance, the #writeProductList macro from the earlier example could use a macro to get the colors for each row; a default macro would be defined globally for the basic colors, but if a template wanted to override the colors used, it could just provide its own version of macro.

Overcoming VTL Shortcomings with VelocityTools

VTL is a flexible language that will meet your needs for most templates; however, it's lacking in a few key areas, namely:

- Formatting numbers

- Formatting dates

- Doing arithmetic with floating-point numbers

- Performing early loop termination

Thankfully, Velocity recognized the need for solutions to these problems and provided a set of tools with the VelocityTools project to overcome them. If you don't already have VelocityTools, refer to Chapter 2 for instructions on how to obtain it.

Before looking at each individual tool, you'll look at what a tool is. Simply put, a *tool* is a class that's accessible using VTL from within your template. In fact, tools are just that—simple classes. You have no special interfaces to be implemented or base classes to be inherited from when building a tool; all you need is a class. Tools are intended to be loaded automatically by some kind of container, and when you use VelocityViewServlet for Web applications, they are. However, since the rest of the examples are going to be run from the command-line, like the previous examples, I'll have to load them and add them to the context myself. You may find that you have to do this in your own applications, especially if they're desktop applications that have no container such as VelocityViewServlet.

Formatting Numbers with NumberTool

For all of these examples, I've used the latest version of VelocityTools available, which is 1.1 RC-1. By the time the book is published, I anticipate that VelocityTools 1.1 will be a final release. However, I don't anticipate any changes affecting the code in this chapter. I won't repeat the API documentation for each of the tools; instead, I'll show you an example of how you can use the tool and then you can check out the API documentation yourself. To get started, create a Java class with the code shown in Listing 3-7.

Listing 3-7. Using NumberTool

```
package com.apress.pjv.ch3;

import java.io.StringWriter;
import java.io.Writer;
import java.util.Locale;

import org.apache.velocity.Template;
import org.apache.velocity.VelocityContext;
import org.apache.velocity.app.Velocity;
import org.apache.velocity.tools.generic.NumberTool;
```

```
public class NumberToolExample {

    public static void main(String[] args) throws Exception{
        // init
        Velocity.init("src/velocity.properties");

        // get the template
        Template t = Velocity.getTemplate("numberTool.vm");

        // create context
        VelocityContext ctx = new VelocityContext();
        ctx.put("number", new NumberTool());
        ctx.put("aNumber", new Double(0.95));
        ctx.put("aLocale", Locale.UK);

        // create the output
        Writer writer = new StringWriter();
        t.merge(ctx, writer);

        // output
        System.out.println(writer);
    }
}
```

Notice that I've added an instance of NumberTool to the context; this makes the tool accessible from my template. Now, create a template with the following code:

```
Integer Formatting:      $number.format("integer", $aNumber)
Currency Formatting:     $number.format("currency", $aNumber)
Number Formatting:       $number.format("number", $aNumber)
Percentage Formatting:   $number.format("percent", $aNumber)

Currency (with Locale): $number.format("currency", $aNumber, $aLocale)
```

As you can see, NumberTool provides four named formats that can be used with the current Locale or, as in the last line of the template, can be used with an arbitrary instance of Locale.

Formatting Dates with DateTool

If your applications require date output, then you certainly need to familiarize yourself with DateTool, which adds excellent date and time formatting support to Velocity. Using DateTool, you can provide formatted output for the current date or access any Calendar or Date object stored in the context and format that as well. Not only that, but DateTool supports formatting based not only on the current Locale but also on any arbitrary Locale instance stored in the context. As with NumberTool, I don't want to repeat the API documentation; instead, I'll give you an example of how DateTool works and then you can check out the API documentation yourself for more details.

To start, create a new Java class with the code shown in Listing 3-8.

Listing 3-8. Using DateTool

```
package com.apress.pjv.ch3;

import java.io.StringWriter;
import java.io.Writer;
import java.util.Calendar;
import java.util.TimeZone;

import org.apache.velocity.Template;
import org.apache.velocity.VelocityContext;
import org.apache.velocity.app.Velocity;
import org.apache.velocity.tools.generic.DateTool;

    public class DateToolExample {

    public static void main(String[] args) throws Exception {
        // init
        Velocity.init("src/velocity.properties");

        // get the template
        Template t = Velocity.getTemplate("dateTool.vm");

        // create context
        VelocityContext ctx = new VelocityContext();
        ctx.put("date", new DateTool());

        Calendar aDate = Calendar.getInstance(TimeZone.getTimeZone("PST"));
        aDate.set(2040, 11, 25);

        ctx.put("aDate", aDate);

        // create the output
        Writer writer = new StringWriter();
        t.merge(ctx, writer);

        // output
        System.out.println(writer);
    }
}
```

Then create the following `dateTool.vm` template:

```
Today's date is:        $date
Today's date is also:  $date.long    #* using property shortcut *#
Today's date is also:  $date.get('long')    #* using full syntax *#
The date and time is:  $date.default $date.short

Another date is:        $aDate
Another date is also:  $date.format('medium', $aDate)
```

When you run the example, you'll get output similar to the following:

```
Today's date is:        21-Feb-2004 11:46:34
Today's date is also:  21 February 2004 11:46:34 GMT
Today's date is also:  21 February 2004 11:46:34 GMT
The date and time is:  21-Feb-2004 11:46:34 21/02/04 11:46

Another date is:        java.util.GregorianCalendar...
Another date is also:  25-Dec-2040 11:46:34

Another date is: $date.toDate("10-Feb-2004 12:00:00")
```

Don't be alarmed if your dates aren't formatted in the same way as mine; the `Locale` for your machine is probably set to something different than mine is.

Performing Floating-Point Arithmetic with MathTool

One of the more annoying deficiencies of VTL is the lack of support for floating-point arithmetic. This can be a real limiting factor for e-commerce sites that often have to perform simple arithmetic on currency values to provide the user with information such as the total of their shopping cart. Fortunately, `MathTool` fills the gap left by VTL. `MathTool` supports most common arithmetic operations and some basic operations such as random number generation. A really useful feature of `MathTool` is that it will parse floating-point numbers from `String` literals, which is good because even with `MathTool`, you still can't have a floating-point literal within your template. In keeping with the rest of the tools, I won't repeat the API documentation here; instead, I'll give you an example (although most of the API is included in this example).

Create the Java class shown in Listing 3-9.

Listing 3-9. Using `MathTool`

```
package com.apress.pjv.ch3;

import java.io.StringWriter;
import java.io.Writer;
```

```java
import org.apache.velocity.Template;
import org.apache.velocity.VelocityContext;
import org.apache.velocity.app.Velocity;
import org.apache.velocity.tools.generic.MathTool;

public class MathToolExample {

    public static void main(String[] args) throws Exception {
        // init
        Velocity.init("src/velocity.properties");

        // get the template
        Template t = Velocity.getTemplate("mathTool.vm");

        // create context
        VelocityContext ctx = new VelocityContext();
        ctx.put("math", new MathTool());
        ctx.put("aNumber", new Double(5.5));

        // create the output
        Writer writer = new StringWriter();
        t.merge(ctx, writer);

        // output
        System.out.println(writer);
    }
}
```

Next, create the `mathTool.vm` template with the following code:

```
$aNumber + 3.2 = $math.add($aNumber, "3.2")
$aNumber - 3.2 = $math.sub($aNumber, "3.2")
$aNumber / 3.2 = $math.div($aNumber, "3.2")
$aNumber * 3.2 = $math.mul($aNumber, "3.2")
$aNumber ^ 3.2 = $math.pow($aNumber, "3.2")

The minimum of $aNumber and 3.2 is $math.min($aNumber, "3.2")
The maximum of $aNumber and 3.2 is $math.max($aNumber, "3.2")

4.45678 rounded to 3 places is $math.roundTo(3, "4.45678")
4.45678 rounded to the nearest integer is $math.roundToInt("4.45678")

$math.random is a random number

$math.random(1, 20) is a random number between 1 and 20
```

Notice that I've used the number 3.2 directly within the template but as a `String` literal, not a numeric literal. This is the only way to pass floating-point numbers that aren't defined in the context to `MathTool`. Running the example will yield output similar to this:

```
5.5 + 3.2 = 8.7
5.5 - 3.2 = 2.3
5.5 / 3.2 = 1.71875
5.5 * 3.2 = 17.6
5.5 ^ 3.2 = 233.97023236799288

The minimum of 5.5 and 3.2 is 3.2
The maximum of 5.5 and 3.2 is 5.5

4.45678 rounded to 3 places is 4.457
4.45678 rounded to the nearest integer is 4

0.1346779786701302 is a random number

10 is a random number between 1 and 20
```

The random numbers should be different in your output and should change each time you run the example.

Performing Advanced Looping with IteratorTool

The `#foreach` directive is one of the most useful directives in VTL, allowing you to create full lists of output with little code. One of the drawbacks of `#foreach` is that you can't exit the loop early. So, if you have 1,000 records and you want to output only 3 and they all appear in the first 20 records, `#foreach` will still go through the other 980 iterations. Using `IteratorTool`, you can overcome this problem and leave a `#foreach` loop early, based on some arbitrary condition. The `IteratorTool` works by wrapping a `Collection` or array and overriding the default behavior for moving to the next item. Using an `IteratorTool`-wrapped `Collection`, you specifically have to request the next item in the list, so when your exit condition is reached, you simply stop requesting any more items. To see this in action, create a Java class with the code shown in Listing 3-10.

Listing 3-10. Looping with IteratorTool

```java
package com.apress.pjv.ch3;

import java.io.StringWriter;
import java.io.Writer;
```

```
import org.apache.velocity.Template;
import org.apache.velocity.VelocityContext;
import org.apache.velocity.app.Velocity;
import org.apache.velocity.tools.generic.IteratorTool;

public class IteratorToolExample {

    public static void main(String[] args) throws Exception {
        // init
        Velocity.init("src/velocity.properties");

        // get the template
        Template t = Velocity.getTemplate("iteratorTool.vm");

        // create context
        VelocityContext ctx = new VelocityContext();
        ctx.put("mill", new IteratorTool());

        // create the output
        Writer writer = new StringWriter();
        t.merge(ctx, writer);

        // output
        System.out.println(writer);
    }
}
```

The name used for the IteratorTool, mill, is recommended in the VelocityTools documentation. Now create the iteratorTool.vm template with the following code:

```
#set($list = ["apple", "bat", "cat", "dog", "egg"])
#set($items = $mill.wrap($list))

#foreach($item in $items)
#if($velocityCount <= 3)
 $items.more()
#end
#end
```

In the first line, I've created a small array, and in the second line I've wrapped this array using IteratorTool. Inside the #foreach loop, I check to see whether the current iteration count is less than or equal to three. If it is, I request the next item in the list using IteratorTool.more(), which will also write the current item to the output stream. When the iteration count is greater than three, I stop requesting new items and the loop exits. Run the example, and you'll get the following the output:

```
apple
bat
cat
```

As you can see, only the first three items are outputted.

Performing Runtime VTL Evaluation with RenderTool

I've included RenderTool for the sake of completeness, but I have yet to find a use
for it. Using RenderTool you can build VTL expressions at runtime and have them
evaluated dynamically. This tool is straightforward to use, and the API has very
few methods. To get started with the example, create a Java class with the code
shown in Listing 3-11.

Listing 3-11. Runtime Evaluation with RenderTool

```java
package com.apress.pjv.ch3;

import java.io.StringWriter;
import java.io.Writer;

import org.apache.velocity.Template;
import org.apache.velocity.VelocityContext;
import org.apache.velocity.app.Velocity;
import org.apache.velocity.tools.generic.RenderTool;

public class RenderToolExample {

    public static void main(String[] args) throws Exception {
        // init
        Velocity.init("src/velocity.properties");

        // get the template
        Template t = Velocity.getTemplate("renderTool.vm");

        // create context
        VelocityContext ctx = new VelocityContext();
        ctx.put("render", new RenderTool());
        ctx.put("str", new String("The One Ring"));
        ctx.put("ctx", ctx);

        // create the output
        Writer writer = new StringWriter();
        t.merge(ctx, writer);
```

```
        // output
        System.out.println(writer);
    }
}
```

The important thing to notice here is that I've placed a reference to context inside the context itself. This will allow me to access the VelocityContext object directly from within my template, something that's required by RenderTool. Next, create a template using the following code:

```
#set($methods = ["length()", "toString()", "toLowerCase()", "toUpperCase()"])
#set($name = '$str')

#foreach($method in $methods)
$render.eval($ctx, "${name}.$method")
#end
```

Notice that when setting the $name variable to $str, I've used single quotes to disable string interpolation for this variable. Otherwise, the $name variable would have the value of $str variable assigned to it and not the value $str. Then in the #foreach loop, I build an expression for the current method and evaluate it using the RenderTool. The output from this example is as follows:

```
12
The One Ring
the one ring
THE ONE RING
```

You can see that each iteration in the #foreach loop executes the current method of the $str object.

Summary

This chapter has looked in detail at all aspects for VTL and its usage. Specifically, you've looked at how to create and access variables, how to access methods and properties of objects, and the syntax shortcuts made available by VTL. You looked at the basic arithmetic support offered by Velocity and also the core set of directives you can use to build your templates. You've seen how to create Velocimacros and how you can create your own reusable library of macros, improving the maintainability of your applications. Lastly, you looked at how you can use VelocityTools to overcome some of the shortcomings in VTL and get greater control over formatting and better support for arithmetic.

In the next chapter, you'll look at a full application built using Velocity, as well as some patterns and practices you can use to make your Velocity applications more maintainable and extensible.

### CHAPTER 4

Introducing Patterns and Best Practices

IN THIS CHAPTER, you'll look at a collection of patterns and best practices that you can use with Velocity to make your applications more easily maintainable and extensible. I also have provided a few hints and tips that I've found useful when developing applications with Velocity. The patterns and practices here should apply to all kinds of applications; the next two chapters look specifically at building stand-alone and Web-based applications with Velocity and at the patterns and practices particular to both.

This chapter is split into three sections, covering the following:

General hints and tips: I'll provide a collection of hints, tips, and code snippets that I've found useful whilst developing Velocity-based applications. Many of these tips are useful only if you're developing applications that are built directly using Velocity, but as you'll see, you can bring them together to provide a cohesive framework.

MVC best practices: Velocity is a great tool for use in an MVC-based application, particularly on the Web. However, you should apply many of the principles of MVC whenever you use Velocity. In this section, I'll address using Velocity for MVC-based applications and show how you can apply the principles of MVC to all Velocity-based applications.

Building a templating framework: Whilst Velocity is a fantastic template engine, it may be that in the future a better solution will present itself. If you build an application that's completely independent of Velocity, migrating to this new technology may be quite a task. In this section, I'll show you how you can build a generic templating framework that will decouple your application from Velocity and also provide a simpler API for creating applications with templating support.

Hints, Tips, and Best Practices

In the following sections, you'll see some general hints and tips you can use to ease the development and maintenance of your Velocity-based applications. Specifically, you'll look at the following:

Context manipulation: The context is a pivotal part of Velocity, and ensuring that you place the correct information in the context can be a nightmare when you have more than a few templates. Also, if you have a particularly large amount of data that needs to be written to the context, the chance of encountering coding errors is quite high. You'll see some simple solutions to these problems.

Runtime instance management: I've touched on this point in previous chapters, and it's quite important if you want your applications to perform acceptably. In this section, I'll present a more detailed look at the issues related to runtime instance management and show how to create a simple solution to the problems related to this matter.

Exception handling: In this section, you'll look at some of the matters related to handling exceptions thrown by the Velocity runtime.

Resource loader practices: Picking a resource loader and configuring it correctly can be a confusing topic. In this section, I'll show you how to choose the correct resource loader for your particular application and how to configure the resource loader appropriately.

VTL techniques: The VTL syntax is quite clean, and you have rarely more than one way to achieve a particular goal. However, you can use a few techniques to make your templates easier to manage and decrease their rendering time.

Using and Manipulating the Context

As I mentioned earlier, the context is a pivotal part of Velocity; without it, you'd have no way to pass data to the Velocity runtime for inclusion in the generated output.

Using Context Rather Than VelocityContext

In most of the examples from the previous chapters, you saw code similar to this when creating a context instance:

```
VelocityContext ctx = new VelocityContext();
```

However, this is bad practice, especially since the Velocity designers went to the trouble of designing Velocity to work with the Context interface rather than the VelocityContext concrete subclass. You should always follow the practice of using the most generic interface or class possible without losing the typing you require. For instance, in this case, the code would be better written as follows:

```
Context ctx = new VelocityContext();
```

In this way, you can easily replace the context implementation with a custom implementation.

Creating a Context Factory

Even if you declare the context as type Context, changing the implementation of the context class will still prove difficult if you have many different classes that create and populate a context. In this case, you can use the Factory pattern to extract the instantiation of the concrete instance to a separate class.

 TIP *If you're unfamiliar with the Factory design pattern, then you should definitely read* Design Patterns: Elements of Reusable Object-Oriented Software *by Gamma, Helm, Johnson, and Vlissides (Addison-Wesley, 1995) by the famous Gang of Four. This is a must-read book for any developer.*

Creating a Factory for context creation is fairly simple: You really need only one method that returns an instance of your chosen Context implementation. Make sure that the return type is declared as Context and not VelocityContext; you don't want to force your custom implementation to derive from VelocityContext, thus losing its single shot at concrete inheritance. Listing 4-1 shows an example of the ContextFactory class that I use in most of my applications.

Listing 4-1. ContextFactory *Class Example*

```
package com.apress.pjv.ch4;

import java.util.Map;

import org.apache.velocity.VelocityContext;
import org.apache.velocity.context.Context;

public class ContextFactory {

    public static Context getInstance() {
        return new VelocityContext();
    }

    public static Context getInstance(Map map) {
        return new VelocityContext(map);
    }
```

```
    public static Context getInstance(Context innerContext) {
        return new VelocityContext(innerContext);
    }

    public static Context getInstance(Map map, Context innerContext) {
        return new VelocityContext(map, innerContext);
    }
}
```

Notice that I've added some additional methods to the ContextFactory class that enable a context to be constructed from a Map instance, as well as enabling context chaining. Now, when creating a Context instance in your code, you simply call the getInstance() method on the ContextFactory class, like so:

```
Context ctx = ContextFactory.getInstance();
```

You may choose to load the name of the Context implementation class from a configuration file and then create the instance using reflection. Using this approach is quite acceptable, but sometimes, such as when you create a custom implementation of Context with nonstandard constructors, you'll need to edit the code in the factory by hand.

Populating the Context

The context can hold any kind of Java Object, which makes it very flexible. However, my preference is to ensure that all Objects I place in the context, besides Strings, Dates, and the primitive wrappers, are JavaBeans. This means that whoever is developing the template can take advantage of the simpler JavaBeans-based syntax when accessing context data. The choice you have when populating the context is whether to copy properties from JavaBeans directly into the context or to place the bean itself into the context. My choice is always to place the bean in the context, as it means that as new properties are added to the bean, there's no need to change the code that populates the context. Also, this method removes any issues that may occur when I want to place the properties of two beans into the context and the beans have properties with the same names. If, however, you want to place values from bean properties directly into the context—maybe you already have a set of templates that have been built this way—then you can reduce the development burden by using introspection to copy the property values dynamically from the bean into the context, as shown in Listing 4-2.

Listing 4-2. The ContextUtils *Class*

```
package com.apress.pjv.ch4;

import java.beans.BeanInfo;
import java.beans.IntrospectionException;
import java.beans.Introspector;
import java.beans.PropertyDescriptor;
import java.lang.reflect.InvocationTargetException;
import java.util.HashMap;
import java.util.Map;

import org.apache.velocity.context.Context;

public class ContextUtils {

    private static Map propertyCache = null;

    static {
        propertyCache = new HashMap();
    }

    public static void addPropertiesToContext(Context ctx, Object bean)
            throws IntrospectionException, IllegalAccessException,
            InvocationTargetException {

        // try to retrieve the properties from the cache
        PropertyDescriptor[] props = (PropertyDescriptor[]) propertyCache
                .get(bean.getClass());

        // no properties in the cache - find them and add them to the cache
        if (props == null) {
            BeanInfo inf = Introspector.getBeanInfo(bean.getClass());
            props = inf.getPropertyDescriptors();

            synchronized (propertyCache) {
                propertyCache.put(bean.getClass(), props);
            }
        }

        // retrieve the property values and add them to context
        for (int x = 0; x < props.length; x++) {
            PropertyDescriptor prop = props[x];

            ctx.put(prop.getName(), prop.getReadMethod().invoke(bean, null));
        }

    }

}
```

Of course, this approach works only if the VTL variables have the same name as the corresponding bean property. If this isn't the case and you're left with a template that requires individual context variables for each value, but the variable names don't match the names of the corresponding JavaBean property, you should consider modifying the template to use a single bean reference internally and then just add the bean to the context.

Try to avoid placing any complex objects in the context and accessing methods on those objects from within the templates. As you'll see when you look at building MVC-based applications with Velocity in the "Using Velocity in an MVC Environment" section, and when building a generic templating engine framework, this passes too much responsibility to the Velocity engine and also increases the coupling between your applications and Velocity.

Runtime Instance Management

As you saw in Chapter 2, you have two mechanisms for interacting with the Velocity runtime. The first is to use the singleton instance maintained by the `Velocity` helper class, and the second is to use individual instances via the `VelocityEngine` class. Unfortunately, neither of these is an ideal solution.

By using the Velocity helper class, you're at the mercy of any other applications loaded into the same JVM that may be using Velocity. For instance, it may be that a servlet container uses Velocity internally for some purpose, or it may be that you're developing a tool that will be used by other applications that use Velocity. In these cases, if your application is sharing the runtime instance managed by the Velocity class with other applications, it's also sharing the configuration for those applications. This can lead to unwanted behavior when the two configurations clash, and either your application or the other application may function incorrectly.

 NOTE *In a Web application context, whether you share the Velocity class with the container will depend on the classloading behavior of your container.*

If you choose to use the `VelocityEngine` class and you create a new instance every time you want to create some output from a template, you lose any benefit of caching that you may gain from your chosen resource loader. What you really need is a way to maintain a singleton instance of the Velocity runtime just for your application. Fortunately, this is quite simple: all you need to do is place a simple wrapper around the `VelocityEngine` class, as shown in Listing 4-3.

Listing 4-3. The VelocityManager *Class*

```
package com.apress.pjv.ch4;

import java.io.IOException;
import java.io.Reader;
import java.io.Writer;
import java.util.Properties;

import org.apache.velocity.Template;
import org.apache.velocity.app.VelocityEngine;
import org.apache.velocity.context.Context;
import org.apache.velocity.exception.MethodInvocationException;
import org.apache.velocity.exception.ParseErrorException;
import org.apache.velocity.exception.ResourceNotFoundException;

public class VelocityManager {

    private static VelocityEngine engine;

    static {
        engine = new VelocityEngine();
    }

    private VelocityManager() {
        // prevent instantiation from outside the class
    }

    public static void init() throws Exception {
        engine.init();
    }

    public static void init(Properties props) throws Exception {
        engine.init(props);
    }

    public static void init(String fileName) throws Exception {
        engine.init(fileName);
    }

    public static void addProperty(String key, Object value) {
        engine.addProperty(key, value);
    }

    public static void clearProperty(String key) {
        engine.clearProperty(key);
    }
```

```java
public static Object getProperty(String key) {
    return engine.getProperty(key);
}

public static void setProperty(String key, Object value) {
    engine.setProperty(key, value);
}

public static void evaluate(Context ctx, Writer writer, String logTag,
        Reader reader) throws IOException, MethodInvocationException,
        ParseErrorException, ResourceNotFoundException {
    engine.evaluate(ctx, writer, logTag, reader);
}

public static void evaluate(Context ctx, Writer writer, String logTag,
        String inString) throws IOException, MethodInvocationException,
        ParseErrorException, ResourceNotFoundException {
    engine.evaluate(ctx, writer, logTag, inString);
}

public static Template getTemplate(String name) throws Exception,
        ParseErrorException, ResourceNotFoundException {
    return engine.getTemplate(name);
}

public static Template getTemplate(String name, String encoding)
        throws Exception, ParseErrorException, ResourceNotFoundException {
    return engine.getTemplate(name, encoding);
}

public static boolean mergeTemplate(String name, Context ctx, Writer writer)
        throws Exception {
    return engine.mergeTemplate(name, ctx, writer);
}

public static boolean mergeTemplate(String name, String encoding,
        Context ctx, Writer writer) throws Exception {
    return engine.mergeTemplate(name, encoding, ctx, writer);
}
}
```

Notice that I've added some simple static helper methods to the class that match the method signatures of the Velocity class. I haven't included all the methods from the VelocityEngine class in the example, but you get the idea. In this way, you can use this class as a direct replacement for the Velocity helper class.

Exception Handling

My biggest annoyance with many tools is the overuse of checked exceptions. This is quite a contentious issue, as the accepted thinking is that checked exceptions are good and that they encourage good programming. In my opinion, they're overused and lead to messy code with an overabundance of try/catch statements.

 TIP *The issue of checked exceptions versus unchecked exceptions is discussed in much more detail in the excellent* Expert One-on-One J2EE Design and Development *by Rod Johnson (Wrox, 2002). As Rod rightly points out, emerging APIs such as JDO use unchecked exceptions almost exclusively for a specific reason.*

Don't get me wrong; there's definitely a case for checked exceptions, but I think that case is much rarer than we're led to believe. Consider a simple example: If a template has an error, the Velocity runtime will throw a `ParseErrorException` or one of its subclasses. Since the template has an error in it, there's not much you can do about it; your application is certainly not going to be able to recover gracefully and magically fix the template before retrying the operation. Yet you're forced to catch the exception and do something with it or let it progress up the call stack. In the trivial examples you've seen so far, letting the exception move up the call stack has been acceptable, but, as you'll see, in order to decouple your applications from Velocity completely, you have to wrap any checked exceptions in a generic framework exception and rethrow them. With unchecked exceptions, you avoid the need for this completely, as client code can remain blissfully unaware of the applications that may occur. Of course, you can still catch unchecked if you need to do so—you're just not forced into doing so when you'd rather just let the exception shoot up the call stack.

You may be thinking that checked exceptions help you build more robust applications by forcing you to catch exceptions that could cause your application to fail. However, this isn't entirely true. In a Web application, the servlet container will catch any uncaught exceptions and handle them to prevent the application from ending abruptly, and you can configure a friendly error page that will be displayed to the user on such an occasion. Looking at the alternative, you could explicitly catch the exception and then display an error page, since the error is unrecoverable. The outcome of both is the same, except that when using checked exceptions, you have to write and therefore maintain more code to reach the same outcome. The same behavior is true of stand-alone applications, except that you'll have to provide the code to catch uncaught errors yourself; this is a job that isn't particularly difficult.

So when are checked exceptions useful? Checked exceptions are useful when there's a real chance that the calling can recover from the exception or when the exception is essentially an alternative return value. An example of this may be where a template is loaded from a remote server. A checked exception would be thrown if the remote server is busy, as the calling code could realistically implement an algorithm to retry ten seconds later. However, in the case where the remote server was completely uncontactable, then an unchecked exception would be thrown, since there's no realistic way that the calling code could recover from that exception. Therefore, you gain no benefit from forcing the code to catch an exception it can't do anything with.

So where does this all fit in with Velocity? Well, unfortunately all Velocity-related exceptions are checked, so you're forced to catch them all at some point. When you look at decoupling your applications from Velocity in the "Using Velocity in an MVC Environment" section, you'll see how you can replace this exception handling behavior with something a little easier to use.

Resource Loader Practices

Resource loaders are a key part of the Velocity engine and, when used correctly, can provide your application with a performance and maintenance boost. In the following sections, you'll look at how to pick the correct resource loader and when it's appropriate to bypass to the resource loader system.

Choosing a Resource Loader

Choosing which resource loader to use can be quite a difficult decision if you're unaware of the repercussions of your decision. However, in my experience it's better to use `FileResourceLoader` or `ClasspathResourceLoader` rather than `JarResourceLoader` and `DataSourceResourceLoader`. The reasons I don't like `JarResourceLoader` are its lack of caching support and it's not a simple job for a nonprogrammer to change a resource that's contained within a JAR file. For a Web application, this can be a real problem because the templates will often be created and maintained by the design team, rather than the development team. My reasons for not liking `DataSourceResourceLoader` are similar—although `DataSourceResourceLoader` supports caching, it's just as complex for a designer to change a template that's stored in a database as it is for a template stored in a JAR file.

Overall, my preference lies with `FileResourceLoader` since it has full support for caching, and changing a template in the stored in the file system is a simple job for a designer. However, `FileResourceLoader` can prove problematic, especially in Web applications, when determining the current folder is difficult and in some cases impossible. In this case, I tend to lean toward `ClasspathResourceLoader`. The only problem with `ClasspathResourceLoader` is that once a template has been cached, it won't be reloaded if it's modified, which can greatly increase the time required to test templates in a Web application, since you have to undeploy the application to make changes. If this is a major problem, see Chapter 10 where I demonstrate how to create a custom resource loader that provides a potential solution to this problem. However, nothing is preventing you from using FileResourceLoader to test your application and ClasspathResourceLoader to deploy it.

Using evaluate() Appropriately

If you have checked out the Velocity JavaDoc you may be aware that by using the evaluate() method of either Velocity or VelocityEngine, you can bypass the resource loader mechanism and provide a template directly to the Velocity runtime using an instance of Reader. By doing this, you're bypassing all the features provided by the Velocity resource management system, including caching and external configuration. In most cases, it's not appropriate to use an instance of Reader—why go to the trouble of creating a FileReader and passing it to Velocity, when you can let the Velocity runtime take care of that for you and get caching support to boot? The only time it's suitable to use a Reader instance is when you want to create the contents of a template dynamically in your code and then have Velocity work on that template. In this case, using an instance of StringReader to pass the template content to Velocity is acceptable. In all other cases, you should either use a prebuilt resource loader or consider implementing your own, as described in Chapter 10.

VTL Techniques

In the following sections, you'll look at a few practices and techniques that you can use to ensure that your Velocity templates perform as well as they can and that they're easily maintainable.

Using Single Quotes Where Possible

In Chapter 3 you looked at the concept of string interpolation, which allowed for String literals in a Velocity template to include VTL variable references, which are then subsequently parsed by the Velocity runtime to be replaced by the corresponding value. To mark a String literal for string interpolation, you use double quotes, and to instruct Velocity not to interpolate a String literal, you use single quotes. Whenever you have a String literal that doesn't contain a VTL variable, always use single quotes to avoid the overhead of parsing that string for variable references.

Separating Reusable Content into Separate Resources

Most applications will use standard content fragments across many different pieces of content. Consider a standard Web application, which has a header at the top of every page and a navigation bar on the left side of every page. If you were to build this Web application using Velocity, you could create a template for each page and include the appropriate VTL and HTML to create the header and navigation bar in each template. However, doing this greatly increases the maintenance burden; imagine what would happen when it comes time to change some of the text in the header—you'd have to make the change in every single template. Not only that, but you have to ensure that every template contains the same VTL markup for the header and the navigation bar—obviously, the chance for errors occurring increases greatly.

Using this method leads to what I consider to be one of the cardinal sins of software development: reuse by cut and paste. This technique should never be used in Java and should never be used in Velocity templates. You should refactor your Velocity templates as aggressively as you should refactor your Java code. In an ideal solution, you'll have no duplication within your templates whatsoever. This may prove difficult, especially when producing HTML output where many of the tags themselves will be duplicated throughout the template, but you certainly shouldn't have big blocks of content that are duplicated in many templates.

 TIP *If you're unfamiliar with the concept of refactoring, then you should read* Refactoring: Improving the Design of Existing Code *by Martin Fowler, et. al. (Addison-Wesley, 1999).*

Using #include Instead of #parse Wherever Possible

In the last tip, you saw that separating reusable pieces of content into separate resources increases the maintainability of your application by allowing you to make changes in a single place. When you're including content fragments into a master template, be sure you use the correct VTL construct for the type of content you're including. If the content fragment contains no VTL markup, then you should always use #include. By using the #parse directive, you're instructing the Velocity runtime that it should parse the fragment for VTL constructs and process them as appropriate. However, if the content fragment contains no VTL, this processing is needless and adds unnecessary overhead to your application.

On the flip side of this, don't be afraid to use #parse when it's necessary. Whether you include the VTL directives directly into the master template or in a content fragment makes no difference to the overall performance of the application, but by repeating the same VTL in multiple templates, you'll be increasing the maintenance burden of the application and increasing the chance of errors creeping into your application.

Avoid Complex Processing

You may be tempted with Velocity to use the excellent support for method invocation and basic arithmetic in order to perform more of the complex processing within your templates. This approach has some fundamental problems. To start with, by moving complex processing into Velocity templates, which essentially form the presentation tier of your application, you're breaking the clear separation of responsibilities that a tiered application gives you. The presentation tier should be responsible for one thing and one thing alone: presenting data. Ideally, the presentation technology will work with a snapshot of the application data and won't take part in any information processing at all. All business logic should be gathered into a central location and should be implemented in a language more suitable to the needs of complex business logic (in this case, Java).

You should also remember that the key benefits of using a technology such as Velocity in the presentation tier are that it's simple and lightweight. By populating the context with complex objects that have methods used to perform business processing, you cause the presentation tier to become overly complex, which can prove counterproductive, especially when you're expecting nondevelopers to work with and build templates.

Another key concern with this approach is that the application becomes closely coupled with Velocity. By delegating business processing to Velocity and thus the presentation tier, you're making it unnecessarily difficult to replace Velocity should a more efficient view technology arise that isn't capable of performing complex processing.

The next two sections discuss this topic in much more detail.

Summarizing VTL

Velocity contains simple but powerful technology, which unfortunately makes it simple to misuse. Whilst there's no incorrect way to use Velocity, some ways are better than others. The techniques and hints included in the previous sections have come from my experience in building applications using Velocity. The practices are by no means complete, but they will provide you with guidelines for 90 percent of the problems you'll solve with Velocity. In the next two sections, you'll investigate how good architectural techniques can help you account for the remaining 10 percent.

Using Velocity in an MVC Environment

When building an application with any kind of user interface, it's useful to follow some kind of coherent model that decouples the data you intend to show from the way in which it's displayed. Thankfully, you have no need to create such a model every time you create an application.

What Is MVC?

Model-View-Controller (MVC) is a standard architectural pattern for developing application interfaces. At a high level, MVC splits the application interface into three parts: the Model, the View, and the Controller. The Model refers to the data that the application manipulates and that can take many forms. In a traditional enterprise application, the Model is likely to be domain-specific, but consider other applications, such as Microsoft Word, in which the document is the Model. The View is the part of the application that displays the Model to the user. As I'm writing this chapter (the Model) using Microsoft Word, I'm viewing it in Print Layout (the View). I can, however, switch the View easily by choosing a new layout from the View menu. In this example, the Word application itself is the Controller, as it receives input in the form of keystrokes and mouse gestures and updates the Model appropriately. The View is then updated to reflect the current state of the Model.

The overriding goal behind MVC is to provide a loose coupling between an application's data and the way in which it's displayed, and this is a goal it has been proven to achieve well.

Depending on the type of application, the View will be generated in a variety of different ways. In the case of Microsoft Word, the View is updated dynamically as the Model changes. In this case, the View registers with the Model and updates its user interface in response to notifications from the Model—this is known as *push MVC*, as the Model is pushing update notifications to the View. Swing-based applications are the perfect example of push-based MVC. Consider the example shown in Listing 4-4.

Listing 4-4. MVC in Swing

```
package com.apress.pjv.ch4;

import java.awt.BorderLayout;

import javax.swing.DefaultListModel;
import javax.swing.JFrame;
import javax.swing.JList;

public class SwingMVC{
```

```
public static void main(String[] args) {
    JFrame frm = new JFrame();
    frm.setTitle("Swing MVC Demo");
    frm.setSize(200, 300);
    frm.getContentPane().setLayout(new BorderLayout());

    JList list = new JList();
    final DefaultListModel model = new DefaultListModel();
    model.addElement("Item 1");
    list.setModel(model);

    frm.getContentPane().add(list);
    frm.show();

    model.addElement("Item 2");
    model.addElement("Item 3");

}
}
```

Notice that once the form is displayed, I can continue to add data to the Model, and the View is updated as soon as the data is added; there's no need to instruct the View to refresh itself.

For a Web application, however, this kind of dynamic update isn't possible, and the Controller will be required to build the Model in its entirety and then pass the Model to the View for rendering—this is known a *pull MVC*, in which the View is given access to the Model and pulls data from it as required.

NOTE   *I have no idea how Microsoft Word is implemented; the described mechanism is just how I would implement it.*

Traditionally, MVC applications are thought of as applications that provide some kind of graphical user interface to the user. However, consider an application that generates personalized e-mail newsletters for a database of subscribers. In this case, the Controller is invoked not by a user action but perhaps by some kind of scheduler. The Model is the newsletter data itself, including the data required for personalization. The View is the e-mail that's generated for each individual subscriber. Whilst this isn't an MVC application in the traditional sense, you can apply the same architectural pattern to ensure that the application is as reusable as possible. For instance, in the application just described, it'd be a simple job to create a new View that would display a nonpersonalized version of the newsletter on the Web or one that would create a PDF version of the newsletter that could be posted to subscribers without e-mail access.

In Chapters 5 and 6, you'll see how you can build MVC applications both for the desktop, using Swing, and for the Web, using a variety of different tools.

Velocity's Role in Generating the View

Whilst Velocity isn't limited to use in an MVC-based architecture, its suitability to the role of the View can't be ignored. Since Velocity has no mechanism for receiving events from the Model, it has no place in a push-based MVC environment, such as Microsoft Word or a Swing application. However, it's ideally suited to a pull-based MVC because of its context-based communication mechanism. In this case, the context acts as the container for the Model, the Controller gathers the Model data and places it into the context, and then a Velocity template will pull the Model data from the context as required.

MVC is a proven architecture for creating simple, maintainable applications that perform well. Whilst Velocity fits the View role well, it can easily violate this role and perform some of the responsibilities of the Model and even the Controller. The reason for this is because a Velocity template is capable of calling any method on any object that resides in its context, a feature that can cause many problems when building an MVC-based application. The following are the Velocity MVC pitfalls:

Loss of View transparency: A key goal of the MVC pattern is to enable an application to easily swap the technology used to produce the View. In this way, the View is defined as a lightweight user interface technology. By relying on some the more advanced features of Velocity, such as method invocation, you increase coupling between the View and the Model, since the Model is relying on the View to perform data processing. This limits the choice of View technologies to those that are capable of performing the data processing.

Unclear division of responsibilities: The role of the View isn't to gather Model data or even to perform any kind of extra processing on that data, other than that required to render the data. By allowing your Velocity templates to load or process data, you're breaking this clear division of responsibility. The case for this can be quite fuzzy; consider the case where you have a list of products and their prices, and you want to display the list along with a total of the prices. Should the Model contain just the list of products and prices, or should it contain the total as well? My preference is to include the total in the Model, rather than rely on the View to perform that processing. You'll see an example of this in the following section.

Increased View complexity: An excellent feature of MVC-based architecture is that it fits in well with multidisciplined development teams. When you have a clear separation between the data and the way in which it's displayed, it's easier for developers and interface designers to work side by side on a project. By moving processing logic into the View, you run the risk of making the View so complex that it prevents interface designers from being able to work directly on the View without help from developers.

However, it's quite simple to ensure that you avoid these issues by limiting the use of Velocity's method invocation ability. If you stick to simple JavaBean properties, not only will you ensure a clean separation between Model and View, but you'll also make it easier for interface designers to work on templates independently of the development team and leave the road clear for migration to, or the addition of, another View technology, should the need arise. You should note that using Velocimacros doesn't fall into the category of features you should avoid. Using macros has no effect whatsoever on external code. Macros aren't used to perform business logic; they're merely used to simplify and increase the reusability of presentation logic.

Appropriate Model Usage

Often a difficult decision when building a Model is just exactly what data it should contain and at what point the Model should be populated. Deciding when to populate the Model will depend on whether you're using push or pull MVC. For push MVC applications, you can populate the Model with data dynamically, refreshing the View each time—this behavior makes push MVC ideal for rich-client scenarios but not so suitable for use with tools such as Velocity. For a pull-based MVC environment, such as Velocity, it's important that the Model is populated with all data before you pass it to the View—in this case, Velocity—for processing. You have no way to hand a context to Velocity, have Velocity start generating the output, add some additional Model data to the context and for Velocity to detect this data, and rerender the View. In this case, you'd have to wait for Velocity to finish generating the first set of output, repopulate the context, and then generate the output again. For this reason, it's important that all Model data is available in the Velocity context before you instruct Velocity to render the View.

Populating the Model with the correct amount of data is pivotal to ensuring that your application can take full advantage of the MVC paradigm. To answer the question of how just much data a Model should contain, you need to look at one of the core goals of designing an MVC-based application—View separation. In a true MVC application, it should be possible to replace a View built using one technology with a View built using another technology, with little or no change to the application code itself. For this to be possible, you should use only those features in your View technology that are likely to be available in the widest selection of other View technologies. Whilst at first this may sound like a bad idea (after all, what's point of using a View technology if you can't advantage of its additional features?), on further inspection you'll see that doing this actually helps to define the clear distinction between view logic, control logic, and business logic. Consider this example: A simple application is required to generate a list of products and their prices, along with the total. One way of achieving this would be to create a `Collection` of `Product` objects and add them to the context, leaving the Velocity template to calculate the total price. Listing 4-5 shows this approach.

Listing 4-5. `ProductList` *Sample Application*

```
package com.apress.pjv.ch4;

import java.io.StringWriter;
import java.io.Writer;
import java.util.ArrayList;
import java.util.Collection;

import org.apache.velocity.Template;
import org.apache.velocity.VelocityContext;
import org.apache.velocity.app.Velocity;
import org.apache.velocity.tools.generic.MathTool;

public class ProductList1 {

    public static void main(String[] args) throws Exception {
        // init
        Velocity.init("src/velocity.properties");

        // get the template
        Template t = Velocity.getTemplate("productList-calcintemp.vm");

        // create context
        VelocityContext ctx = new VelocityContext();

        // add products collection to the context
        Collection products = new ArrayList();
        products.add(new Product("Widget", 12.99));
        products.add(new Product("Wotsit", 13.99));
        products.add(new Product("Thingy", 11.99));
        ctx.put("productList", products);
```

```
        // need MathTool to do in-template calculation
        ctx.put("math", new MathTool());

        // create the output
        Writer writer = new StringWriter();
        t.merge(ctx, writer);

        // output
        System.out.println(writer);
    }
}
```

Notice that I've added an instance of MathTool to the context; without it, the template would be unable to perform arithmetic on the product prices since they're floating-point values. The following code for the template uses the MathTool instance to calculate the total price:

```
#set($totalPrice = 0)
#foreach($product in $productList)
$product.Name      $$product.Price
#set($totalPrice = $math.add($totalPrice, $product.Price))
#end

Total Price: $$totalPrice
```

This approach generates the following output:

```
Widget    $12.99
Wotsit    $13.99
Thingy    $11.99

Total Price: $38.97
```

The output is as desired, but consider what would happen if I wanted to replace the use of Velocity with another View technology, such as JSP. Although JSP is capable of performing arithmetic using scriptlets, this is considered to be bad design, so you shouldn't even consider it a feature of the technology. This leaves me with one option: I have to change not only the code to generate the View but also the code to load the Model, since the Model must now also contain the total price. A better solution in the first place would have been to ignore the arithmetic features of Velocity and refactor the code for generating the total into Java, adding the total price as a parameter in the context, as shown in Listing 4-6.

Listing 4-6. Product List Application

```
package com.apress.pjv.ch4;

import java.io.StringWriter;
import java.io.Writer;
import java.util.ArrayList;
import java.util.Collection;
import java.util.Iterator;

import org.apache.velocity.Template;
import org.apache.velocity.VelocityContext;
import org.apache.velocity.app.Velocity;

public class ProductList2 {

    public static void main(String[] args) throws Exception {
        // init
        Velocity.init("src/velocity.properties");

        // get the template
        Template t = Velocity.getTemplate("productList2.vm");

        // create context
        VelocityContext ctx = new VelocityContext();

        // add products collection to the context
        Collection products = new ArrayList();
        products.add(new Product("Widget", 12.99));
        products.add(new Product("Wotsit", 13.99));
        products.add(new Product("Thingy", 11.99));
        ctx.put("productList", products);

        // calculate total
        Iterator itr = products.iterator();
        double total = 0.00;

        while(itr.hasNext()) {
            Product p = (Product)itr.next();
            total += p.getPrice();
        }

        // add total price to the context
        ctx.put("totalPrice", new Double(total));
```

```
        // create the output
        Writer writer = new StringWriter();
        t.merge(ctx, writer);

        // output
        System.out.println(writer);
    }
}
```

This time there's no need to add an instance of `MathTool` to the context, since the calculation of the total price happens in the Java code and the resultant value is added to the context. Modifying the template to take advantage of the precalculated value results in the following much simpler template:

```
#foreach($product in $productList)
$product.Name      $$product.Price
#end


Total Price: $$totalPrice
```

The output is the same as before, but now it'd be much easier to swap Velocity for a new View technology. The general rule is that the Model should contain a snapshot of the all the dynamic data required by the View and that it shouldn't rely on the View to perform further processing on the Model data for it to be rendered correctly. Following this simple practice will make your applications a lot less brittle and more open to change. You have to remember that the role of the View technology is to generate the View and nothing more—it's the role of the Model to provide the View with all the data it requires to accomplish this.

The Context Isn't the Model

An important issue related to the use of Velocity in an MVC-based environment is that, strictly speaking, the context isn't the Model—it just holds the Model. Whilst it's possible, such as in the previous example, to add pieces of the Model directly to the context, such as the `Collection` or `Products` and the total price, a better solution is to create a class to hold the Model data and add just that class to the context. Before I discuss the benefits of this approach, Listing 4-7 first shows you an example. Using the previous example as a starting point, I simply create a class, `ProductListModel`, to hold the Model data.

Listing 4-7. The ProductListModel *Class*

```java
package com.apress.pjv.ch4;

import java.util.Collection;
import java.util.Iterator;

public class ProductListModel {

    private Collection productList = null;

    private double totalPrice = Double.MIN_VALUE;

    public ProductListModel(Collection aProductList) {
        productList = aProductList;
    }

    public Collection getProductList() {
        return productList;
    }

    public void setProductList(Collection aProductList) {
        productList = aProductList;
        totalPrice = Double.MIN_VALUE;
    }

    public double getTotalPrice() {
        if (totalPrice == Double.MIN_VALUE) {

            totalPrice = 0;
            Iterator itr = productList.iterator();

            while (itr.hasNext()) {
                Product p = (Product) itr.next();
                totalPrice += p.getPrice();
            }
        }

        return totalPrice;
    }
}
```

Instead of adding the Collection of Products and the total price directly into the context, the Collection of Products is passed into the constructor of ProductListModel. The getTotalPrice() method of ProductListModel lazily calculates the total price the first time the property is accessed. Notice that I haven't made the ProductListModel class immutable, even though changing the data in the Model won't be reflected in the output once it's generated. The reason for this is that I don't want to preclude the possibility that this Model object may be used in a push-based MVC environment—if I omit the setters, this wouldn't be possible. Now, when populating the context, all I need to do is add an instance of ProductListModel, as shown in Listing 4-8.

Listing 4-8. Product List Application—Again!

```
package com.apress.pjv.ch4;

import java.io.StringWriter;
import java.io.Writer;
import java.util.ArrayList;
import java.util.Collection;

import org.apache.velocity.Template;
import org.apache.velocity.VelocityContext;
import org.apache.velocity.app.Velocity;

public class ProductList3 {

    public static void main(String[] args) throws Exception {
        // init
        Velocity.init("src/velocity.properties");

        // get the template
        Template t = Velocity.getTemplate("productList-model.vm");

        // create context
        VelocityContext ctx = new VelocityContext();

        // create the product list model
        Collection products = new ArrayList();
        products.add(new Product("Widget", 12.99));
        products.add(new Product("Wotsit", 13.99));
        products.add(new Product("Thingy", 11.99));

        ProductListModel model = new ProductListModel(products);
        ctx.put("model", model);

        // create the output
        Writer writer = new StringWriter();
        t.merge(ctx, writer);

        // output
        System.out.println(writer);
    }
}
```

This approach requires little change to the template; I simply have to access the `productList` and `totalPrice` properties on the `PriceListModel` object as follows, rather than access the variables directly from the context:

```
#foreach($product in $model.productList)
$product.Name     $$product.Price
#end


Total Price: $$model.totalPrice
```

The output produced by this approach is the same as it was in the previous example. You get two clear benefits using this approach. The first is that you're not relying on your View technology to provide a structure like the Velocity context. It's possible that the View technology will require a single object that defines the Model data and that the View will be rendered from that. Since Velocity supports this approach, there's no drawback in doing it (other than the extra code required to create the Model class). The second reason is that it reduces the impact of a change in the Model. When using the first approach, any changes to the Model require changes not only to the template and Model data but also to the Controller, which populates the context with Model data. When using the second approach, only the Model data and template need to be changed—the Controller can be left untouched, reducing the risk of bugs creeping into the Controller and also reducing the maintenance burden. A simple change in the Model shouldn't affect the control flow of the application, so why should it require changes to the Controller class?

Summarizing Velocity and MVC

As you can see from the previous section, Velocity is ideally suited for use in an MVC-based environment. By remembering a few simple guidelines when creating your Velocity-based applications, you'll increase the reusability of your code as well as reducing the future maintenance burden. The following summarizes the best practices:

Use a single Model object: Use a single object to hold all the Model data, and put this object in the Velocity context. This will make any future migrations much simpler, without having a major impact on your use of Velocity. By using this method, you'll also reduce the impact of any future changes to the Model data.

Leverage JavaBeans: When creating your Model object, you should stick to using the JavaBean naming conventions. The benefits for this approach are many, but the main reason is that you can use a much simpler syntax when building templates, which is especially useful in multidisciplined teams.

Avoid technology-specific features: You should have no need to use any of the advanced features of Velocity, such as arithmetic support or method calling support, because this puts too much responsibility on the View and increases coupling between your application and Velocity.

Keep processing out of the View: Any time you find the need to perform some processing in the View other than simply displaying data, you should refactor the behavior and move it into the Model or Controller, depending on which is most appropriate.

Decoupling Velocity

Much of the discussion so far has been related to how you can reduce the coupling between your application and Velocity. Whilst the practices discussed will go some way toward this goal, a change in the View technology still requires changing the code in the Controller. This isn't an ideal solution—it'd be better if the interface to Velocity were hidden behind some kind of abstraction layer. In this way, moving to a new View technology would require changes only to the implementation in the abstraction layer, not client code. Fortunately, it's fairly simple to put something like this together. In the following sections, you'll take a detailed look at providing such an abstraction layer, tying together many of the practices I've discussed so far. At the same time as providing abstraction from Velocity, you can provide a much simpler programming model for client code and reduce the chance of errors creeping into your application.

Design Goals

Before I demonstrate the implementation of the abstraction layer, it's important to define the goals of building such an abstraction layer so you can verify the solution once it's built. The following are the framework's design goals:

Avoid dependency on Velocity: The core goal for building the abstraction layer is to remove all dependencies on Velocity from the client code. This means that when creating output from a template, client code shouldn't require any classes from the Velocity package, and it shouldn't have to handle any Velocity-specific exceptions.

Simplify exception handling: To avoid the need for client applications to handle Velocity specific exceptions, any exceptions that occur will need to be wrapped in a framework exception. Whilst doing this, you can make any unrecoverable exceptions unchecked, reducing the amount of code required in the client.

Provide a typed API: One of my major gripes with Velocity is that the API isn't strongly typed. It relies too much on template names and key names for context parameters, making it easy for coding errors to creep into the software. By hiding the details of this behind a simpler, object-oriented framework, you can reduce the chance for errors and also provide an interface that's simpler to work with for client programmers.

Now that I've defined the goals for the abstraction layer, I'll move onto the implementation.

Framework Overview

The basic framework consists of two interfaces, ModelBean and ContentTemplate, along with two core classes, TemplateFactory and AbstractVelocityContentTemplate. Figure 4-1 illustrates the interaction between these classes and interfaces.

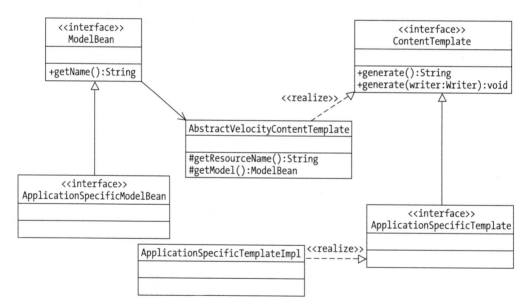

Figure 4-1. Framework overview

The lower portion of this diagram shows how application-specific classes interact with the framework classes. The following sections explain each interface and class in more detail.

The ModelBean Interface

As previously discussed, it's preferable to store all Model data in a single object and pass this object to Velocity. In the framework code, all Model beans implement the following `ModelBean` interface:

```
package com.apress.pjv.ch4;

public interface ModelBean {

    public String getModelName();
}
```

The `getModelName()` method is intended to return the name by which the `ModelBean` can be referenced in the template. In the Velocity context, this will be the name of the `ModelBean` when it's added to the context; in JSP it'd be the name of the `ModelBean` as stored in the request context.

The ContentTemplate Interface

The main interface in the framework is `ContentTemplate`. All template objects that are built will derive from this interface:

```
package com.apress.pjv.ch4;

import java.io.Writer;

public interface ContentTemplate {

    public String generate() throws TemplateException;
    public void generate(Writer writer) throws TemplateException;
}
```

Notice that the interface contains only two methods to generate the output: one to generate the output and place it in a `Writer` instance and the other to generate the output and return it as a `String`. The interface has no mention of anything having to do with the `ModelBean` for this instance. The reason for this will become apparent when you see the framework in action in the "Using the Abstraction Layer" section. You'll also notice that both generates declare a single thrown exception, `TemplateException`, shown in Listing 4-9.

Listing 4-9. TemplateException

```
package com.apress.pjv.ch4;

public class TemplateException extends RuntimeException {

    public TemplateException() {
        super();
    }

    public TemplateException(String msg) {
        super(msg);
    }

    public TemplateException(String msg, Throwable cause) {
        super(msg, cause);
    }

    public TemplateException(Throwable cause) {
        super(cause);
    }
}
```

The TemplateException class inherits from RuntimeException, as it's my experience that an error in generating a template is most often unrecoverable. Of course, a client application is free to catch TemplateException in cases where the exception isn't fatal.

Adding Velocity Support with AbstractVelocityContentTemplate

The AbstractVelocityContentTemplate is an implementation of the ContentTemplate for Velocity templates. When using Velocity as the template engine, template classes in an application inherit from this class, which takes care of the actual generation of the template, as shown in Listing 4-10.

Listing 4-10. AbstractVelocityContentTemplate

```
package com.apress.pjv.ch4;

import java.io.StringWriter;
import java.io.Writer;

import org.apache.velocity.Template;
```

```
import org.apache.velocity.context.Context;

public abstract class AbstractVelocityContentTemplate {

    public void generate(Writer writer) throws TemplateException {
        try {
            VelocityManager.init("src/velocity.properties");

            Template t = VelocityManager.getTemplate(getResourceName());

            // create the context
            Context ctx = ContextFactory.getInstance();

            // populate with model data
            ModelBean model = getModel();
            ctx.put(model.getModelName(), model);

            t.merge(ctx, writer);

        } catch(Exception ex) {
            throw new TemplateException("Unable to generate output", ex);
        }
    }

    public String generate() throws TemplateException {
        Writer w = new StringWriter();
        generate(w);
        return w.toString();
    }

    protected abstract ModelBean getModel();
    protected abstract String getResourceName();
}
```

The AbstractVelocityContentTemplate class provides implementations of the two generate() methods from the ContentTemplate class and declares two protected abstract methods to be implemented by subclasses. These methods are called by the generate() method to complete the generation process. Using this approach means that much of the responsibility for content generation is placed on AbstractVelocityContentTemplate, and the subclass is invoked only at pertinent points.

The AbstractVelocityContentTemplate class invokes the getResourceName() method on the subclass to find the name of the template. The getModel() method accesses the ModelBean instance used to generate the content.

Using the Abstraction Layer

There's not a vast amount to the abstract layer—just four classes and one more that you have yet to see. Building an application using the framework is quite simple and can be broken down into the following four steps:

1. Create interfaces for the templates. Each template in the application should have an interface associated with it that extends the `ContentTemplate` interface. Each template-specific interface will define JavaBean-style properties for setting the Model data for that template.

2. Create concrete implementations of the templates. Once the interface for each template is defined, you can create the concrete implementation of that interface. For templates that are to be processed using Velocity, this concrete implementation will use the `AbstractVelocityContentTemplate` class.

3. Create `ModelBean` classes for each template. Each template needs a class derived from `ModelBean` to hold its Model data. In a Velocity context, an instance of this class will be returned by the `getModel()` method of the template class.

4. Create the client code. Once the template object model is in place, you can create the client code.

Now I'll take you through each step individually so that you fully understand how you use the abstraction layer to build an application. The example I've chosen to use is a simple user profile sheet generator. This application is intended to provide a printable representation of a `UserProfile` object, along with a time stamp to show when the record was printed. The `UserProfile` class is a simple JavaBean with three properties, as shown in Listing 4-11.

Listing 4-11. `UserProfile` *Class*

```
package com.apress.pjv.ch4;

public class UserProfile {

    private String firstName;

    private String lastName;

    private String emailAddress;
```

```
    public String getEmailAddress() {
        return emailAddress;
    }

    public void setEmailAddress(String emailAddress) {
        this.emailAddress = emailAddress;
    }

    public String getFirstName() {
        return firstName;
    }

    public void setFirstName(String firstName) {
        this.firstName = firstName;
    }

    public String getLastName() {
        return lastName;
    }

    public void setLastName(String lastName) {
        this.lastName = lastName;
    }
}
```

Creating Template Interfaces

The client application interacts with the templating engine, be it Velocity or
another, through the interfaces of the templates. Each template has an interface
that derives from ContentTemplate and defines properties for the data required to
render output from the template correctly. The reason for having an interface for
each template and not just accessing the concrete implementation directly from
the client is that this approach would result in the same level of coupling between
the application and the chosen templating technology as using the template engine
directly. For the example, I created the following UserProfileTemplate interface:

```
package com.apress.pjv.ch4;

public interface UserProfileTemplate extends ContentTemplate {

    public UserProfile getUserProfile();

    public void setUserProfile(UserProfile userProfile);
}
```

The purpose of the UserProfileTemplate is to generate a printable output of a UserProfile object. The UserProfile object is part of the Model data for this template, so I've defined the userProfile property on the UserProfileTemplate interface.

Creating Concrete Implementations and ModelBeans

Creating a concrete implementation of the UserProfileTemplate interface for the Velocity engine is actually quite a trivial job. The AbstractVelocityContentTemplate class takes care of all the code for invoking Velocity; all you need to do is to create a class that extends that class and implements the UserProfileTemplate class, providing implementations for the interface methods and for the abstract methods from AbstractVelocityContentTemplate, as shown in Listing 4-12.

Listing 4-12. Implementing AbstractVelocityContentTemplate

```
package com.apress.pjv.ch4;

import java.text.DateFormat;
import java.util.Date;

public class UserProfileTemplateImpl extends AbstractVelocityContentTemplate
        implements UserProfileTemplate {

    private UserProfile userProfile;

    public UserProfile getUserProfile() {
        return userProfile;
    }

    public void setUserProfile(UserProfile userProfile) {
        this.userProfile = userProfile;
    }

    protected String getResourceName() {
        return "userProfile.vm";
    }

    protected ModelBean getModel() {
        String timestamp = DateFormat.getDateTimeInstance().format(new Date());
        return new UserProfileModelBean(userProfile, timestamp);
    }
}
```

Most of the implementation of this class is trivial. I've provided implementations of the getUserProfile and setUserProfile methods, as required by the UserProfileTemplate interface, and also of the getResourceName() and getModel() methods, as required by the AbstractVelocityContentTemplate class. Of these, only the getModel() is of any real interest. The getModel() method returns an instance of UserProfileModelBean, as shown in Listing 4-13.

Listing 4-13. Implementing ModelBean

```
package com.apress.pjv.ch4;

public class UserProfileModelBean implements ModelBean {

    private UserProfile profile;
    private String timestamp;

    public UserProfileModelBean(UserProfile aProfile, String aTimestamp) {
        profile = aProfile;
        timestamp = aTimestamp;
    }

    public String getModelName() {
        return "userProfileModel";
    }

    public UserProfile getUserProfile() {
        return profile;
    }

    public void setUserProfile(UserProfile aProfile) {
        profile = aProfile;
    }

    public String getTimestamp() {
        return timestamp;
    }

    public void setTimestamp(String aTimestamp) {
        timestamp = aTimestamp;
    }

    public String toString() {
        return profile.getFirstName();
    }
}
```

UserProfileModelBean implements the ModelBean interface discussed earlier and provides JavaBean-style properties for the Model data. The UserProfileModelBean defines a property, timestamp, which is used when rendering the output to show the time the output was generated. The important thing about this property is that it's of type String, not Date. The reason for this is that I don't want to rely on Velocity or any other View technology for date formatting. Although it's possible to format dates in Velocity using DateTool, as you saw in Chapter 3, this functionality may not be possible in other View technologies, so it's best to provide the date preformatted. This is quite a contentious point because some would say that it isn't the responsibility of the Model or the Controller to format the time stamp for output. However, my feeling is that for simple values such as dates, numbers, and currency values, it's often better to provide the formatted values as part of the Model, rather than rely on a View technology to perform that formatting.

I mentioned earlier that there was still one class from the framework that I hadn't yet discussed. That class is the TemplateFactory class. This class provides standard factory behavior for creating template instances:

```java
package com.apress.pjv.ch4;

public class TemplateFactory {

    public static UserProfileTemplate getUserProfileTemplate() {
        return new UserProfileTemplateImpl();
    }
}
```

This example of the TemplateFactory class is overly simple; in a real application you'd probably use some kind of external configuration mechanism and create implementation classes on the fly, rather than hard-code the implementation class into the TemplateFactory class. In Chapter 5, I'll present an implementation of TemplateFactory based on this mechanism.

The final part of building the concrete classes is to create the actual template. In this case it's quite simple, as follows:

```
*******************************************
* First Name:    $userProfileModel.UserProfile.FirstName
* Last Name:     $userProfileModel.UserProfile.LastName
* Email Address: $userProfileModel.UserProfile.EmailAddress
*******************************************

Generated By: $userProfileModel.Class.Name
On: $userProfileModel.Timestamp
```

Notice that all the data is accessed via the $userProfileModel variable; this is the name returned from the UserProfileModelBean.getModel() method.

Creating the Client

All that's left now is to create an application that uses these classes. This is actually simple, as the API you've built provides simple, OO-based access to the template and its output, as shown in Listing 4-14.

Listing 4-14. The Client Application

```
package com.apress.pjv.ch4;

public class UserProfileGenerator {

    public static void main(String[] args) throws TemplateException{
        UserProfile up = new UserProfile();
        up.setFirstName("Rob");
        up.setLastName("Harrop");
        up.setEmailAddress("rob@cakesolutions.net");

        UserProfileTemplate upt = TemplateFactory.getUserProfileTemplate();
        upt.setUserProfile(up);

        System.out.println(upt.generate());
    }
}
```

You'll notice that there are no Velocity-specific classes at all. You're free to provide a new implementation of the UserProfileTemplate interface, modify the TemplateFactory.getUserProfileTemplate() method to return an instance of the new implementation, and leverage a new template engine without affecting the client code at all.

Recapping Decoupling

You've now seen how to decouple your applications from Velocity using a simple abstraction layer whilst at the same time providing a much friendlier API for content generation. Whilst this isn't a solution for every problem, it's a simple solution to a problem that can cause maintenance nightmares if you're not careful. The following are the main benefits of this solution:

Totally decoupled from View: Using this solution you can totally decouple your application from the underlying View technology.

Simpler, typed API: Using this solution rather than interacting with Velocity directly means that your client code can interact with a simple, typed API, reducing the chances of errors occurring.

Easier-to-enforce architecture standards: This method enforces strict MVC usage based on the points discussed in this chapter. For instance, using this mechanism it's impossible for a client to add data directly into the Velocity context—it must include all Model data in the `ModelBean`.

However, this solution isn't without the following drawbacks (although they're few and vastly outweighed by the benefits):

An investment in time required to start: You are, of course, free to use the code from this chapter in your own applications, but you'll no doubt require time to document the approach, package for distribution within your organization, and introduce developers to it.

More code required per template: The biggest drawback of this approach is that it requires you to create more code per template—although the code you need to create is simple.

The full code for this solution is available in the download accompanying this book. It can be found at `http://www.apress.com` in the Downloads section.

Summary

This chapter covered a large amount of patterns and practices that are useful for developing Velocity-based applications. If you follow the simple guidelines laid out in this chapter, you'll find that your Velocity-based applications are much easier to extend and maintain. You briefly looked at MVC concepts, a topic I'll expand on in the next two chapters. In Chapter 5, I'll show you how to leverage the framework you built in this chapter to produce a full Swing/Velocity MVC application. In Chapter 6, you'll learn how to build MVC Web applications using VelocityTools, Struts, and Spring.

CHAPTER 5

Creating Stand-Alone Applications with Velocity

BY NOW YOU should have a good grasp of how the underlying Velocity system functions and how you can best utilize Velocity in your applications. However, the examples I've presented so far have been trivial at best, so in this chapter and the next I'll show you how to build full applications with Velocity—for both the desktop and for the Web. In this chapter I'll focus on building an application with Swing and Velocity, and then in the next chapter I'll demonstrate how to use Velocity when building Web applications.

During this chapter I'll build a simple e-mail newsletter application that can be used to send out customized information to Apress customers. Using this application, a member of the marketing team at Apress could keep customers informed of the latest book releases, any new offers, or any upcoming seminars or conferences that Apress may be offering. I'll write the user interface of the application in Swing, and I'll use Velocity to generate the customized e-mail message for each subscriber.

You need to be aware of two main features of the e-mail generations.

First, subscribers can choose whether they want to receive the e-mail in plain text or HTML format. It's also conceivable that in the future Apress may want to offer newsletters that contain embedded Macromedia Flash content, so the software must be able to handle this gracefully.

Second, a subscriber will typically want to receive news on only certain categories of books. For instance, a Java programmer is likely to want to receive updates on Java books as well as books on databases and open source—that Java programmer is unlikely to want to receive updates on books about .NET or Visual Basic. So, the software must be able to generate customized e-mails that go beyond just putting the subscriber's name at the top.

It's important to note that the example in this chapter isn't a complete example of how to create an e-mail marketing tool. For instance, the example in this chapter uses a fixed list of subscribers, whereas a real-life solution would most likely load the subscriber list from a database. In addition, the application provides only rudimentary text editing for the e-mail content, whereas a real-world solution would likely offer some kind of HTML-based editor and then derive the plain-text content from the HTML, perhaps using regular expressions to strip out the HTML tags. Of course, all these things are possible, and you could certainly extend the application in this chapter if you wanted to add any of these features.

Application Overview

Before starting to look at the code, you'll take a quick look at how the finished application looks (see Figure 5-1).

At the top of screen, the user can specify what text should appear in the subject of the message and what the sender address should be. These values default to Apress Newsletter and newsletter@apress.com, respectively.

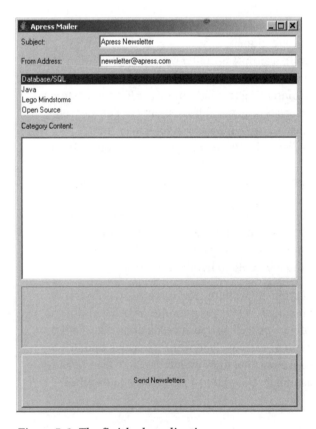

Figure 5-1. The finished application

Underneath this, you have the list of categories. Clicking a category will load the content for that category into the large text area underneath the list box. When the user moves from one category to another, the current content is stored for the category that the user is deselecting, and the stored content for the newly selected category is displayed. Finally, the progress bar and the send button are at the bottom of the screen.

Building the Application

So now that you've seen how the application works, you'll take a look under the hood and examine how it's built. I'll cover the following topics:

Understanding the Domain Object Model: The application needs an object model to represent the data it's manipulating, such as subscriber details and preferences and newsletter content.

Creating the user interface: You'll take a detailed look at how the Swing user interface is assembled and how events in the user interface are linked to actions in the code.

Sending mail with JavaMail: I'll demonstrate how to use the JavaMail API to create and send e-mails.

Interacting with Velocity: You'll see how to use the framework developed in Chapter 4 in the context of a nontrivial example.

Using the VTL templates: To finish the application code, I'll show you the VTL templates used to generate the e-mail content.

Testing the application: Finally, I'll talk you through running the application and taking it for a test drive.

Domain Object Model

The application functions by sending e-mails to subscribers based on their content preferences. Subscribers specify which category or categories of books they're interested in and in what format they want to receive the newsletter. The user of the application can specify content to be included with each category in the newsletter. The combination of the category data, which is fixed between newsletters, and the content for that category, which changes each time a newsletter is sent, forms one section of the newsletter. Depending on their preferences, subscribers will receive one or more of these sections in their preferred format.

The Subscriber Class

In the application, a Subscriber object represents each subscriber. The Subscriber class has no functionality; it's a simple domain object holding data about each subscriber (see Listing 5-1).

Listing 5-1. The Subscriber *Class*

```
package com.apress.pjv.ch5;

public class Subscriber {

    private String firstName = null;

    private String lastName = null;

    private String emailAddress = null;

    private Format preferredFormat = Format.PLAIN_TEXT;

    private Category[] subscribedCategories = null;

    public Subscriber(String firstName, String lastName, String emailAddress,
            Category[] subscribedCategories, Format preferredFormat) {

        this.firstName = firstName;
        this.lastName = lastName;
        this.emailAddress = emailAddress;
        this.subscribedCategories = subscribedCategories;
        this.preferredFormat = preferredFormat;
    }

    public String getEmailAddress() {
        return emailAddress;
    }

    public void setEmailAddress(String emailAddress) {
        this.emailAddress = emailAddress;
    }

    public String getFirstName() {
        return firstName;
    }
```

```java
    public void setFirstName(String firstName) {
        this.firstName = firstName;
    }

    public String getLastName() {
        return lastName;
    }
    public void setLastName(String lastName) {
        this.lastName = lastName;
    }

    public Format getPreferredFormat() {
        return preferredFormat;
    }

    public void setPreferredFormat(Format preferredFormat) {
        this.preferredFormat = preferredFormat;
    }

    public Category[] getSubscribedCategories() {
        return subscribedCategories;
    }

    public void setSubscribedCategories(Category[] subscribedCategories) {
        this.subscribedCategories = subscribedCategories;
    }
}
```

As you can see from Listing 5-1, I've declared five JavaBeans properties for the Subscriber class: FirstName, LastName, EmailAddress, PreferredFormat, and SubscribedCategories. The first three should be fairly self-explanatory, but the other two use classes you haven't seen before, so a little more explanation is required.

The PreferredFormat property represents the format in which subscribers would prefer to receive their e-mail newsletter. As defined in the requirements, this can be either HTML or plain text, but you can add new formats later. It would've been simpler to use an int for each particular format and then use public static final fields to store the possible value. However, a problem arises with this, in that you need to know the MIME type for each format so that the e-mail message can be constructed appropriately. It'd be possible for the code sending the e-mail to decode each int value into the appropriate MIME type. Using this approach has a drawback, in that adding a new format would require changes to the class defining the constant int values and a change to the class that sends the e-mail message. A better approach is to create a Format class and to add a property, ContentType, to the class that returns the appropriate MIME type for a particular format. Listing 5-2 shows the approach I used in the example.

Listing 5-2. The Format *Class*

```
package com.apress.pjv.ch5;

public class Format {

    public static final Format PLAIN_TEXT = new Format("text/plain");
    public static final Format HTML = new Format("text/html");

    private String contentType = null;

    private Format(String contentType) {
        this.contentType = contentType;
    }

    public String getContentType() {
        return contentType;
    }
}
```

You'll notice that the Format class has a private constructor and that the two available formats, HTML and plain text, are declared as static constants. The reason for this is twofold. First, it reduces the chance that the MIME type for one of the formats could be incorrectly specified because of a typing error. Second, this approach will be more efficient than allowing client code to create an instance of the Format class. This approach prevents multiple instances of the Format object being created to represent the same actual format—since there are only two actual formats, there should only ever be two Format objects in the JVM (depending on classloader behavior).

The SubscribedCategories property returns an array of Category objects, each of which represents one of the categories about which the subscriber wants to receive information.

The Category Class

Listing 5-3 shows the code for the Category class.

Listing 5-3. The Category *Class*

```
package com.apress.pjv.ch5;

public class Category {
```

```java
    public static final Category JAVA = new Category("Java",
            "http://www.apress.com/category.html?nID=32");

    public static final Category OPEN_SOURCE = new Category("Open Source",
            "http://www.apress.com/category.html?nID=28");

    public static final Category DATABASE_SQL = new Category("Database/SQL",
            "http://www.apress.com/category.html?nID=42");

    public static final Category LEGO_MINDSTORMS = new Category(
            "Lego Mindstorms", "http://www.apress.com/category.html?nID=46");

    private String name = null;

    private String webLink = null;

    private Category(String name, String webLink) {
        this.name = name;
        this.webLink = webLink;
    }

    public String getName() {
        return name;
    }

    public void setName(String name) {
        this.name = name;
    }

    public String getWebLink() {
        return webLink;
    }

    public void setWebLink(String webLink) {
        this.webLink = webLink;
    }

    public String toString() {
        return name;
    }

    public static Category[] getAllCategories() {
        return new Category[]{Category.DATABASE_SQL, Category.JAVA,
Category.LEGO_MINDSTORMS, Category.OPEN_SOURCE};
    }
}
```

The Category class has two properties: Name and WebLink. The WebLink property provides a hyperlink to that category on the Apress Web site. As with the Format class, Category has a private constructor, and individual instances of Category are declared as static constants. The static method getCategoryList() returns an array of Category objects, one for each category available. Since Apress has a small well-defined list of categories, this approach is acceptable. However, if the list of categories were larger or liable to change often, then it'd be wise to load the categories from a database or some other form of external storage and to use some form of object caching to ensure that only one instance existed for each category.

The SubscriberManager Class

Together the Subscriber, Category, and Format classes effectively describe subscriber and their preferences. However, none of those classes provides a way of getting access to the actual list of subscribers. For this I created the SubscriberManager class (see Listing 5-4).

Listing 5-4. The SubscriberManager *Class*

```
package com.apress.pjv.ch5;

import java.util.ArrayList;
import java.util.List;


public class SubscriberManager {

    public List getSubscribers() {
        List subscribers = new ArrayList();

        subscribers.add(new Subscriber("Rob", "Harrop",
                "rob@cakesolutions.net", new Category[] { Category.JAVA,
                    Category.DATABASE_SQL, Category.LEGO_MINDSTORMS},
                Format.HTML));
        subscribers.add(new Subscriber("Rob", "Harrop", "rob@cakesolutions.net",
                new Category[] { Category.JAVA, Category.DATABASE_SQL,
                    Category.OPEN_SOURCE}, Format.HTML));
        subscribers.add(new Subscriber("Rob", "Harrop", "robh@robharrop.com",
                new Category[] { Category.JAVA}, Format.PLAIN_TEXT));

        return subscribers;
    }
}
```

The implementation of SubscriberManager shown in Listing 5-4 is unrealistic, representing a finite list of subscribers. A more realistic implementation would load the subscribers from some kind of external storage, such as a database. However, for the sake of this example, that would be overly complex, so the simple implementation shown will suffice.

The NewsletterSection Class

The data represented by the Category class is persistent and will rarely change. Certainly you'd expect to see this data included in many different newsletters. However, if this were the only data included in the newsletter, then each one would be the same. The whole purpose of the example application is to communicate new information about the categories to the subscriber. Each newsletter is split into sections, with one section per category. These sections will contain persistent information about the category, such as its name and Web link, but will also contain information about the category that's specific to the particular newsletter. For this purpose, I created the NewsletterSection class, which represents a particular section in a newsletter (see Listing 5-5).

Listing 5-5. The NewsletterSection *Class*

```
package com.apress.pjv.ch5;

public class NewsletterSection {

    private Category category = null;
    private String content = null;

    public NewsletterSection(Category category, String content) {
        this.category = category;
        this.content = content;
    }

    public Category getCategory() {
        return category;
    }

    public void setCategory(Category category) {
        this.category = category;
    }

    public String getContent() {
        return content;
    }
}
```

```
    public void setContent(String content) {
        this.content = content;
    }
}
```

Each `NewsletterSection` class has a corresponding `Category` instance and a `String` instance containing the content for that `Category`.

With the code shown in this section, the application can now represent each subscriber and his or her preferences within the JVM and get access to the list of categories and subscribers. The application also has an effective way of mapping the persistent category data to the transient category content that makes up the individual sections of a newsletter.

User Interface

So far, the application does very little; after all, it has no entry point for the JVM to load the code, and it has no way for the user to interact with the application. In the earlier "Application Overview" section, I demonstrated the mailer application working and showed you the user interface. In this section, I'll show you the code behind the user interface.

NOTE *As you can no doubt tell by now, I'm not a user interface designer. A real-world application would probably have an interface designed by someone with a shred of graphic design skill and some understanding of what makes an application easy to use— and surprisingly that isn't a command-line interface!*

The main entry point to the application is the Mailer class (see Listing 5-6).

Listing 5-6. The `Mailer` *Class*

```
package com.apress.pjv.ch5;

import javax.swing.JFrame;
import javax.swing.SwingUtilities;

public class Mailer {

    public static void main(String[] args) {

        SwingUtilities.invokeLater(new Runnable() {
```

```
        public void run() {
            createAndShowGUI();
        }
    });
}

private static void createAndShowGUI() {
    //Make sure we have nice window decorations.
    JFrame.setDefaultLookAndFeelDecorated(true);

    //Create and set up the window.
    JFrame frame = new JFrame("Apress Mailer");
    frame.setDefaultCloseOperation(JFrame.EXIT_ON_CLOSE);
    frame.setContentPane(new MailerPanel());

    //Display the window.
    frame.pack();
    frame.setVisible(true);
}

}
```

The first point of note in this class is the main() method itself. Rather than call createAndShowGUI() directly, the main method creates an anonymous class that implements the Runnable interface, implementing the run() method to call createAndShowGUI(). This anonymous class is then passed as an argument to the SwingUtilities.invokeLater() method. For those of you who aren't familiar with Swing, the reason for this is that all Swing applications have to be inherently thread safe. This means that the interface should be assembled on the same thread that dispatches the Swing events. The SwingUtilities.invokeLater() method provides a simple way of running a task on the Swing event dispatch thread.

 TIP *Swing is a huge topic and is something that not all Java programmers have used. If you want to learn more about Swing, I recommend the fantastic* Java Swing, Second Edition *(O'Reilly, 2002).*

The createAndShowGUI() method creates a JFrame instance, sets the title and content pane, and then makes the JFrame visible. Most of the actual user interface is created by the MailerPanel class, an instance of which is set as the content pane for the main application window. The MailerPanel class contains a lot of code, so I'll show it piece by piece. To start with, the MailerPanel class imports all the Swing classes required to build the user interface (see Listing 5-7).

Listing 5-7. The First Part of the MailerPanel *Class*

```
package com.apress.pjv.ch5;

import java.awt.Cursor;
import java.awt.GridBagConstraints;
import java.awt.GridBagLayout;
import java.awt.Insets;
import java.awt.event.ActionEvent;
import java.awt.event.ActionListener;
import java.util.Iterator;
import java.util.List;

import javax.swing.JButton;
import javax.swing.JLabel;
import javax.swing.JList;
import javax.swing.JPanel;
import javax.swing.JProgressBar;
import javax.swing.JScrollPane;
import javax.swing.JTextArea;
import javax.swing.JTextField;
import javax.swing.event.ListSelectionEvent;
import javax.swing.event.ListSelectionListener;

public class MailerPanel extends JPanel implements ActionListener {

    private JTextField subjectField = null;

    private JTextField fromAddressField = null;

    private JTextArea categoryContentField = null;

    private JList categoryList = null;

    private JButton sendButton = null;

    private JProgressBar progressBar = null;

    private int selectedCategory = -1;

    private Category[] categories = null;

    private String[] content = null;
```

Notice also that `MailerPanel` class extends the `JPanel` class and implements the `ActionListener` interface. The `JPanel` class is a container for Swing components; by extending this class, you can use the `MailerPanel` class as the main content pane of a `JFrame`, and you can take advantage of the basic implementation provided by `JPanel`. By implementing the `ActionListener` interface, the `MailerPanel` can receive notification of actions from different components—this is useful when you want to detect when the user clicks the send button.

The `MailerPanel` declares nine different private fields. The fields that store Swing components give the `MailerPanel` simple access to the components once they've been added to the content pane. The three remaining fields store the categories and their content and manage the category that the user has selected in the category list.

The actual user interface is assembled when the `MailerPanel` constructor is called (see Listing 5-8).

Listing 5-8. The `MailerPanel` *Constructor*

```
public MailerPanel() {
        super(new GridBagLayout());

        loadData();

        GridBagConstraints c = new GridBagConstraints();
        c.fill = GridBagConstraints.HORIZONTAL;
        c.weightx = 0.5;
        c.weighty = 0.5;
        c.insets = new Insets(5, 5, 5, 5);

        addFieldLabels(c);

        addSubjectField(c);

        addFromAddressField(c);

        addCategoryList(c);

        addCategoryContentsLabel(c);

        addCategoryContentsTextBox(c);

        addProgessBar(c);

        addSendButton(c);

}
```

The first line in the constructor invokes the constructor on the superclass, JPanel, passing as an argument a new instance of GridBagLayout. This will set the layout of the MailerPanel to the GridBagLayout, which allows for precise, grid-based layout of components.

Next, the category list is loaded with a call to loadData():

```
private void loadData() {
    categories = Category.getCategoryList();
    content = new String[categories.length];
}
```

The loadData() method stores the result of the call to Category.getCategoryList() in the categories field and also initializes the content field to a String[] of the same size as the categories field. Back in the constructor, an instance of GridBagConstraints is created, like so:

```
GridBagConstraints c = new GridBagConstraints();
c.fill = GridBagConstraints.HORIZONTAL;
c.weightx = 0.5;
c.weighty = 0.5;
c.insets = new Insets(5, 5, 5, 5);
```

The GridBagConstraints class specifies the location and layout of components when adding them to the GridBagLayout. Now the constructor creates the user interface with calls to private methods, each of which configures a different piece of the user interface. Each of these methods is passed the GridBagConstraints instance. This allows the constructor to provide default settings, such as the insets and fill for the GridBagConstraints, but it also allows each method to supply the layout parameters for each component.

The first method called is the addFieldLabels() method, as follows:

```
private void addFieldLabels(GridBagConstraints c) {
    // labels
    c.gridx = 0;
    c.gridy = 0;
    add(new JLabel("Subject: "), c);

    c.gridx = 0;
    c.gridy = 1;
    add(new JLabel("From Address: "), c);
}
```

This method adds the Subject and From Address labels to the top of the MailerPanel. Notice the use of the gridx and gridy fields of the GridBagConstraints class. By setting these values and then passing the GridBagConstraints instance to the add() method along with each JLabel, I can specify which cell in the grid I want the component to reside. In this case, I'm saying that I want the Subject label to appear in the first row (0) and the first column (0) and that I want the Address label to appear in the second row (1) and the first column (0).

The next call from the constructor is to the addSubjectField() method, like so:

```
private void addSubjectField(GridBagConstraints c) {
    // text fields
    c.gridx = 1;
    c.gridy = 0;

    subjectField = new JTextField();
    subjectField.setText("Apress Newsletter");
    c.ipadx = 150;
    add(subjectField, c);
}
```

This method adds the text field used to enter the message subject to the MailerPanel. Notice that the instance of JTextField created is assigned to the subjectField field. This will give me easy access to the text field and its value later in the code.

Next up is the following call to addFromAddressField():

```
private void addFromAddressField(GridBagConstraints c) {
    c.gridx = 1;
    c.gridy = 1;

    fromAddressField = new JTextField();
    fromAddressField.setText("newsletter@apress.com");
    c.ipadx = 150;
    add(fromAddressField, c);
}
```

This method is similar to the addSubjectField() method, so there's no need for any extra explanation. The next call the constructor makes is to the addCategoryList() method, like so:

```
private void addCategoryList(GridBagConstraints c) {
    c.gridx = 0;
    c.gridy = 2;
    c.gridwidth = 2;
    categoryList = new JList();
    categoryList.setListData(categories);
    categoryList.addListSelectionListener(new ListSelectionListener() {
```

```
            public void valueChanged(ListSelectionEvent event) {
                if (event.getValueIsAdjusting() == false) {
                    updateCategoryContents();
                }
            }
        });
        categoryList.setSelectedIndex(0);
        add(categoryList, c);
    }
```

Most of the code in this method will be familiar to you by now. It configures GridBagConstraints, creates an instance of JList, and assigns that instance to the categoryList field. However, before the JList is added to the MailerPanel, the categories array is set as the source data for the list using the JList.setListData() method. In addition, an anonymous class is created that implements the ListSelectionListener interface, and the valueChanged method is implemented to call the updateCategoryContents() method whenever the value of the list is actually changing, not just when the user is manipulating the list. Finally, before adding the JList to the MailerPanel, the first item in the list is selected, providing a default selection when the user interface is displayed.

Next, the constructor calls addCategoryContentsLabel() and addCategoryContentsTextBox(), like so:

```
private void addCategoryContentsLabel(GridBagConstraints c) {
    // Category Contents Label
    c.gridx = 0;
    c.gridy = 3;
    add(new JLabel("Category Content:"), c);
}
```

```
private void addCategoryContentsTextBox(GridBagConstraints c) {
    c.gridx = 0;
    c.gridy = 4;
    c.ipadx = 250;
    c.ipady = 100;
    categoryContentField = new JTextArea();
    categoryContentField.setLineWrap(true);
    categoryContentField.setWrapStyleWord(true);
    JScrollPane scroller = new JScrollPane(categoryContentField);
    add(scroller, c);
}
```

Both of these methods should look pretty familiar; the only points you should note are the call to JTextArea.setWrapStyleWord(true) and the use of

JScrollPane. Without setting the line wrap style to word wrapping, the JTextArea will wrap a line in the middle of a word, which isn't very user-friendly. You probably noticed the JTextArea instance itself isn't added to the MailerPanel class; instead, an instance of JScrollPane is created with the JTextArea as the inner component and the JScrollPane instance is added to the MailerPanel. This prevents the JTextArea from expanding to take up the whole pane when the text inside it increases.

The final calls of the constructor are to addProgressBar() and addSendButton(), as follows:

```java
private void addProgessBar(GridBagConstraints c) {
    c.gridx = 0;
    c.gridy = 5;
    c.ipady = 40;
    progressBar = new JProgressBar();
    add(progressBar, c);
}

private void addSendButton(GridBagConstraints c) {
    c.gridx = 0;
    c.gridy = 6;
    c.ipady = 30;
    c.ipadx = 100;
    sendButton = new JButton("Send Newsletters");
    sendButton.setActionCommand("send");
    sendButton.addActionListener(this);
    add(sendButton, c);
}
```

Both of these methods should be familiar to you by now; the only point of note is these two lines from addSendButton():

```java
sendButton.setActionCommand("send");
sendButton.addActionListener(this);
```

The call setActionCommand() gives the button a command name, and the call to addActionListener() sets the current MailerPanel instance as the object that will receive notifications when the button is clicked. Using the command name is especially useful when the same ActionListener is used for multiple buttons, as it provides a way to differentiate between the buttons.

The remaining methods in the MailerPanel class handle events from the user interface components. The updateCategoryContents() method is called whenever the value of the category list changes, as follows:

```java
private void updateCategoryContents() {
        if (selectedCategory == -1) {
```

```
            // this is the first-time selection
            selectedCategory = categoryList.getSelectedIndex();
            return;
        }

        saveCurrentContent();

        // display the content for the newly selected category
        categoryContentField.setText(content[categoryList.getSelectedIndex()]);

        // store the new selection
        selectedCategory = categoryList.getSelectedIndex();
    }

    private void saveCurrentContent() {
        // store the content for the previously selected category
        content[selectedCategory] = categoryContentField.getText();
    }
```

The first time the updateCategoryContents() is called, the value of selectedCategory will be -1, so the method simply stores the newly selected index and returns control to the caller. However, after that, the value of selectedCategory will be greater than -1, so the rest of the method is executed. It's important to understand that this method is executed after the value of the listbox has changed. Therefore, the selected index of the list has changed, and the value of the selectedCategory field will be the previously selected index. Using this value as the array index, the saveCurrentContent() method will store the current text from the categoryContentField JTextArea in the content array. In other words, if the Category object for Java is stored at index 1 in the categories array, then the content for the Java category will be stored at index 1 in the content array. Once the saveCurrentCategory() method has executed, the updateCategoryContents() method will get the text for the newly selected category from the content array and set that as the value for the categoryContentField JTextArea. Finally, the new index is stored in the selectedCategory field so that the next time this method is called, the correct category is flagged as the previously selected one.

To receive notifications when the send button is clicked, the MailerPanel class implements the ActionListener interface and is registered as an action listener for the send button. The ActionListener interface has one method, which is actionPerformed(), as follows:

```
public void actionPerformed(ActionEvent event) {
    if (event.getActionCommand().equals("send")) {
        new Thread(new Runnable() {
```

```
        public void run() {
            sendNewsletters();
        }
    }).start();
}
}
```

The `actionPerformed()` method is passed an instance of the `ActionEvent` class by the Swing framework. Using this instance, the `MailerPanel` can determine which action is being performed by checking the value of the `ActionEvent.getActionCommand()` method. In this case, you're looking for the command `send`, which you'll remember was set as the action command for the send button. The `actionPerformed()` method is called from the Swing event dispatch thread, which means that any long-running tasks will interfere with the event processing in the application. To prevent this, I created a new thread to call the `sendNewsletters()` method.

The `sendNewsletters()` method handles the user interface updates before, during, and after the sending process, as well as controlling the sending process for each individual newsletter. The code for `sendNewsletters()` is quite long, so I'll present it in chunks:

```
private synchronized void sendNewsletters() {
    //disable controls
    switchControlState();
```

To start with, `sendNewsletters()` calls the `switchControlState()` method, which disables the send button and the category list if they're enabled and enables them if they're disabled.

```
private void switchControlState() {
    categoryList.setEnabled(!categoryList.isEnabled());
    sendButton.setEnabled(!sendButton.isEnabled());
}
```

Next, the `sendNewsletters()` method sets the cursor to the wait cursor and calls `saveCurrentContent()` to save any content changes for the currently selected category.

```
// show busy cursor
setCursor(new Cursor(Cursor.WAIT_CURSOR));

saveCurrentContent();
```

Next, the `sendNewsletters()` method gets the `List` of subscribers from the `SubscriberManager`. Using this `List`, the maximum and minimum values of the progress bar are configured and then the message subject and from address are retrieved from the corresponding text fields.

```
List subscribers = (new SubscriberManager()).getSubscribers();

progressBar.setMinimum(1);
progressBar.setMaximum(subscribers.size());

String subject = subjectField.getText();
String fromAddress = fromAddressField.getText();
```

The next step in the process is to create an array of NewsletterSection objects, one for each Category object in the category list, like so:

```
NewsletterSection[] sections = new NewsletterSection[categories.length];

for (int x = 0; x < sections.length; x++) {
    sections[x] = new NewsletterSection(categories[x], content[x]);
}
```

Notice how the category and the corresponding content are loaded from the categories and content arrays using the same index. The next-to-last step for the sendNewsletters() method is to iterate over the List of Subscriber objects retrieved from the SubscriberManager and send a newsletter to each one using the NewsletterManager class, like so:

```
Iterator itr = subscribers.iterator();
NewsletterManager manager = new NewsletterManager(fromAddress, subject);

int count = 1;
while (itr.hasNext()) {
    Subscriber s = (Subscriber) itr.next();
    manager.sendNewsletter(sections, s);
    progressBar.setValue(count++);
}
```

Notice that each time a newsletter is sent, the progress bar value is incremented to give the user some visual feedback as to the progress of the sending process. The next section covers the NewsletterManager class in detail; for now, it's enough to know that the NewsletterManager will create the appropriate newsletter content for each subscriber and send it to each subscriber's e-mail address. The final part of the sendNewsletters() method restores the cursor to the default and switches the state of the send button and the category list back to enabled, like so:

```
// restore cursor
setCursor(new Cursor(Cursor.DEFAULT_CURSOR));

// reactivate controls
switchControlState();
```

}

At this point, the application won't actually compile, because there's no imple-mentation for the `NewsletterManager` class. However, you could provide a stub implementation of this class and run the example. If you do this, you should find that the user interface is fully operational—save for the fact that clicking the send button won't actually do anything—but you should be able to add content for each category and switch back and forth between the categories to ensure that the con-tent for each category is being stored appropriately.

Sending the Newsletters

As you saw from the previous section, the logic for actually sending the newsletter resides in the `NewsletterManager.sendNewsletter()` method. The `NewsletterManager` class uses the JavaMail API to construct and send the e-mail message, so you'll need to download it before you can continue with the code. You can download the latest version of JavaMail from `http://java.sun.com/products/javamail/`; I used version 1.3.1 for this book. In addition to JavaMail, you need to download the JavaBeans Activation Framework (JAF), which is used by JavaMail to construct the mail messages. You can obtain JAF from `http://java.sun.com/products/javabeans/jaf/`.

The `NewsletterManager` class declares three instance fields and one constant field (see Listing 5-9).

Listing 5-9. The `NewsletterManager` *Class*

```
package com.apress.pjv.ch5;

import java.util.Properties;

import javax.mail.Address;
import javax.mail.Message;
import javax.mail.MessagingException;
import javax.mail.Session;
import javax.mail.Transport;
import javax.mail.internet.AddressException;
import javax.mail.internet.InternetAddress;
import javax.mail.internet.MimeMessage;
```

```
public class NewsletterManager {

    private static final String SMTP_SERVER = "localhost";

    private Session session = null;

    private Address fromAddress = null;

    private String subject = null;
```

The `SMTP_SERVER` constant holds the address of the SMTP server used to send e-mails. It's likely that this would be a configurable parameter in a real-world application; however, for the sake of this example, a constant will suffice. The `subject` field will store the subject of the message, which, as you saw in `MailerPanel.sendNewsletters()`, is passed to the `NewsletterManager` in the constructor. The session field holds an instance of `javax.mail.Session`, which represents a communication session with the mail server. The `fromAddress` field stores the address to be used as the sender address on the newsletter e-mails.

The `NewsletterManager` constructor requires two arguments: the subject of the message and the sender address (see Listing 5-10).

Listing 5-10. The `NewsletterManager` *Constructor*

```
public NewsletterManager(String fromAddress, String subject)
            throws NewsletterException {
        try {
            this.fromAddress = new InternetAddress(fromAddress);
        } catch (AddressException ex) {
            throw new NewsletterException("Invalid from address", ex);
        }
        this.subject = subject;
    }
```

You'll notice that although the `fromAddress` field is declared as type `javax.mail.Address`, it's instantiated at type `javax.mail.internet.InternetAddress`. The reason for this is that the `Address` class is abstract and serves as the common base class for different kinds of addresses. The `Address` class has two concrete subclasses: `InternetAddress` and `NewsAddress`, used for e-mails and newsgroup addresses, respectively. You should also notice that the constructor for `InternetAddress` throws an `AddressException` if you supply an incorrectly formatted e-mail address. The `NewsletterManager` class catches this exception and wraps it in the `NewsletterException` class (see Listing 5-11).

Listing 5-11. The NewsletterException *Class*

```
package com.apress.pjv.ch5;

public class NewsletterException extends RuntimeException {

    public NewsletterException() {
        super();
    }

    public NewsletterException(String msg) {
        super(msg);
    }

    public NewsletterException(String msg, Throwable rootCause) {
        super(msg, rootCause);
    }

    public NewsletterException(Throwable rootCause) {
        super(rootCause);
    }
}
```

The sendNewsletter() method is where it all happens! In this method, the mail message is constructed, the recipients are configured, and the message is sent. The sendNewsletter() method is quite long, so I'll explain it in chunks. You'll recall from the previous section that the MailerPanel.sendNewsletters() method iterates over the list of subscribers and calls sendNewsletter() once for each subscriber, passing in the Subscriber object and an array of NewsletterSection object representing the newsletter content, like so:

```
public boolean sendNewsletter(NewsletterSection[] sections,
            Subscriber subscriber) throws NewsletterException {
```

The first step taken by the sendNewsletter() method is to create the actual newsletter content:

```
NewsletterTemplate template = NewsletterTemplateFactory.getInstance()
        .getNewsletterTemplate(subscriber.getPreferredFormat());

template.setSections(sections);
template.setSubscriber(subscriber);
```

This is where Velocity enters the equation. The sendNewsletter() method doesn't interact with Velocity directly; instead, it follows the pattern discussed in Chapter 4. It retrieves a template object, in this case an object that implements the `NewsletterTemplate` interface, from the `NewsletterTemplateFactory` and appropriate properties on the `NewsletterTemplate` instance. The next section discusses these classes and interfaces in more detail.

Next up comes the code that sends the actual message. The JavaMail API throws quite a few different exceptions, so this block is wrapped in a try/catch block so that any JavaMail-specific exceptions can be wrapped in a `NewsletterException`. I start by creating an instance of `MimeMessage` and setting the content of the message, like so:

```
try {
    Message msg = new MimeMessage(getMailSession());
    msg.setContent(template.generate(), subscriber.getPreferredFormat()
            .getContentType());
```

The `MimeMessage` constructor is passed an instance of `javax.mail.Session`, which is obtained from the `getMailSession()` method. The code for `getMailSession()` is shown at the end of this section, but it simply ensures that the `Session` object is correctly configured and that all calls to `sendNewsletter()` on the same `NewsletterManager` instance use the same `Session` object. An important call in this block of code is the call to `Message.setContent()`. Here I use the `generate()` method of the template object to provide the content for the message, and I use the `getContentType()` method of the subscribers preferred `Format` object to set the content type.

The remaining code in the `sendNewsletter()` method simply configures the subject, from the address and recipient address of the mail message, and then sends it with a call to `Transport.send()`, as follows:

```
        msg.setSubject(subject);
        msg.setFrom(fromAddress);

        msg.addRecipient(Message.RecipientType.TO, new InternetAddress(
                subscriber.getEmailAddress()));

        Transport.send(msg);
        return true;
    } catch (AddressException e) {
        // invalid address - ignore
        e.printStackTrace();
        return false;
    } catch (MessagingException e) {
        e.printStackTrace();
        throw new NewsletterException("Unable to send newsletter", e);
    }
}
```

Notice that the catch block for the AddressException doesn't rethrow an exception; instead, it simply returns false, indicating that the message wasn't sent. The reason for this is that I don't want an invalid address to stop the entire process. Imagine what would happen if the user left the software to send 1,000 e-mails overnight, only for it to error out on the third one because of an invalid e-mail address. In a real-world application, it'd be likely that some kind of log of invalid addresses would be used so that the user could correct the invalid addresses and attempt to resend the newsletter to those addresses.

For completeness, the following is the code for the getMailSession() method:

```
private Session getMailSession() {
    if (session == null) {
        Properties props = new Properties();
        props.put("mail.smtp.host", SMTP_SERVER);
        session = Session.getDefaultInstance(props);
    }

    return session;
}
```

The code for sending the e-mail messages is relatively short, but the messages are quite basic and don't involve any complex assembly, such as would be required for HTML messages with embedded images or messages with two alternative versions of the content. In the next section I'll show you the last part of the puzzle: content generation using Velocity.

Generating the Newsletter Content

At this point you may be wondering if I've forgotten about Velocity completely. Well, the answer is certainly not. However, I did want to illustrate a point by leaving Velocity until the end of the chapter—the application I've built is completely decoupled from Velocity. I could provide any implementation of the NewsletterTemplate interface used by the sendNewsletter() method; I'm not just limited to using Velocity. This is good application design and doesn't add any additional complexity to the application. However, you aren't interested in another implementation; you're interested in Velocity, so you'll now see how you can provide an implementation of the NewsletterTemplate interface using the framework classes discussed in Chapter 4.

Template Object Model

Listing 5-12 shows the NewsletterTemplate interface.

Listing 5-12. The NewsletterTemplate *Interface*

```
package com.apress.pjv.ch5;

import com.apress.pjv.ch4.ContentTemplate;

public interface NewsletterTemplate extends ContentTemplate {

    public NewsletterSection[] getSections();
    public void setSections(NewsletterSection[] sections);

    public Subscriber getSubscriber();
    public void setSubscriber(Subscriber subscriber);
}
```

As you can see, the NewsletterTemplate interface is pretty basic, but it does inherit some methods from the ContentTemplate interface that were discussed in Chapter 4 (see Listing 5-13).

Listing 5-13. The ContentTemplate *Interface*

```
package com.apress.pjv.ch4;

import java.io.Writer;

public interface ContentTemplate {

    public String generate() throws TemplateException;
    public void generate(Writer writer) throws TemplateException;
}
```

If you recall the example from Chapter 4, it's a trivial job to implement the NewsletterTemplate to use Velocity using the AbstractVelocityContentTemplate class, which provides implementations of the generate() methods that use the Velocity template engine (see Listing 5-14).

Listing 5-14. The AbstractVelocityContentTemplate *Class*

```
package com.apress.pjv.ch4;

import java.io.StringWriter;
import java.io.Writer;
```

```java
import org.apache.velocity.Template;

import org.apache.velocity.context.Context;

public abstract class AbstractVelocityContentTemplate {

    public void generate(Writer writer) throws TemplateException {
        try {
            VelocityManager.init("src/velocity.properties");

            Template t = VelocityManager.getTemplate(getResourceName());

            // create the context
            Context ctx = ContextFactory.getInstance();

            // populate with model data
            ModelBean model = getModel();
            ctx.put(model.getModelName(), model);

            t.merge(ctx, writer);

        } catch(Exception ex) {
            throw new TemplateException("Unable to generate output", ex);
        }
    }

    public String generate() throws TemplateException {
        Writer w = new StringWriter();
        generate(w);
        return w.toString();
    }

    protected abstract ModelBean getModel();
    protected abstract String getResourceName();
}
```

However, the difference between this example and the one from Chapter 4 is that I actually need two implementations of the NewsletterTemplate interface: one for the HTML newsletter and one for the plain-text newsletter. Both of these classes are going to share almost identical implementations—in fact, they only differ in their implementation of AbstractVelocityContentTemplate.getResourceName(). To save duplicating a bunch of code, I created the AbstractNewsletterTemplate class, which provides an implementation of the NewsletterTemplate interface and an implementation of AbstractVelocityContentTemplate.getModel() (see Listing 5-15).

Listing 5-15. The AbstractNewsletterTemplate *Class*

```
package com.apress.pjv.ch5;

import com.apress.pjv.ch4.AbstractVelocityContentTemplate;
import com.apress.pjv.ch4.ModelBean;

public abstract class AbstractNewsletterTemplate
            extends AbstractVelocityContentTemplate
        implements NewsletterTemplate {

    private NewsletterSection[] sections;
    private Subscriber subscriber;

    public NewsletterSection[] getSections() {
        return sections;
    }

    public void setSections(NewsletterSection[] sections) {
        this.sections = sections;
    }

    public Subscriber getSubscriber() {
        return subscriber;
    }

    public void setSubscriber(Subscriber subscriber) {
        this.subscriber = subscriber;
    }

    protected ModelBean getModel() {
        return new NewsletterModelBean(sections, subscriber);
    }
}
```

The getModel() method returns an implementation of the following ModelBean interface shown in Chapter 4:

```
package com.apress.pjv.ch4;

public interface ModelBean {

    public String getModelName();
}
```

Here, this implementation is given by the NewsletterModelBean class (see Listing 5-16).

Listing 5-16. The NewsletterModelBean *Class*

```
package com.apress.pjv.ch5;

import com.apress.pjv.ch4.ModelBean;

public class NewsletterModelBean implements ModelBean {

    private NewsletterSection[] sections = null;

    private Subscriber subscriber = null;

    public NewsletterModelBean(NewsletterSection[] sections,
            Subscriber subscriber) {
        this.sections = sections;
        this.subscriber = subscriber;
    }

    public String getModelName() {
        return "newsletter";
    }

    public NewsletterSection[] getSections() {
        return sections;
    }

    public void setSections(NewsletterSection[] sections) {
        this.sections = sections;
    }

    public Subscriber getSubscriber() {
        return subscriber;
    }

    public void setSubscriber(Subscriber subscriber) {
        this.subscriber = subscriber;
    }
}
```

The next step is to provide two subclasses of AbstractNewsletterTemplate: one for the HTML template and one for the plain-text template. The implementation for these classes is trivial, since most of the code is in the AbstractNewsletterTemplate and AbstractVelocityContentTemplate classes (see Listing 5-17).

Listing 5-17. AbstractNewsletterTemplate *and* AbstractVelocityContentTemplate

```
package com.apress.pjv.ch5;

public class HtmlNewsletterTemplate extends AbstractNewsletterTemplate {

    protected String getResourceName() {
        return "html/newsletter.vm";
    }
}
```

```
package com.apress.pjv.ch5;

public class PlainTextNewsletterTemplate extends AbstractNewsletterTemplate {

protected String getResourceName() {
        return "plainText/newsletter.vm";
    }
}
```

If you recall, the NewsletterManager.sendNewsletter() method obtains an implementation of the NewsletterTemplate from the NewsletterTemplateFactory class (see Listing 5-18).

Listing 5-18. The NewsletterTemplateFactory *Class*

```
package com.apress.pjv.ch5;

public class NewsletterTemplateFactory {

    private static NewsletterTemplateFactory instance;

    static {
        instance = new NewsletterTemplateFactory();
    }

    private NewsletterTemplateFactory() {
        // no-op
    }

    public static NewsletterTemplateFactory getInstance() {
        return instance;
    }

    public NewsletterTemplate getNewsletterTemplate(Format format) {
        if (format == Format.HTML) {
```

```
            return new HtmlNewsletterTemplate();
        } else {
            return new PlainTextNewsletterTemplate();
        }
    }
}
```

Notice that the getNewsletterTemplate() method returns an appropriate imple-mentation based on the Format object supplied as the method argument. The NewsletterTemplateFactory class is the last class needed for the application. The class model that's in place for the template generation provides a model that's sim-ple to code against but is also easy to extend. For instance, you'll remember that at the beginning of the chapter I talked about extending the application so that sub-scribers could receive mailings in Macromedia Flash format. Adding this support to the template generation would be easy; all it requires is a small change to the NewsletterTemplateFactory and a new class, FlashNewsletterTemplate, as follows:

```
public class FlashNewsletterTemplate extends AbstractNewsletterTemplate {

protected String getResourceName() {
        return "flash/newsletter.vm";
    }
}
```

Of course, I could quite easily rip out the Velocity support altogether and pro-vide completely different implementations of the NewsletterTemplate interface.

Velocity Templates

With all the Java code complete, all that's left is to create the Velocity templates and run the software. The plain-text template is the simplest, so I will start with that one (see Listing 5-19).

Listing 5-19. The Plain-Text Template

```
Hi, $newsletter.Subscriber.FirstName $newsletter.Subscriber.LastName, ➥
and welcome to the
Apress Monthly Newsletter!

We have a great selection of new books for you this week:

#foreach($section in $newsletter.Sections)
#set($include = false)
```

```
#foreach($cat in $newsletter.Subscriber.SubscribedCategories)
#if($cat == $section.Category)
#set($include = true)
#end
#end
#if($include)
-------------------------------------------
$section.Category.Name
-------------------------------------------

$section.Content

View more details about $section.Category.Name at: $section.Category.WebLink.

#end
#end
-------------------------------------------
To unsubscribe from this newsletter, visit: http://www.apress.com/unsubscribe/ ➥
$newsletter.Subscriber.EmailAddress
```

Most of this code will look familiar; the only part that may throw you is this:

```
#set($include = false)
#foreach($cat in $newsletter.Subscriber.SubscribedCategories)
#if($cat == $section.Category)
#set($include = true)
#end
#end
```

This code will run for each NewsletterSection object in the model and will check to see if the subscriber is subscribed to the category represented by the NewsletterSection. If so, the $include variable is set to true, and the content will be included; otherwise, $include is false and the content will be excluded. Another way of achieving this would have been to add an isSubscribedToCategory(Category) method to the Subscriber object and have Velocity call that—either way the outcome is the same.

For the most part, the HTML template is similar; the only real difference is the obvious one—layout is achieved using HTML tags (see Listing 5-20).

Listing 5-20. The HTML Template

```
<html>
<head>
<title>A P R E S S . C O M | Books for Professionals, by Professionals
...</title>
<base href="http://www.apress.com">
</head>
<body text="#000000" vLink="#333399" link="#333399" leftmargin="0"
background="/img/v1/bkgd.gif" topmargin="0"
marginheight="0" marginwidth="0">
<table cellspacing="0" cellpadding="0" width="780" border="0">
  <tbody>
    <tr valign="top" align="left">
      <td> <table cellspacing="0" cellpadding="0" width="166" border="0">
          <tbody>
            <tr valign="top" align="left">
              <td valign="top" align="left" width="166" height="109">
               <a href = "/">
                 <img src="/img/v1/aMod.gif" height="118"
                          width="166" border="0">
                </a><br />
               </td>
            </tr>
          </tbody>
        </table></td>
      <td> <table cellspacing="0" cellpadding="0" width="614" border="0">
          <tbody>
            <tr valign="top" align="left">
              <td valign="top" align="left" width="614" height="40">
                <img height="40" src="/img/v1/top.gif" alt=""
                          width="614" border="0"><br />
              </td>
            </tr>
          </tbody>
        </table>
        <table cellspacing="0" cellpadding="0" width="614" border="0">
          <tbody>
            <tr valign="top" align="left">
              <td valign=top align=left width="614" height="45">
                     <img height="45" src="/img/v1/mid.gif" alt=""
                             width="614" border="0">
```

```
                    <br />
                    </td>
                </tr>
            </tbody>
        </table>
        <table cellspacing="0" cellpadding="0" width="614" border="0">
            <tbody>
                <tr valign="top" align="left">
                    <td valign="top" align="left" width="614" height="24">
                    <img height="24" src="/img/v1/bot.gif" alt=""
                            width="614" border="0"><br /> </td>
                </tr>
            </tbody>
        </table>
        <!-- Start of Newsletter Content -->
        <h1>Hi, $newsletter.Subscriber.FirstName
$newsletter.Subscriber.LastName,
and welcome to the Apress Monthly Newsletter!</h1>
        <h2>We have a great selection of new books for you this week:</h2>
        <table border="0">
            #foreach($section in $newsletter.Sections)
            #set($include = false)
            #foreach($cat in $newsletter.Subscriber.SubscribedCategories)
            #if($cat == $section.Category)
            #set($include = true)
            #end
            #end

            #if($include)
            <tr>
                <td style="text-weight:bold; text-decoration:underline" bgcolor>
                        $section.Category.Name
                    </td>
            </tr>
            <tr>
                <td>$section.Content</td>
            </tr>
            <tr>
                <td><br>
                    View more details about $section.Category.Name, click
                    <a href="$section.Category.WebLink">here</a>.
```

```
        <hr>
      </tr>
      #end #end
    </table>
    <h3>To unsubscribe from this newsletter, click
<a href="http://www.apress.com/unsubscribe/$newsletter.Subscriber.EmailAddress">
        here</a></h3>.
    <!-- End of Newsletter Content --> </td>
  </tr>
 </tbody>
</table>
</body>
</html>
```

Most of the HTML code has been taken from the Apress Web site; the only fragment of real interest is the bit between the `<!-- Start of Newsletter Content-->` and `<!-- End of Newsletter Content-->` comments.

That's all the code required for the application completed. Now all that remains is to test the application.

Running the Example

Now that you have all the code, you can test the application. Make sure that the SMTP server specified in `NewsletterManager` and the e-mail addresses specified in `SubscriberManager` are valid for your environment.

To run the application, Unix users should execute the following command:

```
java -cp "lib/mail.jar:lib/activation.jar:lib/velocity-dep-1.4.jar:build/." ➥
com.apress.pjv.ch5.Mailer
```

If you're using a Windows operating system, you should swap the colons separating the paths for semicolons.

When the application first loads, you get the main screen with Database/ SQL option preselected in the category list, as shown in Figure 5-2.

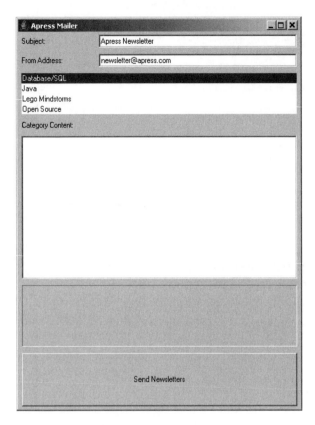

Figure 5-2. Application at startup

Enter some text in the text area, and then swap to another category. You should repeat this process until all the categories have some content, as shown in Figure 5-3.

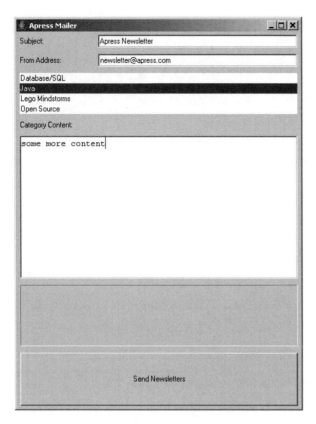

Figure 5-3. Adding category content

Now all that remains to do is click send and watch the progress bar as the mails are sent. When you receive the mail, you should see something like what's shown in Figure 5-4 for the plain-text mails.

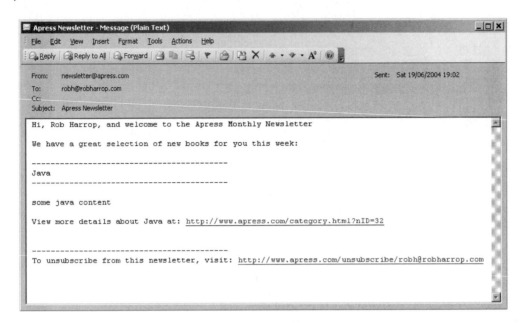

Figure 5-4. Plain-text e-mail

HTML mails look a bit more enticing, as shown in Figure 5-5.

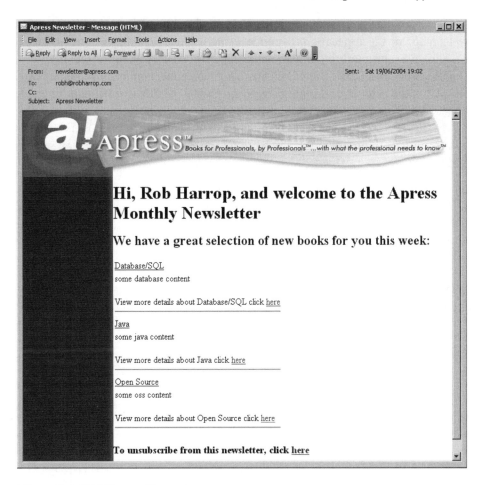

Figure 5-5. HTML e-mail

Summary

In this chapter you saw how you can use Velocity when building nontrivial applications. You haven't seen, however, a vast amount of Velocity code—this is mainly because of the framework discussed in Chapter 4. You saw how easy it is to extend the templating capabilities of the application to include new message formats and how it's possible to replace the templating implementation completely without affecting the application itself.

Applications that are built on top of Velocity should have little Velocity-specific code, reducing the application's dependency on the Velocity engine. In the example shown in this chapter, only one class, `AbstractVelocityContentTemplate`, contains Velocity-specific code. Even though the example application has only two templates, the benefits of this abstraction are clear—consider the benefits for an application with many more templates.

In the next chapter, you'll see how you can use Velocity to build Web-based applications both on its own and in conjunction with frameworks such as Struts and Spring.

### CHAPTER 6

Creating Web Applications with Velocity

VELOCITY IS MOST commonly associated with Web applications, and for good reason. Velocity offers one of the most effective methods for building the user interface for a Web application. Velocity is especially useful in multidisciplined teams where designers and developers work together on the same project. Often designers will find JSP too intimidating and difficult to understand, whereas Velocity templates are easy to learn and read, especially when producing HTML, because white space isn't such as issue.

This chapter covers two distinct topics. First, I'll discuss the basic support for Web applications offered by the standard Velocity distribution and the additional support provided by the VelocityTools project. Second, I'll demonstrate how you can use Velocity in conjunction with two different MVC frameworks, Struts and Spring, to produce full Web applications.

Whilst it's possible to build whole applications on top of the VelocityServlet supplied with the standard Velocity distribution, this isn't a practical approach. VelocityServlet offers only basic control over the Velocity runtime, and it lacks the advanced MVC features of the likes of Struts and Spring. Instead, Velocity is best used in conjunction with these technologies, acting as the View component while your application takes care of the Model and while Struts and Spring take care of the Controller.

Using VelocityServlet

On its own, the standard Velocity distribution offers limited support for building Web applications—in the form of the abstract VelocityServlet class. It's possible to build entire applications with VelocityServlet, just as it's possible to build entire applications on top of HttpServlet. However, as you'll see during the course of this chapter, you have more elegant solutions for building Web applications that use Velocity as the View technology. Having said that, you shouldn't preclude the use of VelocityServlet for developing simple, focused applications that require no navigation—for instance, an RSS aggregator. In this case, the application has a single URI, and using a framework such as Struts or Spring would be overkill.

Creating Hello World with VelocityServlet

Building a servlet on top of VelocityServlet is similar to building a servlet on top of the HttpServlet class. The main difference is that VelocityServlet implements the main methods required by HttpServlet and provides a more specific handleRequest() method for your code to implement. In addition, the VelocityServlet class provides several utility methods that can interact with the Velocity runtime.

Creating a HelloWorldServlet that uses VelocityServlet is a simple job; in fact, more work goes into the configuration and deployment than goes into the actual coding. To start with, I created the template that will create the desired output, like so:

```
Hello $name $!req.getParameter("lastName")
```

This should look familiar to you at this point. Notice that as well as outputting the value of the $name variable, I also have a silent reference to $req.getParameter("lastName"). The VelocityServlet class will automatically add the current HttpServletRequest and HttpServletResponse objects to the context under the names req and res respectively. The next step is to create the servlet code itself. As of version 1.1 of Velocity, you can override two methods on the VelocityServlet class to process each request.

```
Template handleRequest(Context)
Template handleRequest(HttpServletRequest, HttpServletResponse, Context)
```

The first method is the older of the two, and it offers the least amount of control. You can still retrieve the HttpServletRequest and HttpServletResponse in the body of the handleRequest(Context) method using this:

```
HttpServletRequest request =
(HttpServletRequest)context.get(VelocityServlet.REQUEST);
HttpServletResponse response =
(HttpServletResponse)context.get(VelocityServlet.RESPONSE);
```

The main difference in these two methods lies in the handling of null and invalid return values. The first method treats a null or invalid return value as an error, which means you can return only valid Template objects, which Velocity will then output. The second method allows null return values and treats them as an indication that the servlet has handled the request in some other way, perhaps with a redirect or by writing directly to the response stream.

It's generally better to use the latter of the two methods, as it offers the most flexibility in the future, and it also saves you from having to retrieve the request and response objects from the context on every request. The implementation of handleRequest() for the HelloWorldServlet is quite simple (see Listing 6-1).

Listing 6-1. Implementing handleRequest()

```java
package com.apress.pjv.ch6;

import javax.servlet.http.HttpServletRequest;
import javax.servlet.http.HttpServletResponse;

import org.apache.velocity.Template;
import org.apache.velocity.context.Context;
import org.apache.velocity.servlet.VelocityServlet;

public class HelloWorldServlet extends VelocityServlet {

    public Template handleRequest(HttpServletRequest request,
            HttpServletResponse response, Context context) {

        String name = "World";

        if (request.getParameter("name") != null) {
            name = request.getParameter("name").toString();
        }

        context.put("name", name);

        Template t = null;

        try {
            t = getTemplate("helloWorld.vm");
        } catch (Exception ex) {
            log("Unable to find the template helloWorld.vm");
        }

        return t;
    }
}
```

This code is simple enough to require little explanation; the only point of note is the use of getTemplate() method to retrieve a Template instance. The VelocityServlet superclass is responsible for configuring and managing the

Velocity runtime. Using the getTemplate() method, your servlet can retrieve a Template using the resource loaders configured in the current runtime instance.

Configuring the HelloWorldServlet has three stages: the first is to create a Velocity configuration file; the second is to create the web.xml file for the Web application, and the third is to package the application for deployment. Creating the Velocity configuration file is just like creating any standard Velocity configuration file; in fact, for the example code you'll find in the download, I used the same property file for every chapter. For Web applications I prefer to use the ClasspathResourceLoader, since I know my application will always be able to access the classpath. This requires the following small change to my master properties file:

```
resource.loader = file, class

# Classpath Resource Loader (used for chapter 6)
class.resource.loader.class = ➥
org.apache.velocity.runtime.resource.loader.ClasspathResourceLoader
class.resource.loader.cache=true
class.resource.loader.modificationCheckInterval=1
```

The next step is to create the web.xml file for the Web application, like so:

```
<?xml version="1.0" encoding="UTF-8"?>
<!DOCTYPE web-app PUBLIC '-//Sun Microsystems, Inc.//DTD Web Application 2.3//EN'
'http://java.sun.com/dtd/web-app_2_3.dtd'>
<web-app>
    <!-- Simple HelloWorldServlet -->
    <servlet>
        <servlet-name>helloWorld</servlet-name>
        <servlet-class>com.apress.pjv.ch6.HelloWorldServlet</servlet-class>
        <init-param>
            <param-name>properties</param-name>
            <param-value>/velocity.properties</param-value>
        </init-param>
    </servlet>
    <!-- Mapping for Hello World -->
    <servlet-mapping>
        <servlet-name>helloWorld</servlet-name>
        <url-pattern>/helloWorld/*</url-pattern>
    </servlet-mapping>
</web-app>
```

The important thing to notice here is that the `<servlet>` section for the
`HelloWorldServlet` has an `<init-param>` entry that specifies the location of the
properties file containing the Velocity configuration. This is picked up by the
`VelocityServlet` class (the superclass of `HelloWorldServlet`) and is used to load
in the configuration.

The final step is to package the files for deployment to the servlet container. I used Ant to create a WAR file and to ensure that all the files sit in the
correct locations inside the WAR file.

```
<target name="ch6-war"  depends="compile">
        <war destfile="pjv.war" webxml="${ch6.web}/web.xml">
            <classes dir="${dir.build}">
                <include name="**/*.class" />
            </classes>
            <classes dir="${ch6.templates}">
                <include name="**/*.vm" />
            </classes>
            <classes dir="${ch6.data}">
                <include name="**/*.xml" />
            </classes>
            <lib dir="${dir.lib}">
                <include name="**/*.jar" />
            </lib>
            <fileset dir="${dir.src}">
                <include name="velocity.properties" />
            </fileset>
            <webinf dir="${ch6.web}">
                <exclude name="web.xml" />
                <include name="**/*.xml" />
            </webinf>
        </war>
    </target>
```

Notice that the templates are placed in the `classes` directory—which
makes them accessible at the root of the classpath—just what's needed by the
`ClasspathResourceLoader`.

I used Apache Tomcat 5.0.18 to deploy the servlet. You can download the latest version of Tomcat from `http://jakarta.apache.org/tomcat`, or alternatively,
you can use your favorite servlet container. Once you've deployed the Web application, point your browser at the correct location. For Tomcat, this will most
likely be `http://localhost:8080/pjv/helloWorld`. Your output should look similar
to Figure 6-1.

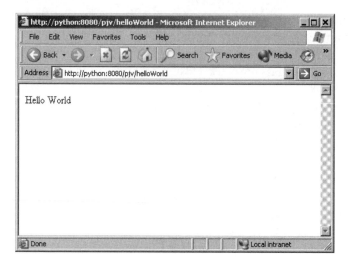

Figure 6-1. HelloWorldServlet *in action*

Now try providing values for name and lastName on the querystring, as shown in Figure 6-2.

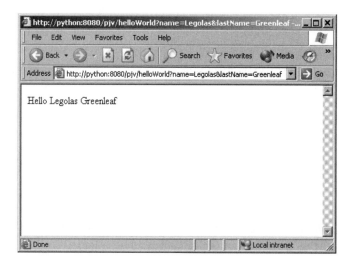

Figure 6-2. More HelloWorldServlet

In Figure 6-2, you can see that instead of World the value Legolas has now been outputted—the servlet code controlled this. Notice also that the value Greenleaf now appears at the end of the output—this is from the silent reference to $req.getParameter("lastName") in the template code.

Using Further VelocityServlet Extensions

The VelocityServlet class has several methods other than the handleRequest()
methods that can be overridden to modify the behavior of your servlet. Table 6-1
describes these methods.

Table 6-1. Additional Hook Methods on VelocityServlet

Method Name	Purpose
createContext(HttpServletRequest, HttpServletResponse)	Overriding this method allows you to add data to or remove data from the Context instance that's passed to the handleRequest() method.
error(HttpServletRequest, HttpServletResponse)	The error() method is invoked whenever an uncaught exception occurs during the doRequest() method. By overriding this method, you can provide a catchall exception handler to prevent your users from seeing a stack trace and so that you can log the stack trace for further inspection.
loadConfiguration(ServletConfig)	By overriding this method, you can add to or completely replace the standard configuration behavior of the VelocityServlet.
mergeTemplate(Template, Context, HttpServletResponse)	Using this method, you can replace the standard template processing behavior. This may be useful if you want to ensure that some content is always included in the context or you want to manipulate the content after the merge.
requestCleanup(HttpServletRequest, HttpServletResponse, Context)	This method is called at the end of the request-processing sequence. Overriding this method allows you to clean up any resources that you may have created during a request or to perform any other end-of-process tasks.
setContentType(HttpServletRequest, HttpServletResponse)	If it's likely that you will be generating the same type of content in each request, you can override this method to set the content type on a request-by-request basis.

Of course, the VelocityServlet class has more methods, but these are the
only ones that are documented hook points. Overriding other methods may
have adverse side effects, either straightaway or when you upgrade to another
version of Velocity.

Easier Views with VelocityViewServlet

Whilst it's quite simple to build a Web application with the VelocityServlet class, it isn't the ideal solution for building full applications because there's no real support for handling navigation and complex actions. The other drawback of VelocityServlet is that it requires you to write code for every single template in your application—you have no way simply to place a template in your Web application and have VelocityServlet pick it up straightaway. Fortunately, the Velocity team recognized this drawback and added the VelocityViewServlet to VelocityTools to solve these problems. VelocityViewServlet brings the following interesting features to the table:

- **Direct processing of VTL templates**: With VelocityViewServlet you can directly reference your Velocity templates as URLs, removing the need to write specific request-handling logic for each template.

- **First-class support for tools**: VelocityViewServlet adds additional support for tools that allow them to be loaded automatically into the context of each template.

- **An excellent set of prebuilt tools**: In addition to providing a simple method to link your own tools into the template context, VelocityViewServlet introduces an interesting set of additional prebuilt tools.

By leveraging tool support it's possible to build complex applications using VelocityViewServlet. You should note, however, that this isn't the preferred mechanism for building Web applications with Velocity. Using this approach is analogous to building an application using just JSP. No central controller is managing navigation and user flow, and business logic in the form of calls to tool methods is intermixed with presentation logic. Tools are ideal, however, for replacing some of the advanced presentational logic that's available with JSP tags. If you're migrating an application from JSP to Velocity, using tools in place of tags should ease that migration somewhat.

Creating Hello World with VelocityViewServlet

Building the Hello World application with VelocityViewServlet requires absolutely no Java code whatsoever. It simply requires a template and the correct configuration of the VelocityViewServlet in the Web application. The template code for this example is slightly more complex, since I now need to check the value of the name querystring parameter in the Velocity template.

```
#set ($name = "World")
#if($request.getParameter("name"))
```

```
#set($name = $request.getParameter("name"))
#end
Hello $name $!request.getParameter("lastName")
```

Notice that I am able to reference the current request object directly in my template through the $request variable. VelocityViewServlet exposes the request, response, session, and servlet context objects in the variables: $request, $response, $session, and $application.

NOTE *You've probably noticed the annoying discrepancy in naming between the* VelocityServlet *and* VelocityViewServlet *classes.* VelocityServlet *uses* $req *and* $res *for the request and response, and* VelocityViewServlet *uses* $request *and* $response. *Be careful of this when building your applications—it can lead to annoying errors.*

The context that's passed to templates via VelocityViewServlet not only searches the inner context for data but also performs an exhaustive search of request, session, and application scope for the data. As you'll see later, this makes VelocityViewServlet invaluable for use in Struts-based applications. To configure the VelocityViewServlet, you just need to add <servlet> and <servlet-mapping> entries to web.xml.

```
<!-- VelocityViewServlet -->
<servlet>
    <servlet-name>velocityTools</servlet-name>
    <servlet-class>
        org.apache.velocity.tools.view.servlet.VelocityViewServlet
    </servlet-class>
    <init-param>
        <param-name>org.apache.velocity.properties</param-name>
        <param-value>/velocity.properties</param-value>
    </init-param>
    <load-on-startup>2</load-on-startup>
</servlet>
<!-- Map *.vm files to Velocity -->
<servlet-mapping>
    <servlet-name>velocityTools</servlet-name>
    <url-pattern>*.vm</url-pattern>
</servlet-mapping>
```

Notice that in a similar vein to VelocityServlet, I specify the location of the properties file, only this time the parameter name is different. The mapping declared will map all requests for resources ending with .vm to the

VelocityViewServlet. All you need to do to get this example running is package the application in the same way you did for the HelloWorldServlet example, deploy it, and point your browser at http://localhost:8080/pjv/helloWorldTools.vm; you should be presented with a screen like that shown in Figure 6-3.

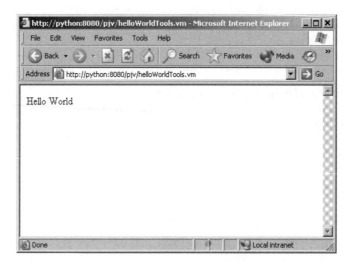

Figure 6-3. VelocityViewServlet *in action*

Try adding the querystring parameter for name and lastName—the output will change accordingly.

Using the Toolbox

In Chapter 3 you saw the use of tools to provide additional functionality from within a Velocity template. The VelocityViewServlet takes the concept of tools a step further and introduces a managed container for tools called the Toolbox. The Toolbox is an externally configured set of Tools that's automatically placed in the context of any template that's accessed through the VelocityViewServlet.

Along with the Toolbox, the VelocityViewServlet introduces an additional set of tools that can prove useful for building your applications. See Table 6-2 for an explanation of the Tools available.

Table 6-2. `VelocityViewServlet` *Tools*

Tool Name	Usage
AbstractSearchTool	Provides a standard API for search tools that are used within Velocity templates. Check the API documentation if you're interested in building an implementation for your application.
CookieTool	Provides methods for creating and manipulating cookies.
ImportTool	Use this tool to import text from a given resource, specified by a URL, into the current template.
LinkTool	This tool provides an excellent set of methods for manipulating links and is useful for building links when you don't know the context path in advance.
ParameterParser	This tool provides convenience methods for parsing POST and GET parameters.
ViewRenderTool	This is an extension of the `RenderTool` for use with the Toolbox.

To load tools into your templates using the Toolbox, you need to create a Toolbox configuration file. Toolbox configuration files are simple, small XML files that simply declare each Tool with a name, a scope value, and an implementing class (see Listing 6-2).

Listing 6-2. Toolbox Config File

```xml
<?xml version="1.0"?>
<toolbox>
    <tool>
        <key>cookie</key>
        <scope>request</scope>
        <class>org.apache.velocity.tools.view.tools.CookieTool</class>
    </tool>
    <tool>
        <key>import</key>
        <scope>session</scope>
        <class>org.apache.velocity.tools.view.tools.ImportTool</class>
    </tool>
    <tool>
        <key>link</key>
        <scope>request</scope>
        <class>org.apache.velocity.tools.view.tools.LinkTool</class>
    </tool>
```

```
<tool>
    <key>params</key>
    <scope>request</scope>
    <class>org.apache.velocity.tools.view.tools.ParameterParser</class>
</tool>
</toolbox>
```

To make the VelocityViewServlet aware of the Toolbox configuration, you
need to add an additional <init-param> entry to the <servlet> definition in web.xml.

```
<init-param>
    <param-name>org.apache.velocity.toolbox</param-name>
    <param-value>/WEB-INF/toolbox.xml</param-value>
</init-param>
```

Now you're ready to start using the tools declared in your Toolbox from within
your templates. Accessing the tools is just like accessing any variables from within
a template. The following is an example of the CookieTool, ImportTool, LinkTool, and
ParameterParser tools in action. I'll explain each tool in order.

```
<html>
    <head>
        <title>Toolbox Demo</title>
    </head>
    <body>
        ## add a cookie
        $cookie.add("myCookie", "someValue")

        #set($cookies = $cookie.getAll())
        <h2>You have the following cookies:</h2>
        {<br>
        #foreach($ck in $cookies)
            $ck.name=$ck.value<br>
        #end
        }
```

The CookieTool allows you manipulate the cookies for the current user. Using
CookieTool.add(), you can create a new cookie for the user, and you can retrieve
all the user's cookies with CookieTool.getAll(). CookieTool.getAll() returns an
array of Cookie objects that can access information about the cookies. You should
note that in Listing 6-2, the cookie added using the call to CookieTool.add() won't
appear in the list until you refresh the page.

ImportTool is the easiest to use of all the supplied tools.

```
<h2>Here is a nice message:</h2>
$import.read("helloWorldTools.vm")
```

ImportTool has a single method, read(), that accepts a single String argument for the URL of the resource you want to import. In the previous code, I imported the helloWorldTools.vm template from the previous example, but I could just as easily have used http://www.amazon.com to import the Amazon home page into my content.

One of the most useful Tools supplied with VelocityViewServlet is the LinkTool. Using this tool, you can construct links to other pages within your application without having to worry about issues such as parameter encoding and context paths.

```
<h2>Here are some interesting links</h2>

<a href="
    $link.setURI("helloWorldTools.vm") ➡
.addQueryData("name", "James T. Kirk")">
    Say Hello</a><br>

<a href="
    $link.setURI("http://www.apress.com/category.html").➡
addQueryData("nID", "32")">
    Java Books at Apress</a><br>

$link.contextURL<br>
$link.contextPath<br>
```

Most of the methods in the LinkTool class return the current LinkTool instance so that they can be chained together to support complex URLs. The most basic method of LinkTool is setURI(), which sets the base URI for the link. In the previous examples, I've added querystring parameters using the addQueryData() method. You should notice that the value for the first link contains spaces—the LinkTool will take care of encoding this correctly. The contextURL and contextPath properties provide information about the URL of the current template. The LinkTool has many more methods for creating and managing links—check the API documentation for more information.

ParameterParser provides utility methods for reading parameters from the querystring. ParameterParser provides getXXX() methods where XXX is the data type you want to read. Support is provided for boolean, double, int, Number, and String data types. ParameterParser also provides support for supplying a default value and for readings arrays of values from the querystring.

```
<h2>Here are some parameters</h2>
p1 = $params.getString("p1", "--unspecified--")<br>
p2 = $params.getInt("p2", 0)<br>
p3 = <br>
{<br>
#foreach($i in $params.getInts("p3"))
    $i<br>
```

```
        #end
        }
    </body>
</html>
```

In the previous example, you can see that I've specified a default value when reading the p1 and p2 parameters from the querystring. When reading the p3 parameter, I've read it as an array of `ints`—this is to support querystrings such as: `?p3=1&p3=9&p3=7`.

Try deploying this sample template and accessing it with different querystring parameters such as `http://localhost:8080/pjv/toolbox.vm?p1=hello&p2=123f&p3=1&p3=2&p3=3`, and you should see something like Figure 6-4.

Figure 6-4. Using the Toolbox

As you can see, the tools supplied with VelocityViewServlet provide a lot of useful functionality for free. However, sometimes you want some functionality that isn't supplied by the standard tools. In the next section you'll see how to build a custom tool and deploy it in the Toolbox.

Using Custom Tools

Building custom tools is quite simple—as you saw in Chapter 3, they're just plain classes. Some of the tools supplied with the VelocityViewServlet implement an additional interface, ViewTool, but this isn't necessary for building your own tools.

Listing 6-3 is a simple tool that generates random messages (mainly movie quotes!).

Listing 6-3. The RandomMessageTool *Class*

```
package com.apress.pjv.ch6;

import java.util.Random;

public class RandomMessageTool {

    private static String[] MESSAGES = new String[] { "Hello World!",
            "May the Force be with you",
            "If I'm reading this right, and I'd like to think that I am...",
            "Core Purge!",
            "Welcome back Mr. Anderson - we missed you...",
            "I will fong you!",
            "One Ring to rule them all!"};

    private Random rnd = null;

    public RandomMessageTool() {
        rnd = new Random();
    }

    public String generateMessage() {
        int index = rnd.nextInt(MESSAGES.length);
        return MESSAGES[index];
    }
}
```

The code is simple and shouldn't require any explanation. To add this tool to the Toolbox, you simply add another <tool> entry to toolbox.xml, like so:

```
<tool>
    <key>randomMessage</key>
    <class>com.apress.pjv.ch6.RandomMessageTool</class>
</tool>
```

Accessing this tool from a template is just like accessing any other tool:

```
Hello Visitor, here is the thought for your visit: ➥
$randomMessage.generateMessage()
```

When you access this template, you'll get something similar to Figure 6-5 (although your message may by different).

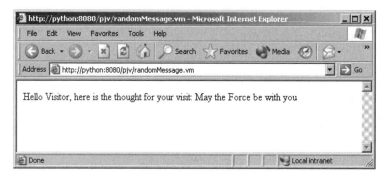

Figure 6-5. Custom tools in the Toolbox

Summarizing Servlets

As you can see from the previous examples, Velocity and VelocityTools have substantial support for producing Web content included; however, they have little support for any of the other features required when building a Web application of any size, such as separation of content and logic and centralized flow control. For these features, you need to couple Velocity with a framework that does support the required features. In the next part of the chapter, I'll demonstrate how you can use Velocity in conjunction with both the Struts and the Spring frameworks to create a full Web application.

Building a Web Application

In this section you'll look at how to build a Web application that uses Velocity as the View technology. Velocity is an excellent View technology that can be used with any of the many different Web application frameworks available. To demonstrate this effectively, I'll build the Web tier twice, once using Struts and once using Spring. Both versions of the Web application will use the same data access logic—exactly the same business logic and exactly the same set of Velocity templates. The only change will be the Web application framework.

The application I'll build is the basis of an e-commerce Web site—Gimli's Widgetarium. I won't build the entire application, since that would probably take a book all to itself; instead, I'll concentrate on just the product catalog and shopping cart to illustrate the use of Velocity.

The data access layer code for the sample application is written using Hibernate, and I have used MySQL as the database although using Hibernate means you can easily change the database if you like. I've used plain old Java objects for the business tier and then framework-specific classes for the Web tier.

NOTE   *For those of you who aren't familiar with Hibernate, it's a high-performance Object Relational Mapping (ORM) tool, written entirely in Java. Hibernate has recently become a part of the JBoss group of projects and continues to be one of the more popular open-source libraries. The reason for using Hibernate in the example was that it requires much less code than straight JDBC!*

I won't spend too much time going into the details of MySQL and Hibernate—you can find more details at `http://www.mysql.com` and `http://www.hibernate.org`, respectively.

Creating the Database

If you don't have MySQL installed on your machine, you should download the latest version from `http://www.mysql.com`. You'll find full installation instructions for your environment on the Web site as well.

The Widgetarium database has only two tables: one for storing products and the other one for storing categories. Each product fits into only one category, but each category will almost certainly have more than one product.

To create the database on your machine, create an SQL script with the code shown in Listing 6-4.

Listing 6-4. SQL Script for Widgetarium

```
DROP DATABASE IF EXISTS widgetarium;
CREATE DATABASE widgetarium;

USE widgetarium;
```

```
DROP TABLE IF EXISTS Categories;
CREATE TABLE Categories (
    CategoryId INTEGER PRIMARY KEY,
    Name VARCHAR(64) NOT NULL
);

DROP TABLE IF EXISTS Products;
CREATE TABLE Products (
    ProductId INTEGER PRIMARY KEY,
    Name VARCHAR(64) NOT NULL,
    Description VARCHAR(255) NULL,
    Price DECIMAL(10,2) NOT NULL,
    CategoryId INTEGER NOT NULL
);

GRANT ALL ON widgetarium.* TO 'gimli'
IDENTIFIED BY 'pwd';
GRANT ALL ON widgetarium.* TO 'gimli'@'localhost'
IDENTIFIED BY 'pwd';
GRANT ALL ON widgetarium.* TO 'gimli'@'localhost.localdomain'
IDENTIFIED BY 'pwd';

FLUSH PRIVILEGES;

INSERT INTO Categories VALUES(0, 'Widgets');
INSERT INTO Categories VALUES(1, 'Wotsits');
INSERT INTO Categories VALUES(2, 'Thingys');

INSERT INTO Products
VALUES(1, 'Standard Widget',
 'A standard widget with no useful features', 12.99, 0);
INSERT INTO Products
VALUES(2, 'Professional Widget', 'A widget for professionals', 14.99, 0);
INSERT INTO Products
VALUES(3, 'Developer Widget', 'Development use only widget', 2.99, 0);
INSERT INTO Products
VALUES(4, 'Enterprise Widget', 'Less extra value - lots extra cost', 18.99, 0);
INSERT INTO Products
VALUES(5, 'Community Widget', 'Widget code included!!!', 5.99, 0);

INSERT INTO Products
VALUES(6, 'Standard Wotsit',
'A standard wotsit with no useful features', 12.99, 1);
INSERT INTO Products
```

```
VALUES(7, 'Professional Wotsit', 'A wotsit for professionals', 15.99, 1);
INSERT INTO Products
VALUES(8, 'Developer Wotsit', 'Development use only wotsit', 3.99, 1);
INSERT INTO Products
VALUES(9, 'Enterprise Wotsit', 'Less extra value - lots extra cost', 21.99, 1);
INSERT INTO Products
VALUES(10, 'Community Wotsit', 'Wotsit code included!!!', 6.99, 1);

INSERT INTO Products
VALUES(11, 'Standard Thingy',
'A standard thingy with no useful features', 18.99, 2);
INSERT INTO Products
VALUES(12, 'Professional Thingy', 'A thingy for professionals', 12.99, 2);
INSERT INTO Products
VALUES(13, 'Developer Thingy', 'Development use only thingy', 1.99, 2);
INSERT INTO Products
VALUES(14, 'Enterprise Thingy', 'Less extra value - lots extra cost', 14.99, 2);
INSERT INTO Products
VALUES(15, 'Community Thingy', 'Thingy code included!!!', 2.99, 2);
```

Save the script file as data.sql and then run the script from the mysql command-line utility using the following command:

```
\. data.sql
```

Make sure that the user you logged into MySQL has the appropriate permissions and that the script file is accessible. If you choose to use a different database, you may need to tweak the script a little to get it working. To check that the script has executed correctly, you should log out of MySQL and attempt to log back in with the following command:

```
mysql --user=gimli --password=pwd
```

If you can't log in, you should check that the GRANT statements from the script are correct and that they executed successfully. As a final check, run the SHOW DATABASES command and check that the list contains the widgetarium database.

Creating the Data Access Layer

An important part of any application is the data access layer. The data access layer for the Widgetarium system is implemented using the Hibernate ORM tool, but this implementation is decoupled from the rest of the application using an interface. The business tier operates against the interface and is unaware of how the data access layer is implemented. You achieve this decoupling by using classes that follow the Factory pattern to create implementation instances, rather than allowing business tier code to create data access objects directly.

 NOTE *During this section, I'll discuss many design patterns. If you're unfamiliar with these design patterns, you should read* Core J2EE Patterns, *Second Edition (Prentice Hall, 2003) and/or* Patterns of Enterprise Architecture *(Addison-Wesley, 2002).*

The interface for the main Data Access Object (DAO) is the `ProductCatalogDAO` interface.

```
package com.apress.pjv.ch6;

import java.util.List;

public interface ProductCatalogDAO {

    public List getAllProducts();
    public List getProductsInCategory(Category category);
    public Product getProduct(int productId);
}
```

As you can see, the interface has only three methods, and the method names are fairly self-explanatory as to the purpose of each method. The `Product` and `Category` classes are Java object representations of the corresponding data in the database. The `Product` class contains properties that correspond to the fields of the Products table, and the only difference is that the category property is of type `Category`, not `int`—this mapping will be taken care of by Hibernate (see Listing 6-5).

Listing 6-5. The `Product` *Class*

```
package com.apress.pjv.ch6;

public class Product {

    private Integer productId;

    private String name;

    private String description;

    private Double price;
```

```java
    private Category category;

    public Product() {

    }

    public Category getCategory() {
        return category;
    }

    public void setCategory(Category category) {
        this.category = category;
    }

    public String getDescription() {
        return description;
    }

    public void setDescription(String description) {
        this.description = description;
    }

    public String getName() {
        return name;
    }

    public void setName(String name) {
        this.name = name;
    }

    public Double getPrice() {
        return price;
    }

    public void setPrice(Double price) {
        this.price = price;
    }

    public Integer getProductId() {
        return productId;
    }

    public void setProductId(Integer productId) {
        this.productId = productId;
    }
}
```

The Category also has properties corresponding to the fields in the database, but these properties are read-only, and Hibernate will never read a Category object from the database. The reason for this is that the Category class is little more than an enum. The Category has no business meaning beyond classifying a grouping of Products. Each Product in the Widget category doesn't need its own instance of Category representing the Widget category—instead, all Products in a Category can share the same instance.

Hibernate has full support for enums using the PersistentEnum interface, which declares a single method toInt(), but Hibernate also requires that classes that implement PersistenEnum provide a static fromInt(int) method as well. Listing 6-6 shows the code for the Category class.

Listing 6-6. Category *Class*

```
package com.apress.pjv.ch6;

import net.sf.hibernate.PersistentEnum;

public class Category implements PersistentEnum {

    public static final Category WIDGET = new Category(0, "Widgets");

    public static final Category WOTSIT = new Category(1, "Wotsits");

    public static final Category THINGY = new Category(2, "Thingys");

    public static final Category[] ALL_CATEGORIES = new Category[] { WIDGET,
            WOTSIT, THINGY};

    private int categoryId;

    private String name;

    private Category(int categoryId, String name) {
        this.categoryId = categoryId;
        this.name = name;
    }

    public int toInt() {
        return categoryId;
    }

    public int getCategoryId() {
        return categoryId;
    }

    public String getName() {
```

```
        return name;
    }

    public static Category fromInt(int id) {
        switch (id) {
        case 0:
            return WIDGET;
        case 1:
            return WOTSIT;
        case 2:
            return THINGY;
        default:
            throw new RuntimeException("Unknown category code");
        }
    }
}
```

Notice that all the possible values for the `Category` class are stored as public constants. This may seem strange at first, especially when you consider that the data is stored in the database and could just as easily be loaded from there. This is until you realize that you could simply remove the Categories table altogether from the database, which would have no adverse effect on the code. Using this approach is a difficult architectural decision, but it's one that can give your application a noticeable performance boost by reducing object creation overhead and memory consumption.

The next step is to create a Hibernate implementation of the `ProductCatalogDAO` interface. Before you can write any Java code, however, you need to create the Hibernate mapping definitions. The mapping definitions tell Hibernate how it should map your Java classes to your database. You only need to create a mapping for the `Product` class, because Hibernate can take care of the `Category` class via the `PersistentEnum` interface—and as I said earlier, the table in the database doesn't need to be there.

 TIP   *Although you don't need the Categories table for this example, it can prove useful if you have other applications that need to be supported by the database such as reporting or archiving. Another benefit is that if your database fully supports foreign keys, then it can check that the correct* `CategoryId` *values are being entered into the database.*

Hibernate mapping files are created in XML, and using the mapping file you can configure not only simple mappings but also complex relationships such as one-to-many and many-to-many. The topic of Hibernate mappings is outside the scope of this book—however, Hibernate does benefit from an excellent PDF manual that you can download from the Web site, which explains mapping in some detail. The `Product` mapping, which is stored in the `Product.hbm.xml` file, is quite simple, as there are no relationships to map.

```xml
<?xml version="1.0"?>
<!DOCTYPE hibernate-mapping PUBLIC "-//Hibernate/Hibernate Mapping DTD//EN"
"http://hibernate.sourceforge.net/hibernate-mapping-2.0.dtd">
<hibernate-mapping>
    <class name="com.apress.pjv.ch6.Product" table="Products">
        <id name="productId" type="int" unsaved-value="null">
            <generator class="assigned"/>
        </id>
        <property name="name" type="string"/>
        <property name="description" type="string"/>
        <property name="price" type="double"/>
        <property name="category" column="categoryId"
                        type="com.apress.pjv.ch6.Category"/>
    </class>
</hibernate-mapping>
```

Most of the mapping should be self-explanatory. The `<id>` tag specifies which of the properties on the `Product` class is the ID of the object. Since the property name is the same as the column name, you have no need to specify the column name. The `<generator>` tag tells Hibernate how the value for `productId` is derived. If your database uses autoincrement or sequence features, you can instruct Hibernate to use those. The `<property>` tags map the properties on the `Product` class to the columns in the Products table. Since most of the properties have the same name as the corresponding column, you have no need to specify a column name. Notice that the mapping for the `category` property has the column name and that the type is set to `Category`. Hibernate will take care of switching between the integer value in the `categoryId` column and an instance of `Category` using the `PersistentEnum` interface.

Hibernate also requires a main configuration file, also written in XML, where the database connection details are stored along with the paths to the mapping files (see Listing 6-7).

Listing 6-7. Main Hibernate Config File

```xml
<?xml version='1.0' encoding='utf-8'?>
<!DOCTYPE hibernate-configuration
PUBLIC "-//Hibernate/Hibernate Configuration DTD//EN"
"http://hibernate.sourceforge.net/hibernate-configuration-2.0.dtd">

<hibernate-configuration>

    <session-factory>
```

```
        <property
name="connection.driver_class">org.gjt.mm.mysql.Driver</property>
        <property name="connection.pool_size">15</property>

        <property name="connection.url">
                jdbc:mysql://localhost:3306/widgetarium
        </property>
        <property name="connection.username">gimli</property>
        <property name="connection.password">pwd</property>
        <property name="connection.autoReconnect">true</property>
        <property
name="dialect">net.sf.hibernate.dialect.MySQLDialect</property>

        <!-- Mapping files -->
        <mapping resource="Product.hbm.xml"/>


    </session-factory>

</hibernate-configuration>
```

You aren't limited to specifying the connection details in this file—you can use a JNDI connection instead if you prefer. With this in place, you're almost ready to create the DAO implementation, but you don't want to expose calling code to the HibernateExceptions that will be thrown by the Hibernate framework if any errors occur; instead, you want to wrap these in an application exception that reduces the coupling to Hibernate (see Listing 6-8).

Listing 6-8. The DataAccessException *Class*

```
package com.apress.pjv.ch6;

public class DataAccessException extends RuntimeException {

    public DataAccessException() {
        super();
    }

    public DataAccessException(String msg) {
        super(msg);
    }
    public DataAccessException(String msg, Throwable rootCause) {
        super(msg, rootCause);
    }

    public DataAccessException(Throwable rootCause) {
        super(rootCause);
    }
}
```

In keeping with my previous comments about checked versus unchecked exceptions, the DataAccessException class is a subclass of RuntimeException, making it unchecked. My thinking is that if your database throws an error, you're unlikely to be able to recover—so why force calling code to catch an exception it can do nothing with?

Now, finally, you can create the ProductCatalogDAOHibernateImpl class that implements the ProductCatalogDAO interface using Hibernate. The class is quite long, so I'll explain it method by method (see Listing 6-9).

Listing 6-9. Implementing ProductCatalogDAO *with Hibernate*

```
package com.apress.pjv.ch6;

import java.util.List;

import net.sf.hibernate.HibernateException;
import net.sf.hibernate.Query;
import net.sf.hibernate.Session;
import net.sf.hibernate.SessionFactory;
import net.sf.hibernate.cfg.Configuration;

public class ProductCatalogDAOHibernateImpl implements ProductCatalogDAO {

    private SessionFactory sessionFactory = null;

    public ProductCatalogDAOHibernateImpl() {
        try {
            sessionFactory = new Configuration().configure()
                    .buildSessionFactory();
        } catch (HibernateException e) {
            throw new DataAccessException(
                    "Unable to configure hibernate framework", e);
        }
    }
}
```

First up is the class constructor, where the SessionFactory is configured. The SessionFactory interface provides access to the important Session interface, which is used to execute queries against the datastore. An implementation of SessionFactory is retrieved using the Configuration class, which will configure the SessionFactory based on the XML configuration file you created earlier. By default, the Configuration class looks in the root of the classpath for a file named hibernate.cfg.xml, but you can change this by passing in a different file path to the configure() method.

NOTE *Working with Hibernate sessions is the most complex part of using Hibernate. The implementation in the* `ProductCatalogDAOHibernateImpl` *class is the simplest but will also lead to poor performance in an application with high throughput. You should read the Hibernate document for a detailed discussion of some techniques for optimizing session performance.*

Notice that any `HibernateExceptions` are wrapped as a `DataAccessException` and rethrown. Next, you have the `getSession()` method, which returns an implementation of the `Session` interface.

```
private Session getSession() throws DataAccessException {
    try {
        return sessionFactory.openSession();
    } catch (HibernateException e) {
        throw new DataAccessException("Could not create session", e);
    }
}
```

This retrieves the `Session` object using the `SessionFactory.openSession()` method, catching any errors and wrapping them. The `closeSession()` method follows a similar pattern.

```
private void closeSession(Session session) throws DataAccessException {
    try {
        session.close();
    } catch (HibernateException e) {
        throw new DataAccessException("Unable to close hibernate session",
                e);
    }
}
```

Again, the code performs a simple operation but also encapsulates the error-handling code. Using this approach for the `getSession()` and `closeSession()` methods means that the rest of the methods in the class will have uniform handling of any errors that should occur when trying to manipulate the `Session`.

The `closeSession()` method is the last of the internal helper methods. Each of the remaining methods implements one of the required methods from the `ProductCatalogDAO` interface. The first method is `getAllProducts()`.

```
public List getAllProducts() {
    Session session = getSession();
    try {
```

```
            Query query = session
                        .createQuery("SELECT p FROM Product AS p ORDER BY p.name");
            return query.list();
        } catch (HibernateException ex) {
            throw new DataAccessException("Unable to retrieve all products", ex);
        } finally {
            closeSession(session);
        }
    }
}
```

In the first line, an implementation of Session is obtained using the getSession()
method. Next the code enters a try/catch/finally block to perform the actual operations. Any HibernateExceptions are caught and rethrown as DataAccessExceptions.
This finally ensures that the closeSession() method is always called to close the
Session object.

The main point of interest in this method is the use of the Query interface.
The code itself is fairly self-explanatory: An implementation of the Query interface is obtained from the Session and then is executed to return a List using
the Query.list() method. The interesting part is the syntax of the query string.
Whilst at first it looks like the query is written in SQL, it's in fact written in
Hibernate Query Language (HQL). HQL shares many similarities in syntax with
SQL, but the main difference is that HQL operates on the object model, not on
the database. You'll notice that the SELECT statement operates on Product (the
class) not Products (the table). HQL provides a powerful abstraction and has
many more features than those shown here—again, check the Hibernate manual for a full rundown.

Next up you have getProductsInCategory().

```
public List getProductsInCategory(Category category) {
    Session session = getSession();
    try {
        Query query = session
                    .createQuery(
                    "SELECT p FROM Product AS p WHERE "
                    + "p.category = :category ORDER BY p.name");
        query.setEnum("category", category);

        return query.list();
    } catch (HibernateException ex) {
        throw new DataAccessException("Unable to retrieve products", ex);
    } finally {
        closeSession(session);
    }
}
```

This method is similar to the getAllProducts() method, and the main difference is the use of a named parameter, :category, in the querystring and the use of Query.setEnum() to give it a value. The Query interface has many setXXX() methods for setting the values of named parameters using different data types—setEnum() is used when the value is a PersistentEnum.

The last method is getProduct().

```
public Product getProduct(int productId) {
    Session session = getSession();
    try {
        Query query = session
                .createQuery("SELECT p FROM Product AS p"
                                    + " WHERE p.productId = :productId");
        query.setInteger("productId", productId);
        return (Product)query.uniqueResult();
    } catch (HibernateException ex) {
        throw new DataAccessException("Unable to retrieve product", ex);
    } finally {
        closeSession(session);
    }
}
}
```

This should look familiar by now—the noticeable difference is that instead of calling Query.list() to return a List containing the query results, you call Query.uniqueResult(), which will return a single result as an Object. The resultant Object is then cast to Product and returned to the caller.

That concludes the code for the Hibernate implementation of ProductCatalogDAO; all that remains for the data tier is to create a factory class to create instances of ProductCatalogDAOHibernateImpl.

```
package com.apress.pjv.ch6;

public class DAOFactory {

    private static DAOFactory instance = null;
    private ProductCatalogDAO productCatalogDAO = null;

    static {
        instance = new DAOFactory();
    }

    private DAOFactory() {
        this.productCatalogDAO = new ProductCatalogDAOHibernateImpl();
    }
```

```
    public static DAOFactory getInstance() {
        return instance;
    }

    public ProductCatalogDAO getProductCatalogDAO() {
        return this.productCatalogDAO;
    }
}
```

The DAOFactory class is a basic implementation of the Factory pattern. Any class that wants an implementation of the ProductCatalogDAO interface will obtain one with a call to DAOFactory.getProductCatalogDAO(). The calling code doesn't need to be aware of the implementation class, which is important if you want to keep your application components loosely coupled.

Creating the Business Tier

There's actually little to the business tier in this application. It would've been much simpler for the Web application to obtain an implementation of ProductCatalogDAO from the DAOFactory and use that directly. However, if I wanted to add some business logic, I'd be left with the choice of either adding the logic to the data tier or creating the business tier and rewriting the Web tier—changes to the business logic would be affecting other tiers. I prefer to make the effort up-front to add the business tier and have the Web tier use that.

For the business tier, I used a similar pattern to the data tier: I have an interface for the business methods, an implementation, and a factory class to enable the Web tier to obtain the correct implementation.

The StoreManager interface contains only three methods, which map one-to-one with the methods in the ProductCatalogDAO interface.

```
package com.apress.pjv.ch6;

import java.util.List;

public interface StoreManager {

    public List getProductList();
    public List getProductList(Category category);
    public Product getProduct(int productId);
}
```

The implementation of the StoreManager class uses the ProductCatalogDAO developed in the previous section, but it could just as easily use another method, such as EJB entity beans, like so:

```
package com.apress.pjv.ch6;

import java.util.List;

public class StoreManagerPOJOImpl implements StoreManager {

    private ProductCatalogDAO dao = null;

    public StoreManagerPOJOImpl() {
        dao = DAOFactory.getInstance().getProductCatalogDAO();
    }

    public List getProductList() {
        return dao.getAllProducts();
    }

    public List getProductList(Category category) {
        if (category == null) {
            return getProductList();
        } else {
            return dao.getProductsInCategory(category);
        }
    }

    public Product getProduct(int productId) {
        return dao.getProduct(productId);
    }

}
```

As you can see, the methods in the StoreManagerPOJOImpl class map directly to the methods in the ProductCatalogDAO interface. However, adding additional business logic would be a simple job and would affect only the business tier. Classes in the Web tier can obtain an implementation of the StoreManager interface using the StoreManagerFactory class, like so:

```
package com.apress.pjv.ch6;

public class StoreManagerFactory {

    private static StoreManagerFactory instance = null;
    private StoreManager impl = null;

    static {
        instance = new StoreManagerFactory();
    }
```

```
        private StoreManagerFactory() {
            impl = new StoreManagerPOJOImpl();
        }

        public StoreManager getStoreManager() {
            return impl;
        }

        public static StoreManagerFactory getInstance() {
            return instance;
        }
    }
```

That's all there is to the business logic for this application. It's likely that your applications will contain much more complex logic than this—but the basic architectural pattern will be the same.

Creating Cart Classes

The classes that implement the cart don't really fit into the business tier, since the business tier most likely doesn't care how the order details are gathered from the user. Also, the cart classes are going to be coupled to the Web tier—there would be no need to use a shopping cart to process orders that were received as an EDI or cXML file.

The CartItem class represents each item that's stored in the cart (see Listing 6-10).

Listing 6-10. CarItem *Class*

```
package com.apress.pjv.ch6;

import java.io.Serializable;

public class CartItem implements Serializable {

    private Product product = null;

    private int quantity;

    public CartItem(Product product, int quantity) {
        this.product = product;
        this.quantity = quantity;
    }
```

```
    public Product getProduct() {
        return this.product;
    }

    public int getQuantity() {
        return this.quantity;
    }

    public void setQuantity(int newQuantity) {
        this.quantity = newQuantity;
    }

    public double getSubTotal() {
        return product.getPrice().doubleValue() * this.quantity;
    }
}
```

Each CartItem class has an associated Product class and a quantity value. You'll also notice that I've added the getSubTotal() method, which calculates the subtotal of this particular CartItem—this method will come in handy when presenting a summary of the cart to the user.

The Cart class represents the cart itself (see Listing 6-11).

Listing 6-11. Cart *Class*

```
package com.apress.pjv.ch6;

import java.io.Serializable;
import java.util.Collection;
import java.util.HashMap;
import java.util.Map;

import javax.servlet.http.HttpSession;

public class Cart implements Serializable {

    private Map items = null;

    private static final String SESSION_KEY = "__CART";

    private Cart() {
        items = new HashMap(8);
    }
```

```
public void addItem(Product product, int quantity) {
    addItem(new CartItem(product, quantity));
}

public void addItem(CartItem cartItem) {
    Integer key = cartItem.getProduct().getProductId();

    if(items.containsKey(key)) {
      CartItem currItem = (CartItem)items.get(key);
      cartItem.setQuantity(cartItem.getQuantity() + currItem.getQuantity());
    }

    items.put(key, cartItem);
}

public void removeItem(Product product) {
    removeItem(product.getProductId());
}

public void removeItem(int productId) {
    removeItem(new Integer(productId));
}

private void removeItem(Integer productId) {
    items.remove(productId);
}

public Collection getItems() {
    return items.values();
}

public static Cart fromSession(HttpSession session) {
    Cart c = (Cart)session.getAttribute(SESSION_KEY);

    if(c == null) c = new Cart();

    return c;
}

public static void storeInSession(HttpSession session, Cart cart) {
    session.setAttribute(SESSION_KEY, cart);
}
}
```

Internally, the Cart class stores the CartItems in a HashMap. The reason for choosing the HashMap over something such as ArrayList is that it's simpler to retrieve a CartItem by the ID of the Product it represents. This is useful in the addItem() method, which won't add two CartItems for the same Product; instead, it will combine the quantities of the two CartItems and keep the resultant CartItem in the HashMap. Using HashMap internally is an implementation detail; for this reason the getItems() method returns a Collection of just the CartItems—there's no need for classes that want to manipulate the list items directly to work with the HashMap; they simply need a list.

The Cart class also encapsulates the logic for storing the Cart in and retrieving the Cart from an HttpSession. Since the Cart class has a private constructor, the only way Web tier code can obtain a Cart instance is by using fromSession(), which will create a new instance if one doesn't exist in the session.

Creating the Velocity Templates

The templates used to create the output are the same for both the Struts and the Spring application. The entry point into the application is the Product List screen, which is created by the productList.vm template (see Listing 6-12).

Listing 6-12. The Product List Template

```
<html>
    <head>
        <title>Product List</title>
    <head>
    <body>
        <h2>Product List</h2>
        <form method="POST" action="/pjv/store/productList">
            <select name="category">
                <option value="-1">All</option>
                #foreach ($category in $categories)
                    <option
value="$category.categoryId">$category.name</option>
                #end
            </select>
            <input type="submit" name="filter" value="filter">
        </form>
        <hr>
        #foreach ($product in $products)

        <a href="/pjv/store/productDetail?pID=$product.productId"
            style="font-size:14pt">
```

```
        $product.name
        </a><br>

        $product.price

        <a href="/pjv/store/addToCart?pID=$product.productId">[Add To Cart]<a>

        <br><br>
        #end
    </body>
</html>
```

This template iterates over the $categories variable to output a list of categories as <option> elements of a <select> form control. This is to support the filtering capability of the Product List page. Selecting a category name and clicking the filter button will redisplay the page with the filtered product list. The product list is produced by iterating over the $products variable. The output of this template looks like Figure 6-6.

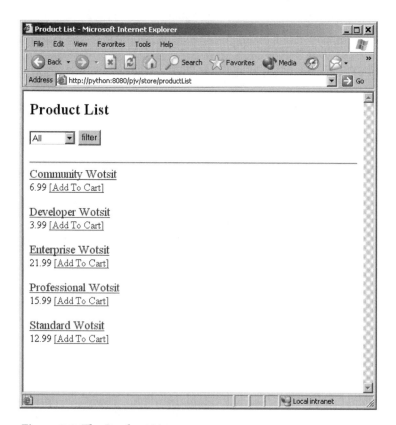

Figure 6-6. The Product List screen

Clicking any of the product names takes the user to the Product Detail screen, and clicking Add To Cart will add one of those products to the cart and display the current contents of the cart.

The productDetail.vm template creates the Product Detail screen (see Listing 6-13).

Listing 6-13. The Product Details Template

```
<html>
    <head>
        <title>$product.name</title>
    </head>
    <body>
        <div style="background-color:Navy; color:White; font-size: 22pt">
        $product.name</div><br>
        <i>$product.description</i><br>
        <br>
        <span style="color: Red;">&pound;$product.price</span>
        <a href="/pjv/store/addToCart?pID=$product.productId">[Add To Cart]<a>
        <br>
        <a href="/pjv/store/pfProductDetail?pID=$product.productId"
                target="_blank">
        [print friendly]</a>
    </body>
</html>
```

This template is simple—it uses the $product variable stored in the context to output the product details. It also creates an Add To Cart link and a link to the printer-friendly version of the Product Detail screen. The output produced by this template looks like Figure 6-7.

Figure 6-7. The Product Detail screen

The pfProductDetail.vm template produces the Print Friendly Product Detail screen and is almost identical to the productDetail.vm template (see Listing 6-14).

Listing 6-14. The Print Friendly Product Detail Template

```
<html>
    <head>
        <title>$product.name</title>
    </head>
    <body>
        <div style="font-size: 22pt">$product.name</div><br>
        <i>$product.description</i><br>
        <br>
        <span>&pound;$product.price</span>
        <br>
        <a href="/pjv/store/pfProductDetail?pID=$product.productId"
            target="_blank">[print friendly]</a>
    </body>
</html>
```

The main differences between this template and the `productDetail.vm` template are the formatting and the lack of a link to the Print Friendly Product Detail screen (no need to link to the current page!). The output for this template looks like Figure 6-8.

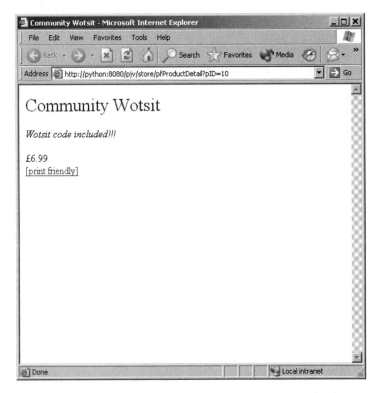

Figure 6-8. The Print Friendly Product Detail screen

The final template is for the Cart Contents screen. The `cart.vm` template renders the contents of the user's cart and provides links to increase the quantity of each item and to remove the item (see Listing 6-15).

Listing 6-15. The Cart Template

```
<html>
    <head>
        <title>Your Cart</title>
    </head>
    <body>
    <h1>Your Cart</h1>
    #if($cart.items.size() > 0)
        <table border="1" cellspacing="1">
        <tr>
```

```
            <th>Product Name</th>
            <th>Price</th>
            <th>Quantity</th>
            <th>Sub Total</th>
            <th> </th>
            <th> </th>
        </tr>
        #foreach($cartItem in $cart.items)
        <tr>
            <td>
            <a href="/pjv/store/productDetail?pID=$cartItem.product.productId"
                style="font-size:14pt">
                $cartItem.product.name</a></td>

            <td>$cartItem.product.price</td>

            <td>$cartItem.quantity</td>

            <td>$cartItem.subTotal</td>

            <td>
            <a href="/pjv/store/addToCart?pID=$cartItem.product.productId"
                style="font-size:14pt">
                [add another]</a></td>

            <td>
            <a href="/pjv/store/removeFromCart?pID=$cartItem.product.productId"
                style="font-size:14pt">
                [remove]</a></td>
        </tr>
        #end
        </table>
    #else
        <i>No items in cart</i>
    #end
    <br>
    <a href="/pjv/store/productList">[back to product list]</a>
    </body>
</html>
```

The code for the cart.vm template should all look familiar, but you should
note the use of the #if directive to check the number of items in the cart. If the
cart contains zero items, then the template will output the message "No items in
cart" instead of an empty table. The output of this template looks like Figure 6-9.

Figure 6-9. The Cart Contents screen

That is the last of the templates; all that remains is to create the Struts and Spring implementations.

Using Velocity with Struts

This is where it starts to get really interesting! I'm not even going to try to cover Struts in detail in this section. If you're unfamiliar with Struts, then I recommend you visit the Web site at http://jakarta.apache.org/struts and invest in a good book such as *Pro Jakarta Struts* (Apress, 2004) written by John Carnell and Rob Harrop (I'm not biased, by the way!).

You can download the latest version from the Web site—I used version 1.1 for this example. Struts leverages the VelocityViewServlet for its Velocity support, so you can simply use template names as the paths for your ActionForward declarations. Any data you place in either session or request, as is the common way with Struts, will be available to your templates that are processed by the VelocityViewServlet. This means that you can create your Struts-based applications in exactly the same way as you would if you were using JSP—there are no special requirements placed on your Struts Actions.

NOTE *For all the examples, I've excluded any code to verify querystring arguments. In a real application, you'd certainly want to validate arguments passed in over the querystring, but in this case I think it'll only overcomplicate the examples.*

Using the ProductListAction Class

The ProductListAction class is responsible for retrieving the appropriate model, passing it to Velocity, and then redirecting the user to the correct template. As with all Struts Actions, the actual template name is contained in the configuration, so it's quite simple to change the ProductListAction class to use a completely different view, perhaps JSP or XMLC (see Listing 6-16).

Listing 6-16. ProductListAction

```
package com.apress.pjv.ch6.struts;

import java.util.List;

import javax.servlet.http.HttpServletRequest;
import javax.servlet.http.HttpServletResponse;

import org.apache.struts.action.Action;
import org.apache.struts.action.ActionForm;
import org.apache.struts.action.ActionForward;
import org.apache.struts.action.ActionMapping;

import com.apress.pjv.ch6.Category;
import com.apress.pjv.ch6.StoreManager;
import com.apress.pjv.ch6.StoreManagerFactory;

public class ProductListAction extends Action {

    public ActionForward execute(ActionMapping mapping, ActionForm form,
            HttpServletRequest request, HttpServletResponse response)
            throws Exception {

        Category c = null;
        if (request.getParameter("category") != null) {
            int id = Integer.parseInt(request.getParameter("category"));

            if (id >= 0) c = Category.fromInt(id);
        }
```

```
    StoreManager mgr = StoreManagerFactory.getInstance().getStoreManager();
    List products = mgr.getProductList(c);

    request.setAttribute("categories", Category.ALL_CATEGORIES);
    request.setAttribute("products", products);

    return mapping.findForward("success");
    }
}
```

Nothing special going on here; if a category parameter is included in the request, then a list of products in that category is stored in the request scope; otherwise the whole list of products is retrieved. In addition to the product list, the entire list of categories is stored in request scope as well. Finally, the method returns an ActionForward instance, which will be retrieved from the configuration using the key success.

The configuration for this action is quite simple:

```
<action type="com.apress.pjv.ch6.struts.ProductListAction" path="/productList">
    <forward name="success" path="/productList.vm"/>
</action>
```

The class is configured to handle any requests for the /productList URI (note that this is relative to servlet mapping for the Struts servlet). The success ActionForward is mapped to the productList.vm template.

Using the ProductDetailAction Class

The ProductDetailAction class processes requests for both the Product Detail and Print Friendly Product Detail pages. The configuration will take care of mapping the correct request URI to the correct template (see Listing 6-17).

Listing 6-17. ProductDetailAction

```
package com.apress.pjv.ch6.struts;

import javax.servlet.http.HttpServletRequest;
import javax.servlet.http.HttpServletResponse;

import org.apache.struts.action.Action;
import org.apache.struts.action.ActionForm;
import org.apache.struts.action.ActionForward;
import org.apache.struts.action.ActionMapping;

import com.apress.pjv.ch6.Product;
import com.apress.pjv.ch6.StoreManager;
import com.apress.pjv.ch6.StoreManagerFactory;
```

```
public class ProductDetailAction extends Action {

    public ActionForward execute(ActionMapping mapping, ActionForm form,
            HttpServletRequest request, HttpServletResponse response)
            throws Exception {

        StoreManager mgr = StoreManagerFactory.getInstance().getStoreManager();

        Product p = null;
        if (request.getParameter("pID") != null) {
            int id = Integer.parseInt(request.getParameter("pID"));

            if (id >= 0) p = mgr.getProduct(id);
        }

        request.setAttribute("product", p);

        return mapping.findForward("success");
    }
}
```

The code is fairly simple; an instance of Product is retrieved using the ID specified in the pID. This instance is stored in request scope, and an instance of ActionForward is retrieved from the configuration using the "success" key and is returned to the caller.

This class has two entries in the configuration, one for the Product Detail screen and the other for the Print Friendly Product Detail screen.

```
<action type="com.apress.pjv.ch6.struts.ProductDetailAction"
                path="/productDetail">
        <forward name="success" path="/productDetail.vm"/>
</action>
<action type="com.apress.pjv.ch6.struts.ProductDetailAction"
                path="/pfProductDetail">
        <forward name="success" path="/pfProductDetail.vm"/>
</action>
```

As you can see, the only differences are the request URI and the template mapped to the success ActionForward.

Using the AddToCartAction Class

The AddToCartAction class is responsible for adding an item to the user's cart and then forwarding the user to the Cart Contents page (see Listing 6-18).

Listing 6-18. AddToCartAction

```java
package com.apress.pjv.ch6.struts;

import javax.servlet.http.HttpServletRequest;
import javax.servlet.http.HttpServletResponse;

import org.apache.struts.action.Action;
import org.apache.struts.action.ActionForm;
import org.apache.struts.action.ActionForward;
import org.apache.struts.action.ActionMapping;

import com.apress.pjv.ch6.Cart;
import com.apress.pjv.ch6.Product;
import com.apress.pjv.ch6.StoreManager;
import com.apress.pjv.ch6.StoreManagerFactory;

public class AddToCartAction extends Action {

    public ActionForward execute(ActionMapping mapping, ActionForm form,
            HttpServletRequest request, HttpServletResponse response)
            throws Exception {

        StoreManager mgr = StoreManagerFactory.getInstance().getStoreManager();

        Product p = null;
        if (request.getParameter("pID") != null) {
            int id = Integer.parseInt(request.getParameter("pID"));

            if (id >= 0) p = mgr.getProduct(id);
        }

        Cart cart = Cart.fromSession(request.getSession());
        cart.addItem(p, 1);
        Cart.storeInSession(request.getSession(), cart);

        return mapping.findForward("success");
    }
}
```

Most of this code should look familiar; the important part to look at is the interaction with the Cart class. The configuration for this class is slightly different than for the classes you've seen so far.

```xml
<action type="com.apress.pjv.ch6.struts.AddToCartAction" path="/addToCart">
    <forward name="success" path="/store/showCart" contextRelative="false"/>
  </action>
```

You should notice that the success `ActionForward` isn't mapped to a Velocity template; instead, it's mapped to the request URI /store/showCart. This URI is mapped to the `ShowCartAction` class. So why couldn't I just map to cart.vm template? The reason is that the `ShowCartAction` performs some specific setup code before forwarding the user to the cart.vm template, and I didn't want to duplicate this code in the `AddToCartAction` class.

Using the RemoveFromCartAction Class

The `RemoveFromCartAction` class processes any requests to remove an item from the cart (see Listing 6-19).

Listing 6-19. RemoveFromCartAction

```
package com.apress.pjv.ch6.struts;

import javax.servlet.http.HttpServletRequest;
import javax.servlet.http.HttpServletResponse;

import org.apache.struts.action.Action;
import org.apache.struts.action.ActionForm;
import org.apache.struts.action.ActionForward;
import org.apache.struts.action.ActionMapping;

import com.apress.pjv.ch6.Cart;

public class RemoveFromCartAction extends Action {

    public ActionForward execute(ActionMapping mapping, ActionForm form,
            HttpServletRequest request, HttpServletResponse response)
            throws Exception {

        int id = Integer.parseInt(request.getParameter("pID"));

        Cart cart = Cart.fromSession(request.getSession());
        cart.removeItem(id);
        Cart.storeInSession(request.getSession(), cart);

        return mapping.findForward("success");
    }
}
```

Configuring this class is similar to the configuration for `AddToCartAction`.

```
<action type="com.apress.pjv.ch6.struts.RemoveFromCartAction"
                path="/removeFromCart">
    <forward name="success" path="/store/showCart"
                        contextRelative="false"/>
</action>
```

Again, I've mapped the success ActionForward to the URI for the
ShowCartAction class.

Using the ShowCartAction Class

The ShowCartAction class is the simplest of all the Struts Action classes (see
Listing 6-20).

Listing 6-20. ShowCartAction

```
package com.apress.pjv.ch6.struts;

import javax.servlet.http.HttpServletRequest;
import javax.servlet.http.HttpServletResponse;

import org.apache.struts.action.Action;
import org.apache.struts.action.ActionForm;
import org.apache.struts.action.ActionForward;
import org.apache.struts.action.ActionMapping;

import com.apress.pjv.ch6.Cart;

public class ShowCartAction extends Action {

    public ActionForward execute(ActionMapping mapping, ActionForm form,
            HttpServletRequest request, HttpServletResponse response)
            throws Exception {

        Cart cart = Cart.fromSession(request.getSession());
        request.setAttribute("cart", cart);

        return mapping.findForward("success");
    }
}
```

It should be noted that there's no need to place the Cart object in the request
scope. Instead, I could access it directly from the session. However, in this case
I have a specific name for the Cart variable, $cart, and the cart is bound to the

session as __CART, so this way I make the Cart available using the correct variable name. The configuration class simply maps the success ActionForward to the cart.vm template.

```
<action type="com.apress.pjv.ch6.struts.ShowCartAction"
            path="/showCart">
    <forward name="success" path="/cart.vm"/>
</action>
```

All that's left for the Struts version of the application is to create the struts-config.xml file and to configure the Struts servlet in the web.xml file.

Configuring the Application

The first step in configuring the application is to create the struts-config.xml file. You've already seen most of the content for this file—Listing 6-21 shows the code for the completed file.

Listing 6-21. struts-config.xml

```
<?xml version="1.0" encoding="ISO-8859-1" ?>

<!DOCTYPE struts-config PUBLIC

 "-//Apache Software Foundation//DTD Struts Configuration 1.1//EN"

 "http://jakarta.apache.org/struts/dtds/struts-config_1_1.dtd">
<struts-config>
    <action-mappings>
        <action type="com.apress.pjv.ch6.struts.ProductListAction"
                    path="/productList">
            <forward name="success" path="/productList.vm"/>
        </action>
        <action type="com.apress.pjv.ch6.struts.ProductDetailAction"
                    path="/productDetail">
            <forward name="success" path="/productDetail.vm"/>
        </action>
        <action type="com.apress.pjv.ch6.struts.ProductDetailAction"
                    path="/pfProductDetail">
            <forward name="success" path="/pfProductDetail.vm"/>
        </action>
        <action type="com.apress.pjv.ch6.struts.AddToCartAction"
                    path="/addToCart">
```

```
                <forward name="success" path="/store/showCart"
                              contextRelative="false"/>
        </action>
        <action type="com.apress.pjv.ch6.struts.RemoveFromCartAction"
                     path="/removeFromCart">
                <forward name="success" path="/store/showCart"
                              contextRelative="false"/>
        </action>
        <action type="com.apress.pjv.ch6.struts.ShowCartAction"
                     path="/showCart">
                <forward name="success" path="/cart.vm"/>
        </action>
    </action-mappings>
    <controller
        processorClass="org.apache.struts.action.RequestProcessor"
locale="false"/>
</struts-config>
```

The last step is to add the appropriate `<servlet>` and `<servlet-mapping>` definitions to the web.xml file.

```
<servlet>
        <servlet-name>struts</servlet-name>
        <servlet-class>org.apache.struts.action.ActionServlet</servlet-class>
        <init-param>
            <param-name>config</param-name>
            <param-value>/WEB-INF/struts-config.xml</param-value>
        </init-param>
        <load-on-startup>1</load-on-startup>
    </servlet>
<servlet-mapping>
        <servlet-name>struts</servlet-name>
        <url-pattern>/store/*</url-pattern>
    </servlet-mapping>
```

Now all you need to do is package up the application and deploy it to your servlet container. All the code is included in the download, including an Ant build script to create a WAR file to deploy the application.

Try the application to make sure it's functioning correctly—you should be able to filter the product list, view product details, and add and remove products from the cart.

Using StrutsTools

Before moving onto the Spring implementation of the application, I want to point out some additional tools that are available as part of the VelocityTools project specifically for use with Struts (see Table 6-3).

Table 6-3. Tools for Struts Included in VelocityTools

Tool Name	Description
ActionMessagesTool	This tool provides methods for working with Struts ActionMessages.
ErrorsTool	This tool provides methods for manipulating Struts error messages.
FormTool	Using this tool, you can create HTML forms for use in Struts applications without relying on the Struts HTML JSP tag library.
MessageTool	Use this tool to work with internationalized content in your Struts application.
StrutsLinkTool	This tool provides methods for creating links to Struts Actions and Forwards without the need for the Struts HTML JSP tag library. This tool extends the standard LinkTool available in VelocityTools.
SecureLinkTool	This tool serves the same purpose as the StrutsLinkTool but works for SSL links.
TilesTool	Provides a mechanism to interact with the Tiles framework from within your Struts applications.
ValidatorTool	Provides a method to work with the Validator framework.

Using Velocity with the Spring Framework

As with Struts, I don't want to go into too much detail on the Spring Framework. Spring is an absolutely huge topic, much bigger even than Struts. Spring isn't just a Web framework, but it also includes a complete Aspect Oriented Programming (AOP) framework, an Inversion of Control (IoC) container, and convenience APIs for many different technologies including EJB, JDBC, and even Hibernate and Struts. Typically, I'd use Spring throughout an application, not just in the Web tier; however, it works just as well for the Web tier.

To find out more information about Spring and to download the latest version of the framework, visit http://www.springframework.org. I use version 1.0 of the Spring Framework for this example.

The Java code for the Spring version of the application is much simpler than the code for the Struts version. Much of the code is the same, but rather than having separate classes for each action, each action corresponds to a single method in the same class, which is a subclass of the MultiActionController class (see Listing 6-22).

Listing 6-22. StoreActionController

```
package com.apress.pjv.ch6.spring;

import java.util.HashMap;
import java.util.List;
import java.util.Map;

import javax.servlet.ServletException;
import javax.servlet.http.HttpServletRequest;
import javax.servlet.http.HttpServletResponse;

import org.springframework.web.bind.RequestUtils;
import org.springframework.web.servlet.ModelAndView;
import org.springframework.web.servlet.mvc.multiaction.MultiActionController;

import com.apress.pjv.ch6.Cart;
import com.apress.pjv.ch6.Category;
import com.apress.pjv.ch6.Product;
import com.apress.pjv.ch6.StoreManager;

public class StoreActionController extends MultiActionController {

    private StoreManager storeManager = null;

    public void setStoreManager(StoreManager storeManager) {
        this.storeManager = storeManager;
    }

    private Map getModel() {
        Map model = new HashMap();
        return model;
    }

    public ModelAndView handleProductList(HttpServletRequest request,
            HttpServletResponse response) throws ServletException {
```

```
        Category c = null;
        int id = RequestUtils.getIntParameter(request, "category", -1);

        if (id >= 0) c = Category.fromInt(id);

        List products = storeManager.getProductList(c);

        Map model = getModel();
        model.put("categories", Category.ALL_CATEGORIES);
        model.put("products", products);

        return new ModelAndView("productList.vm", model);
    }

    public ModelAndView handleAddToCart(HttpServletRequest request,
            HttpServletResponse response) throws ServletException {

        Product p = null;

        int id = RequestUtils.getIntParameter(request, "pID", -1);

        if (id >= 0) p = storeManager.getProduct(id);

        Cart cart = Cart.fromSession(request.getSession());
        cart.addItem(p, 1);
        Cart.storeInSession(request.getSession(), cart);

        return handleShowCart(request, response);
    }

    public ModelAndView handleRemoveFromCart(HttpServletRequest request,
            HttpServletResponse response) throws ServletException {
        int id = RequestUtils.getIntParameter(request, "pID", -1);

        Cart cart = Cart.fromSession(request.getSession());
        cart.removeItem(id);
        Cart.storeInSession(request.getSession(), cart);

        return handleShowCart(request, response);
    }

    public ModelAndView handleProductDetail(HttpServletRequest request,
            HttpServletResponse response) throws ServletException {
        return handleProductDetailInternal(request, response,
                "productDetail.vm");
    }
```

```
    public ModelAndView handlePrintFriendlyProductDetail(
            HttpServletRequest request, HttpServletResponse response)
            throws ServletException {
        return handleProductDetailInternal(request, response,
                "pfProductDetail.vm");
    }

    private ModelAndView handleProductDetailInternal(
            HttpServletRequest request, HttpServletResponse response,
            String viewName) throws ServletException {

        int id = RequestUtils.getIntParameter(request, "pID", -1);

        Product p = null;

        if (id >= 0) p = storeManager.getProduct(id);

        return new ModelAndView(viewName, "product", p);
    }

    public ModelAndView handleShowCart(HttpServletRequest request,
            HttpServletResponse response) throws ServletException {
        Cart cart = Cart.fromSession(request.getSession());

        Map model = getModel();
        model.put("cart", cart);

        return new ModelAndView("cart.vm", model);
    }
}
```

You should note that this isn't the only way of building Web applications with Spring—you have many different ways of creating controllers in the Spring framework; this is just one of them. Since most of the methods contain similar code to the corresponding Struts Actions, I'll just explain one of the methods so you can get an idea of how Spring works.

The handleShowCart() method retrieves the user's cart from the session using the Cart class.

```
public ModelAndView handleShowCart(HttpServletRequest request,
        HttpServletResponse response) throws ServletException {
    Cart cart = Cart.fromSession(request.getSession());

    Map model = getModel();
    model.put("cart", cart);
```

```
            return new ModelAndView("cart.vm", model);
    }
```

Next, an instance of HashMap is retrieved using the getModel() method, and the Cart is added to the HashMap. This is one of the big differences between Struts and Spring. In Struts, the data is added into the request or session scope, but in Spring, you add the data to a Map, and Spring will take care of the rest. The final step is to return an instance of the ModelAndView class, which links the name of the view, in this case cart.vm, to the model data—Spring will then load the view and pass it the data based on the configuration options you set.

Although there isn't as much Java code for the Spring version of the application, there's much more configuration to do. First, you may have noticed that none of the methods in the StoreActionController uses StoreManagerFactory to load an implementation of StoreManager—in fact, the StoreManagerFactory class isn't used in the StoreActionController at all. Instead, I've a created a property on the StoreActionController so that the StoreManager implementation can be set by an external class:

```
private StoreManager storeManager = null;

    public void setStoreManager(StoreManager storeManager) {
        this.storeManager = storeManager;
    }
```

Second, I can then use Spring's IoC capabilities to set the value of this property dynamically. In the Spring applicationContext.xml file, I declare a bean that I'll then use to set this property of the StoreActionController.

```
<?xml version="1.0" encoding="UTF-8"?>
<!DOCTYPE beans PUBLIC "-//SPRING//DTD BEAN//EN"
"http://www.springframework.org/dtd/spring-beans.dtd">

<beans>
    <!-- StoreManager Implementation -->
    <bean id="storeManager"
        class="com.apress.pjv.ch6.StoreManagerPOJOImpl" lazy-init="true"/>
</beans>
```

The next step is to create the configuration for the Spring servlet. The Spring servlet requires some specific configuration beans to be set to use Velocity (see Listing 6-23).

Listing 6-23. Configuring Velocity in Spring

```xml
<?xml version="1.0" encoding="UTF-8"?>
<!DOCTYPE beans PUBLIC "-//SPRING//DTD BEAN//EN"
"http://www.springframework.org/dtd/spring-beans.dtd">
<beans>
    <!-- View Resolver -->
    <bean id="viewResolver"
 class=
"org.springframework.web.servlet.view.velocity.VelocityViewResolver">
        <property name="viewClass">
            <value>org.springframework.web.servlet.view.velocity.VelocityView
            </value>
        </property>
    </bean>
    <bean id="velocityConfig"
class=
"org.springframework.web.servlet.view.velocity.VelocityConfigurer">
        <property name="configLocation">
            <value>velocity.properties</value>
        </property>
    </bean>
```

The viewResolver bean is a special bean that Spring uses to determine
how it should resolve the view names returned in the ModelAndView objects. The
VelocityViewResolver class requires that another bean of type VelocityConfigurer
be present in the current context. You can give this bean any name you like—
I chose the name velocityConfig. Notice that I set the configLocation of the
VelocityConfigurer to velocity.properties, so the Spring version of the application is using the same configuration as the Struts application. The next step in
the configuration is to configure the StoreActionController and the URL mappings (see Listing 6-24).

Listing 6-24. Spring Controller Configuration

```xml
<!-- Multi Action Controller to handle store actions -->
    <bean id="storeController"
        class="com.apress.pjv.ch6.spring.StoreActionController">
        <property name="methodNameResolver">
            <ref local="storeControllerResolver"/>
        </property>
        <property name="storeManager">
            <ref bean="storeManager"/>
        </property>
```

```
        </bean>
        <!-- Method Resolver for the Store Controller-->
        <bean id="storeControllerResolver"
class=
"org.springframework.web.servlet.mvc.multiaction.PropertiesMethodNameResolver">
            <property name="mappings">
                <props>
                    <prop key="/productList">handleProductList</prop>
                    <prop key="/addToCart">handleAddToCart</prop>
                    <prop key="/removeFromCart">handleRemoveFromCart
                            </prop>
                    <prop key="/showCart">handleShowCart</prop>
                    <prop key="/productDetail">handleProductDetail
                            </prop>
                    <prop key="/pfProductDetail">handlePrintFriendlyProductDetail
                            </prop>
                </props>
            </property>
        </bean>
        <!-- Manage URL to Controller Mappings -->
        <bean id="urlMapping"
class="org.springframework.web.servlet.handler.SimpleUrlHandlerMapping">
            <property name="mappings">
                <props>
                    <prop key="/productList">storeController</prop>
                    <prop key="/addToCart">storeController</prop>
                    <prop key="/removeFromCart">storeController</prop>
                    <prop key="/showCart">storeController</prop>
                    <prop key="/productDetail">storeController</prop>
                    <prop key="/pfProductDetail">storeController</prop>
                </props>
            </property>
        </bean>
</beans>
```

The urlMapping bean is a special bean that's used by the Spring servlet to
map requests to controller instances. In this case, I've mapped all the URLs to
the storeController bean. The storeController bean is an instance of the
StoreActionController class. Notice that I have set two properties on this bean.
The storeManager property is set to the storeManager bean that I configured
previously—Spring will ensure that this property is set before my action handler
methods are called. In this way, I can easily change the implementation of
StoreManager used by the Controller. The methodNameResolver property is set to
the storeControllerResolver bean. This bean maps each of the request URLs to

the appropriate handler method. The `MultiActionController` (the superclass of `StoreActionController`) uses this bean to determine which methods need to be invoked for each request. At first, this configuration can appear intimidating, but you soon get to grips with it, and it offers an excellent level of flexibility for configuring the application behavior without changing the Java code.

The final step is to add the appropriate configuration options to the `web.xml` file.

```
<context-param>
<param-name>contextConfigLocation</param-name>
<param-value>/WEB-INF/applicationContext.xml</param-value>
 </context-param>
<!-- Spring Context Loader -->
<servlet>
<servlet-name>context</servlet-name>
<servlet-class>org.springframework.web.context.ContextLoaderServlet
</servlet-class>
    <load-on-startup>1</load-on-startup>
</servlet>
<!-- Spring Dispatcher -->
<servlet>
    <servlet-name>spring</servlet-name>
    <servlet-class>org.springframework.web.servlet.DispatcherServlet
    </servlet-class>
    <load-on-startup>2</load-on-startup>
</servlet>
<!-- Store Mapping -->
<servlet-mapping>
        <servlet-name>spring</servlet-name>
    <url-pattern>/store/*</url-pattern>
</servlet-mapping>
```

The `contextConfigLocation` `<context-param>` is used by the Spring `ContextLoaderServlet` to load the application's context configuration into the VM. The `ContextLoaderServlet` will monitor the configuration file for changes and reload the configuration as appropriate.

 NOTE *You may be wondering why I've split the context configuration into two files. The reason for this is that I have put all the Web-specific configuration into the servlet configuration and all the Web-independent configuration into the application configuration. In this way I'm free to reuse the application configuration with other non-Web-based user interfaces.*

The main servlet is the `DispatcherServlet`, which is mapped to the request URI `/store/*`. Try deploying this version of the application and working your way through it—it should function just the same as the Struts application; after all, both versions share the same data and business logic along with the same set of templates.

Summary

I've covered a lot of different concepts in this chapter. To start, I demonstrated how to use the `VelocityServlet` and `VelocityViewServlet` classes to build Web content. I took a detailed look at the `VelocityViewServlet` Toolbox and at the tools available as part of the VelocityTools project. In the second part of the chapter, I built the basic components of a full Web application, including data access, business logic, and presentation, with Velocity. Finally, I used these components to implement two versions of the same Web application: one using Struts and the other using Spring.

You should now have a clear understanding of what goes into building a Web application with Velocity; you should also have a clear idea about which framework you'll be using in conjunction with Velocity. Struts has enjoyed great success and is well integrated with Velocity, making for a proven solution to your Web applications. In contrast, Spring is the new kid on the block and is yet to experience the same level of adoption as Struts. However, I urge you to look at Spring, as it promises to be a viable solution for your entire application, not just the Web tier.

CHAPTER 7

Using Velocity and Anakia

SO FAR YOU'VE SEEN how you can use Velocity to build your applications but not how you can use Velocity to improve other areas of the development process. In this chapter, I'll show you how to use Velocity and Anakia to ease the burden of creating documentation within your project.

So what is Anakia? Well, put simply, Anakia is a tool for transforming XML data using familiar Velocity concepts. Anakia is built as an Ant task and uses JDOM and Velocity to manipulate the XML input and to produce textual output. Using Anakia to transform XML content is typically a lot simpler than using XSL, although Anakia is not quite as powerful as XSL.

Anakia was originally created as a replacement for Stylebook and is used for creating static Web sites based on XML content. Whilst you can create any kind of output using Anakia and use it for any purpose, it's really intended as a documentation tool for software development projects. The following are the main features of Anakia:

Ant integration: Anakia runs as an Ant task, which makes it perfect for integration into software development projects. Using the Anakia task you can integrate the documentation creation process into your build process.

Simple VTL syntax: The style sheets used to transform the XML are written in VTL. This means you can use all the familiar VTL constructs to transform the XML content—no need to learn the complex XSL syntax.

JDOM for XML: The decision to use JDOM for the XML content rather than standard DOM was particularly inspired. Reading XML content using DOM is difficult enough in Java and would be a nightmare in VTL. The JDOM simple object model is a perfect complement to VTL.

File set processing: Rather than working on files individually, Anakia works on sets of XML files, applying the same transformations to each XML file to produce a distinct output file.

Shared project data: A feature that goes hand in hand with Anakia's ability to work on sets of input files is the ability to define an XML file that contains data to be included in every output file. When creating a style sheet, you have access to the XML of the current file and the XML of the shared project file.

As you can see from the feature set, Anakia is clearly suited to building documentation or project Web sites for software development projects. In fact, the documentation for the Velocity and the Jakarta sites was created using Anakia—the process used is documented at `http://jakarta.apache.org/site/` `jakarta-site2.html`.

In the first part of this chapter, I'll present some simple examples to give you a feel for how Anakia works. Next, I'll briefly introduce JDOM, and I'll compare code written using Java and JDOM with code written using Anakia and Velocity so you're able to see the similarities between the two. Then, I'll detail the Anakia Ant task, how it establishes the Velocity context for your style sheets, and what data is available in that context. Finally, I'll present a full demonstration and build the documentation for a full project using Anakia.

Getting Started

Before you get started with the examples, you need to make sure you have all the required tools. You will of course need to obtain Ant from `http://ant.apache.org`; I used version 1.6.1 for the examples in this chapter. You can find instructions for installing Ant in the download. If you're unfamiliar with Ant, you should definitely check out the Web site and pick up a copy of *Ant: The Definitive Guide* (O'Reilly, 2002). Anakia itself is included in the standard Velocity distribution, but you'll need to download JDOM, which isn't included in the download at all. You can obtain JDOM from `http://www.jdom.org`; I used beta 9 for the examples in this chapter.

 CAUTION   *At the time of writing, the current version of the JDOM is actually beta 10. However, some classes in beta 10 have been moved to different packages, causing an incompatibility with Velocity 1.4.*

Creating Hello World with Anakia

In keeping with the rest of the book, and indeed almost all computer books ever, the first example will be the ubiquitous Hello World example. To create output using Anakia, you need at least three files: a style sheet, an Ant build script, and at least one input file. The input file must be a well-formed XML document, but it doesn't have to adhere to any particular schema, so you're free to use whatever flavor of XML you like. For the purposes of this example I'll keep the XML simple.

```
<root>
    <msg>Hello World!</msg>
</root>
```

In this XML document I have the document element, in this case <root>. The <root> element has a single child, <msg>, which contains the text *Hello World!* This file is saved as helloWorld.xml. The VTL code required to extract the text from the <msg> tag is simple.

```
$root.getChild("msg").getText()
```

You're probably wondering where the $root variable comes from and what kind of object it is—well, don't worry about that for now. I'll get to that later, so for now just know that this fragment of VTL will read the text from the <msg> tag.

NOTE *If one of the nodes in your VTL expression doesn't exist, then no error is thrown. Instead, the raw VTL is included in the output stream. For instance, if you change the name of the node in the previous example from* msg *to* msg1, *then Velocity will treat the line* $root.getChild("msg").getText() *as static output.*

The style sheet is saved as helloWorld.vsl (the .vsl extension being the recommended extension for Anakia style sheets). The last piece of the puzzle is the Ant build script (see Listing 7-1).

Listing 7-1. Ant Build Script

```
<project name="Pro Jakarta Velocity" basedir="." default="helloWorld">

    <!-- properties for build -->
    <property name="dir.src" value="src" />
    <property name="dir.lib" value="lib" />
    <property name="dir.build" value="build" />

    <!-- classpath -->
    <path id="project.classpath">
        <pathelement path="${dir.build}" />
        <fileset dir="${dir.lib}" includes="*.jar" />
    </path>

    <!-- Chapter 7 specific properties/tasks -->
    <property name="anakia.class" value="org.apache.velocity.anakia.AnakiaTask" />
    <property name="ch7.xml" value="src/xml/ch7" />
    <property name="anakia.output" value="anakia-output" />

    <taskdef classname="${anakia.class}"
                            name="anakia" classpathref="project.classpath" />
```

```
<!-- Chapter 7 Specific Targets -->
<target name="anakia-setup">
    <mkdir dir="${anakia.output}" />
</target>

<!-- Hello World example -->
<target name="helloWorld" depends="anakia-setup"
                    description="Anakia Hello World Example">
    <anakia basedir="${ch7.xml}/helloWorld"
        destdir="${anakia.output}"
        extension=".html"
        excludes="**/*.html"
        includes="**/*.xml"
        style="helloWorld.vsl"
        velocityPropertiesFile="${dir.src}/velocity.properties"/>
</target>
</project>
```

I've used the same build script for all the examples in the book, so the build script in Listing 7-1 is a subset of what's included in the download. The first important point to note is the use of the `<taskdef>` tag to define the Anakia task.

```
<taskdef classname="${anakia.class}"
                    name="anakia" classpathref="project.classpath" />
```

Notice that I've used the `${anakia.class}` property for the class name, which is set to `org.apache.velocity.anakia.AnakiaTask` earlier in the script. It's important to note that I've set the `classpathref` property of the `<taskdef>` tag to refer to the classpath used by the whole project. This classpath must include all the Velocity classes, the Velocity dependency classes, and the JDOM classes. If you don't set this classpath value correctly, Ant will be unable to find the `AnakiaTask` class or any of its dependencies. The easiest way I've found of doing this is to place all the JAR files in the project's `lib` directory and then build a path for the classpath in the Ant script.

```
<path id="project.classpath">
    <pathelement path="${dir.build}" />
    <fileset dir="${dir.lib}" includes="*.jar" />
</path>
```

Of course, if you don't want to distribute the Velocity and JDOM classes with your application, then you can use a separate directory and a separate `<path>` for the `AnakiaTask` classpath. The `helloWorld` `<target>` depends on the `anakia-setup`

<task> that simply ensures that the directory for the output files exists. The main purpose of the helloWorld <target> is to execute the Anakia task.

```
<anakia basedir="${ch7.xml}/helloWorld"
          destdir="${anakia.output}"
          extension=".html"
          excludes="**/*.html"
          includes="**/*.xml"
          style="helloWorld.vsl"
          velocityPropertiesFile="${dir.src}/velocity.properties"/>
```

Don't worry too much about each individual attribute on the <anakia> tag just yet; they're explained in detail in the "The Anakia Ant Task" section. However, you should be aware that the file paths in the examples are the paths used in the code in the download. If you have problems getting this example to work, you should download the example code and check out the correct directory structure. It's also important that the folder containing the helloWorld.xml file is configured as a location for templates in the velocity.properties file. Now you can run the example using the command ant helloWorld. This should yield the following output in a file called helloWorld.html:

```
Hello World!
```

That was quite a lot of code just to generate the desired output, but it illustrates how Anakia works. The transformation defined in the helloWorld.vsl file was applied to the input file, helloWorld.xml, to render the output file helloWorld.html. The real power of Anakia comes when you have a bunch of moderately complex XML files that need to have the same transformation applied to them. In this case, the amount of code needed to perform the transform using Anakia is much less than the code required to create the output using Java.

Introducing JDOM

In the previous example, you saw the following code in the VTL style sheet:

```
$root.getChild("msg").getText()
```

Whilst the VTL code is clear, what isn't clear is just what the type of the $root variable is. As I mentioned earlier, Anakia uses JDOM to read the XML input and make the data available to your style sheets. The $root variable is actually an instance of org.jdom.Element that represents the root node of the input XML.

NOTE *You should note that the* $root *variable is always called* $root, *irrespective of the name of the root element in your XML. So whilst the root element of the XML document in the Hello World example is* <root>, *I could have changed it to* <foo>, *and the variable in the style sheet would still be* $root.

JDOM offers a greatly simplified API for working with XML data in Java. Working with XML data in Java is quite a complex process, especially if you want to operate on arbitrary pieces of XML that have no DTD defined. Consider the example of Hello World implemented using Java API for XML Processing (JAXP) and DOM (see Listing 7-2).

Listing 7-2. Hello World Using JAXP

```
package com.apress.pjv.ch7;

import javax.xml.parsers.DocumentBuilder;
import javax.xml.parsers.DocumentBuilderFactory;

import org.w3c.dom.Document;
import org.w3c.dom.Element;
import org.w3c.dom.Node;
import org.w3c.dom.NodeList;

public class HelloWorldJAXP {

    public static void main(String[] args) throws Exception {

        DocumentBuilder builder = DocumentBuilderFactory.newInstance()
                .newDocumentBuilder();

        Document doc = builder.parse("src/xml/ch7/helloWorld/helloWorld.xml");

        Element jaxpRoot = doc.getDocumentElement();

        // Can't use root.getFirstChild() in case
        // of whitespace!
        NodeList nodes = jaxpRoot.getElementsByTagName("msg");

        Element msgElement = (Element) nodes.item(0);

        // can't use msgElement.getNodeValue()
        // it returns null!

        nodes = msgElement.getChildNodes();
```

```
        for (int x = 0; x < nodes.getLength(); x++) {
            Node node = nodes.item(x);

            if (node.getNodeType() == Node.TEXT_NODE) {
                System.out.println(node.getNodeValue());
                break;
            }
        }
    }
}
```

The reason for the relative complexity of this example is due to the complexity of the DOM API. DOM is a standard API governed by the W3C and is designed to be largely language neutral. The DOM API also enforces a strict tree model, so whilst you and I may consider the text *Hello World!* to be the value of the <msg> element in the sample XML, DOM considers it to be a child node. JDOM simplifies things somewhat; consider the implementation of Hello World using JDOM (see Listing 7-3).

Listing 7-3. Hello World Using JDOM

```
package com.apress.pjv.ch7;

import org.jdom.Document;
import org.jdom.Element;
import org.jdom.input.SAXBuilder;

public class HelloWorldJDOM {

    public static void main(String[] args) throws Exception {
        SAXBuilder builder = new SAXBuilder();
        Document doc = builder.build("src/xml/ch7/helloWorld/helloWorld.xml");

        Element jdomRoot = doc.getRootElement();
        System.out.println(jdomRoot.getChild("msg").getText());
    }
}
```

Not only is there substantially less code, it's also much easier to decode the JDOM version. The JDOM API tends to work more like you and I, as Java developers, think. As if this simplicity alone wasn't enough to justify the usage of JDOM as the XML tool of choice for Velocity, JDOM handles collections of nodes and elements in a much more Java-like manner. Consider the following line from the JAXP example:

```
NodeList nodes = jaxpRoot.getElementsByTagName("msg");
```

The NodeList class represents a list of XML nodes, but it has absolutely no relation to the Java Collection Framework classes, so writing something such as the following would be invalid:

```
List nodes = jaxpRoot.getElementsByTagName("msg");
```

The main problem with this approach is that it then becomes impossible to iterate over collections of nodes using the standard Velocity collection support. In stark contrast to the approach taken by DOM, JDOM uses collections that implement standard Java Collection interfaces such as List. So, using JDOM, you could write something like this:

```
List nodes = jdomRoot.getChildren();
```

The use of standard Java Collection interfaces makes JDOM ideal for use in Anakia because it makes it simple to iterate over sets of nodes in a style sheet. Consider the following XML:

```
<people>
    <person firstName="Rob" lastName="Harrop"/>
    <person firstName="Scott" lastName="McNealy"/>
    <person firstName="Larry" lastName="Ellison"/>
    <person firstName="Bill" lastName="Gates"/>
    <person firstName="Marc" lastName="Fleury"/>
</people>
```

The previous XML quite clearly depicts a list of people and their names. If I wanted to transform this into a bulleted list within HTML, I could use the following VTL style sheet:

```
<html>
    <head>
        <title>Person List</title>
    </head>
    <body>
        <ul>
            #foreach($person in $root.getChildren())
                <li>$person.getAttribute("lastName").getValue() ,
                    $person.getAttribute("firstName").getValue()</li>
            #end
        </ul>
    </body>
</html>
```

Notice that I've called the getChildren() method of the $root variable and that I'm able to use the resultant List in a VTL #foreach directive. Within the #foreach loop, I'm able to use the standard methods of the org.jdom.Element class to access the attributes on each <person> element. In turn I use the getValue() method of the org.jdom.Attribute class to get the attribute value. I'm sure you'll agree that the combination of the concise VTL syntax and the simple JDOM API makes for an easy-to-use XML transformation solution.

For the trivial Hello World example, it's much simpler to write the code in Java directly; however, as the input and output get more complex, it becomes simpler to use Anakia over a straight Java approach. For instance, consider the previous example rewritten to use JDOM directly from Java (see Listing 7-4).

Listing 7-4. Hello World Using JDOM Directly from Java

```
package com.apress.pjv.ch7;

import java.util.Iterator;

import org.jdom.Document;
import org.jdom.Element;
import org.jdom.input.SAXBuilder;

public class HelloPeopleJDOM {

    public static void main(String[] args) throws Exception {
        SAXBuilder builder = new SAXBuilder();
        Document doc = builder.build("src/xml/ch7/helloPeople/helloPeople.xml");

        StringBuffer output = new StringBuffer();

        // create the basic HTML output
        output.append("<html>\n").append(
                "<head>\n<title>\nPerson List</title>\n</head>\n").append(
                "<body>\n").append("<ul>\n");

        Iterator itr = doc.getRootElement().getChildren().iterator();

        while (itr.hasNext()) {
            Element elem = (Element) itr.next();

            output.append("<li>");
            output.append(elem.getAttribute("lastName").getValue());
            output.append(", ");
            output.append(elem.getAttribute("firstName").getValue());
            output.append("</li>\n");
        }
```

```
        // create the end of the HTML output
        output.append("</ul>\n</body>\n</html>");

        System.out.println(output.toString());
    }
}
```

As you can see, the Anakia method is much more straightforward and is more accessible to nonprogrammers. The Anakia method also requires no extra code to add additional files, whereas you need to write additional code to process multiple files using the Java approach.

I've touched only briefly on the use of JDOM. Since most of what you can do in Anakia is governed by what you can do with JDOM, I recommend you come to grips with the JDOM API. You'll find that Brett McLaughlin's *Java and XML*, Second Edition (O'Reilly, 2001), is an excellent reference—which isn't surprising since he's heavily involved in the project.

The Anakia Ant Task

In the previous examples you used the Anakia Ant task without really knowing what the tag attributes meant. You can use ten attributes to control the behavior of the Anakia task (see Table 7-1).

Table 7-1. AnakiaTask *Tag Attributes*

Name	Description
basedir	Path to the directory holding the input XML files. You can put XML files in subdirectories of this path, and they will be put in the appropriate subdirectory of the output directory.
destdir	Path to the folder to where the output files should be written.
extension	The file extension to use for the output files. Specifying an extension of .html will result in the output file of index.xml to be called index.html. The default value for extension is .html.
style	This is the filename of the style sheet. It's relative to the path specified in either templatePath or velocityPropertiesFile.

(continues)

Table 7-1. AnakiaTask *Tag Attributes (continued)*

Name	Description
projectFile	The filename of the projectwide input file. Use this to make a set of data available for all input files. This file is resolved in the same way as the style sheet.
excludes	An Ant path expression specifying which files should be excluded from the input set.
includes	An Ant path expression specifying which files should be included in the input set.
lastModifiedCheck	Setting this to true will cause Anakia to check the last modified dates of the input files, style sheets, and project file. If the files are unchanged, the output will not be regenerated. Setting this to false will cause Anakia to regenerate all output regardless of changes made to the input. The default value for this attribute is true.
velocityPropertiesFile	Specifies the path to the Velocity configuration file. The configuration file should set up the resource loaders appropriately to enable Anakia to load the style sheet specified by the style attribute.
templatePath	This parameter can be specified as an alternative to velocityPropertiesFile. Use this parameter to specify the path to the directory containing the style sheet file. This value should be either an absolute path or a path relative to the build file.

In the previous examples I've used the velocity.properties file to configure a resource loader to load the style sheets. You may find it easier to use the templatePath attribute instead, since you can keep all the information to process the Anakia task in one file.

Avoid setting the lastModifiedCheck attribute to false unless you absolutely need to do so. If you have a lot of input files that change rarely, you'll find that keeping the lastModifiedCheck attribute set to true will save you a lot of time during the build cycle.

Anakia Context Data

Anakia prepopulates the Velocity context for the style sheet with a substantial amount of data that can be useful when creating your output (see Table 7-2).

Table 7-2. Anakia Context Data

Variable	Description
$root	You've already seen the $root variable in action; it holds the root element of the input XML.
$project	The $project variable holds the root element of the project XML file specified using the projectFile attribute of the Anakia Ant tag.
$relativePath	This object contains a String that's the path to the base directory relative to the current input file. The documentation incorrectly states that this parameter is the path of the XML file relative to the base directory.
$date	A java.util.Date object representing the current date.
$escape	Using the $escape.getText() method will escape all HTML or XML content so that it can be displayed in an HTML page.
$treeWalk	The allElements($element) method of the $treeWalk variable is used to build a tree of JDOM elements starting at $element. This method is now deprecated in favor of using $element.selectNodes('//').
$xpath	The $xpath.applyTo('path', $root) expression selects the nodes specified in the XPath expression from the $root element. This method is deprecated in favor of $element.selectNodes().
$xmlout	The $xmlout.outputString($element, true) expression is used to output the XML representation of an element's children; using $xmlout.outputString($element) will output the element itself and its children. Both of these methods are deprecated in favor of $element.content and $element respectively.

Those of you who are familiar with JDOM may be wondering where the methods selectNodes() and getContent() on the Element class came from. Well, they come from the fact that the elements in the style sheets are represented by a subclass of org.jdom.Element, specifically, org.apache.velocity.anakia.AnakiaElement. This class provides a few useful additions to the Element class, including the methods listed and a useful override to toString() that outputs the Element's XML representation.

Before I move on to you show you real usage of Anakia, I want to show you these context objects in action. Consider the following <anakia> task tag:

```
<!-- Context example -->
    <target name="contextExample"
                depends="anakia-setup" description="Anakia Context
```

```
Example">
        <anakia basedir="${ch7.xml}/contextExample"
            destdir="${anakia.output}"
            extension=".html"
            excludes="**/stylesheets/**"
            includes="**/*.xml"
            projectFile="./stylesheets/project.xml"
            style="./style.vsl"
            templatePath="${ch7.xml}/contextExample/stylesheets"/>
    </target>
```

Notice that I've used `templatePath` instead of `velocityPropertiesFile` and that I've configured a project XML file and the style sheet to sit in the same directory. The `excludes` attribute is set to exclude everything in the `stylesheets` directory—this will prevent the `project.xml` file from being treated as an individual input file. The XML for the project file is quite simple:

```
<project>
    <name>Context Example Project</name>
</project>
```

The XML for the input file is also quite simple:

```
<document>
    <sections>
        <section name="header">This is the header</section>
        <section name="body">This is the middle section</section>
        <section name="footer">This is the footer</section>
    </sections>
</document>
```

So now I have two XML files: one that will be available to the style sheet for every input file and a single individual input file. The style sheet simply uses the context objects discussed previously along with familiar VTL concepts.

```
Today's Date is $date <BR>
The path to this file is $relativePath<br>

The Project Name Is: $project.getChild('name').getTextTrim()
<br>

These are the sections:<br>
#foreach($section in $root.getChild('sections').getChildren())
    $section.getAttribute('name').getValue()<br>
#end
```

```
#set($footer = $root.selectNodes("sections/section[@name='footer']"))
The footer section content is: $footer.get(0).getText()<br><br>

The XML for the footer node is $escape.getText($footer.toString())<br><br>

The XML for the whole input is:
<br>$escape.getText($root.content.toString())
```

The output produced from this style sheet is as follows:

```
Today's Date is Fri Apr 09 13:39:43 BST 2004 <BR>
The path to this file is .<br>

The Project Name Is: Context Example Project
<br>

These are the sections:<br>
    header<br>
    body<br>
    footer<br>

The footer section content is: This is the footer<br><br>

The XML for the footer node is &lt;section name=&quot;footer&quot;&gt;This is the
footer&lt;/section&gt;<br><br>

The XML for the whole input is:
<br>&lt;document&gt;
    &lt;sections&gt;
        &lt;section name=&quot;header&quot;&gt;This is the
header&lt;/section&gt;
        &lt;section name=&quot;body&quot;&gt;This is the middle section
                        &lt;/section&gt;
        &lt;section name=&quot;footer&quot;&gt;This is the
footer&lt;/section&gt;
    &lt;/sections&gt;
&lt;/document&gt;
```

The interesting piece of code to notice is the XPath query that allowed me to select just the <section> element whose name attribute was set to footer. Furthermore, the selectNodes() method returns an instance of org.apache.velocity.anakia .NodeList. Using this class you can access each element using its index as shown in the style sheet. You should also note that the XML representations have been correctly escaped for display in HTML using the $escape object.

That pretty much covers how Anakia works; now I'll finish up with a slightly more realistic example using multiple input files.

Documenting Your Project

As I mentioned earlier in the chapter, Anakia is primarily suited to creating documentation and project Web sites for software development projects and is used to great effect already within the Jakarta project. In this section I'll show you how to use Anakia effectively to produce project documentation.

The first place to start is with the build script.

```
<anakia basedir="${ch7.xml}/simpleProject"
    destdir="${anakia.output}/simpleProject"
    extension=".html"
    excludes="**/stylesheets/**"
    includes="**/*.xml"
    projectFile="./stylesheets/project.xml"
    style="site.vsl"
    templatePath="${ch7.xml}/simpleProject/stylesheets"/>
```

This should be familiar by now; I've defined a project file, project.xml, and a style sheet, site.vsl. The style sheet is loaded from the path indicated in the templatePath attribute. The next step is to create the project.xml file. In the project file I want to control data that will appear on every page of the documentation site—namely, project name and navigation.

```
<project>
    <name>Gimli's Widgetarium Documentation</name>
    <menu header="User Documentation">
        <item href="about/index.html">About</item>
        <item href="gettingStarted/index.html">Getting Started</item>
    </menu>
    <menu header="Developer Documentation">
        <item href="manual/index.html">Manual</item>
        <item href="javadoc/index.html">JavaDoc</item>
    </menu>
</project>
```

The navigation defined in the project.xml file is split into individual menus, each of which contains menu items that I want to render as links in the output. Notice that I've added hyperlink references to the <item> tags for each of the four menu items. The next files to look at are the input files, all of which follow the same basic structure.

```
<document>
    <properties>
            <author email="robh@cakesolutions.net">Rob Harrop</author>
    </properties>
    <sections>
        <section header="Gimli's Widgetarium">
            This is the documentation for Gimli's Widgetarium
        </section>
        <section header="Latest News">
            There is <b>No News</b>.
        </section>
    </sections>
</document>
```

You can see the code for the rest of the files in the download. The files are organized into a hierarchical structure, as in Figure 7-1.

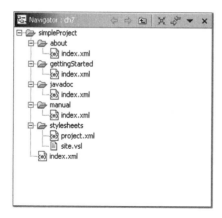

Figure 7-1. Input directory structure

You'll notice that the hierarchical structure reflects hyperlink references in the project.xml file. You'll also notice that in the previous example file I've embedded HTML directly within one of the section tags.

```
<section header="Latest News">
        There is <b>No News</b>.
    </section>
```

My intention is that the content in these sections can be produced using any normal HTML. The final piece in the puzzle is the style sheet. Most of the output is created using macros that are declared at the top of the style sheet file and then accessed from the HTML template at the bottom of the file. Listing 7-5 shows the basic HTML template with the macro calls.

Listing 7-5. HTML Template with Macro Calls

```
<html>
    <head>
        <title>#makeHeader()</title>
        <style type="text/css">
            .pageHeader {
                background-color: Navy;
                color: White;
                font-size: 18pt;
            }
            .sectionHeader {
                background-color: Navy;
                color: White;
                font-size: 12pt;
            }
            .menuHeader {
                font-weight: bold;
            }
        </style>
        #makeProperties()
    </head>
    <body>
        <table border="0" width="100%">
            <tr>
                <td colspan="2" class="pageHeader">#makeHeader()</td>
            </tr>
            <tr>
                <td width="200">#makeMenu()</td>
                <td>#makeDoc()</td>
            </tr>
        </table>
    </body>
</html>
```

The template itself is quite simple, but you can play with the format to your heart's content. The macros do the bulk of the content generation. The first macro used is the #makeHeader macro, which produces the text at the top of each page and the text for displaying in the browser title bar.

```
#macro (makeHeader)
$project.getChild("name").getText()
#end
```

As you can see, the #makeHeader macro is simple—it just outputs the text contained in the <name> element from the project.xml file. The next macro used is #makeProperties, which outputs some simple <meta> tags at the top of the HTML file based on the content of the <properties> tag in every input file.

```
#macro (makeProperties)
#set($author = $root.getChild("properties").getChild("author"))
<meta name="author" value="$author.getTextTrim()">
<meta name="email" value="$author.getAttributeValue("email")">
#end
```

If you wanted, you could reuse the information contained in the <properties> tag and add it to the visible output, or you could add more document properties, perhaps some keywords to support searching or a version identifier. Next up you have #makeMenu.

```
#macro (makeMenu)
#foreach($menu in $project.selectNodes("menu"))
    <span class="menuHeader">$menu.getAttributeValue("header")</span><br>
    #foreach($item in $menu.getChildren())
    <a href="$relativePath/$item.getAttributeValue("href")">$item.getTextTrim()
    </a><br>
    #end
#end
#end
```

As you can see, this macro is much more complex than the previous two. First, the macro obtains a list of <menu> elements and iterates over them using the #foreach directive. Second, within each iteration, the macro will iterate over the list of child elements for each <menu> element and render a hyperlink based on the href attribute of the <item> element. Notice that all the hyperlinks are prefixed with the output of $relativePath, which for any of the files in the subdirectories (such as about) will be ... This is the path to the base directory relative to the input file, not (as the documentation says) the path to the input file relative to the base directory, which would be ./about/. The final macro is #makeDoc, which renders the content of the input file in the body of the output.

```
#macro (makeDoc)
#foreach($section in $root.selectNodes("sections/section"))
    <div class="sectionHeader">$section.getAttributeValue("header")</div>
    $section.content
#end
#end
```

This macro is much simpler than the last, simply iterating over the `<section>` tags in the input file, outputting the section header and then writing the inner content of the tag straight to the output. This method allows for HTML tags to be embedded in each section.

All that remains is to execute the build script with the command `ant simpleProject` and then watch as the content is generated. Once the build script has completed, you'll be left with an output directory structure that looks something like Figure 7-2.

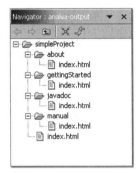

Figure 7-2. Output directory structure

Check out the output in the browser and marvel at the splendid design skills (see Figure 7-3).

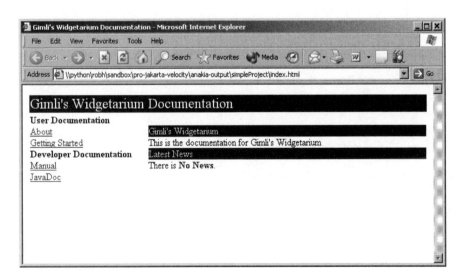

Figure 7-3. Sample output from Anakia

Try the navigation and then check out the source code; be sure to notice that the links are correct because of using `$relativePath`.

Summary

That's all there is to Anakia—which is probably what makes it so useful. Anakia is a genuinely useful tool, especially if you're like me and you like the site-generation capabilities of Maven but you're just so attached to Ant that it would require major surgery to decouple you from your build tool. I've found that Anakia is particularly useful when you couple the output without other documentation such as JavaDoc, Java2HTML, and JUnit reports. If you put a little bit of effort in, you can create a shell Ant script and style sheet that you can use for every one of your projects. For some help with the layout of your site, you should check out the Style project at `http://www.tigris.org`, which provides a really smooth CSS style sheet that's specifically designed for use in systems such as this.

In the next chapter, I'll demonstrate a selection of additional tools that leverage Velocity. I'll demonstrate Texen, a text-generation tool in a similar vein to Anakia; DVSL, a prototype XML transformation tool that's intended as a replacement for XSL; and Veltag, a JSP tag library for using Velocity within JSP pages.

CHAPTER 8

Using Additional
Velocity Tools

IN THE PREVIOUS CHAPTER, you saw how to use Anakia to manipulate XML input files to create textual output. Anakia is perhaps the most developed of the Velocity tools, but it isn't the only one available. In this chapter, I'll demonstrate three additional tools that you can put to a wide variety of uses. First, I'll discuss the Veltag project, which enables you to embed Velocity content directly in JSP pages. Second, I'll demonstrate Texen, a text-generation tool for Ant in a similar vein to Anakia. Texen powers the source code–generation capabilities of the Torque utility in the Jakarta Turbine project. The third and final tool covered in this chapter is Declarative Velocity Style Language (DVSL)—a Velocity-based alternative to XSL. DVSL offers a more feature-rich alternative to XSL than Anakia, but it isn't currently reliable.

Using Veltag

The Veltag project was created to ease the conversion between JSP and Velocity and, more importantly, to open Velocity to those who are locked into JSP. Veltag is implemented as a JSP tag that you use to embed Velocity content directly into a JSP page. In keeping with the rest of the book, I'll start with a basic example to introduce Veltag before moving onto something a bit more involved.

Building Veltag

Before you can get started with Veltag, you need to obtain the code and build the JAR file. The standard binary and source distributions of Velocity don't include either the Veltag JAR file or the source code. To obtain the source code, you need to obtain the Velocity code directly from the CVS repository. If you don't have a CVS client installed, visit http://www.cvshome.org to obtain the client for your platform. Once you've obtained the client, you need to log into the Apache CVS server with the following command:

```
cvs -d :pserver:anoncvs@cvs.apache.org:/home/cvspublic login
password: anoncvs
```

Once you're logged in, you can download the Velocity module with the following command:

```
cvs -d :pserver:anoncvs@cvs.apache.org:/home/cvspublic checkout jakarta-velocity
```

A new directory called `jakarta-velocity` will be created in your current directory. Once the CVS checkout is complete, change to the `contrib/temporary/veltag` directory. Veltag comes with two build files—one that uses Jakarta JJar to download and build the code on the fly and the other that builds the code you received from CVS. The easiest way to build Veltag is to use the code you obtained from CVS. Before you run Ant, however, you need to change some of the details in the build file. Veltag depends on the Velocity and Servlet APIs and, as such, requires the appropriate classes to build. Open the `build_nojjar.xml` file, and modify these two properties appropriately for your environment:

```
<!-- The pathname of the "servlet.jar" JAR file -->
  <property name="servlet.jar" value="lib/javax.servlet.jar"/>

  <!-- The pathname of the "velocity.jar" JAR file -->
  <property name="velocity.jar" value="lib/velocity-dep-1.4-rc1.jar"/>
```

Now save your changes to the build file, and run the following command:

```
ant -buildfile build_nojjar.xml jar
```

You may get some warnings about the use of deprecated APIs—don't worry; your build will still function. The Veltag JAR file will now be available in the `contrib/temporary/veltag` directory.

Creating Hello World with Veltag

I assume at this point you're familiar with how to use a JSP tag in your JSP pages—if you aren't, then I recommend you read *Beginning JSP 2: From Novice to Professional* (Apress, 2004). Using Veltag is ridiculously easy—if you can use JSP and Velocity, then there isn't much else to say. Here is the classical Hello World example using Veltag:

```
<%@ taglib uri="/WEB-INF/tlds/veltag.tld" prefix="vel" %>
<html>
<head>
```

```
        <title>Veltag - Hello World</title>
</head>
<body>
    <vel:velocity>
        #set($name = "World")
        Hello $name
    </vel:velocity>
</body>
</html>
```

Notice that I'm able to embed standard VTL constructs within the
<vel:velocity> tag. Deploy this to your servlet container, and point your browser
at the JSP page—your results should look like Figure 8-1.

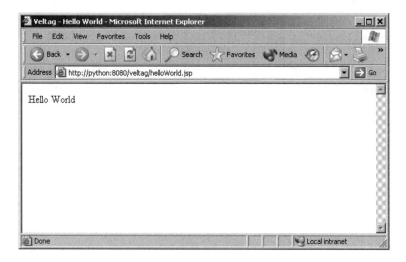

Figure 8-1. Hello World with Veltag

If you're unsure how to deploy a JSP page with tag libraries to your servlet
container, the build script available in the code download will create a WAR file
of all the examples in this chapter.

Examining a More Complex Example

The Hello World example is pretty trivial; it has no data processing and no variable data. Indeed, it would have been simpler to create the page as a simple

HMTL file. However, you can access any of the data stored in page, request, session, or application scope automatically from within your application. So, if you have some object stored in request scope called foo, then you can access that object inside the <vel:velocity> tag using $foo. When trying to resolve an object reference, Veltag will search page, request, session, and application scope (in that order). So, if you have two objects called foo, one in page scope and one in session scope, then the $foo variable will refer to the object in page scope. The ability to easily access data stored in the four scopes comes in handy if you use something such as Struts, which populates the request and session scope with model data. If you aren't using Struts, then you can opt to populate the scopes manually using a servlet controller, or you can use the <jsp:useBean> tag to load JavaBeans from a JSP page.

That's the theory behind the use of scopes in Veltag; now you'll see an example. This example shows how to use both servlet-populated scopes and JSP-populated scopes. The FooServlet class creates two instances of Foo and stores one in request scope and the other in session scope. Once the objects are stored in the correct scopes, the servlet redirects the user to the appropriate view (see Listing 8-1).

Listing 8-1. The FooServlet *Class*

```
package com.apress.pjv.ch8;

import java.io.IOException;

import javax.servlet.RequestDispatcher;
import javax.servlet.ServletException;
import javax.servlet.http.HttpServlet;
import javax.servlet.http.HttpServletRequest;
import javax.servlet.http.HttpServletResponse;

public class FooServlet extends HttpServlet {

    protected void doGet(HttpServletRequest request,
            HttpServletResponse response) throws ServletException, IOException {
        process(request, response);
    }

    protected void doPost(HttpServletRequest request,
            HttpServletResponse response) throws ServletException, IOException {
        process(request, response);
    }
```

```
private void process(HttpServletRequest request,
        HttpServletResponse response) throws ServletException, IOException {

    // add a Foo to the request scope
    Foo foo = new Foo();
    foo.setValue("I am a request scope bean");
    request.setAttribute("servletFoo", foo);

    // add a Foo to the session scope
    foo = new Foo();
    foo.setValue("I am a session scope bean");
    request.getSession().setAttribute("servletFoo", foo);

    // now display the view page
    String viewName = this.getInitParameter("viewName");
    RequestDispatcher dispatcher = request.getRequestDispatcher(viewName);
    dispatcher.forward(request, response);
    }
}
```

Notice that the view path is loaded from the servlet configuration; the reason for this will become apparent in the next section. The Foo class is just a simple JavaBean.

```
package com.apress.pjv.ch8;

public class Foo {

    private String value;

    public String getValue() {
        return this.value;
    }

    public void setValue(String value) {
        this.value = value;
    }
}
```

In the veltag.jsp JSP file I create four beans using the <jsp:useBean> tag, storing one in each of the four different scopes. Then I use <jsp:setProperty> to give each of the four beans a different value for the value property. With those beans set, Veltag outputs the value of the four beans set in the JSP page and the servletFoo bean set in FooServlet (see Listing 8-2).

Listing 8-2. Using Veltag with JavaBeans

```
<%@ taglib uri="/WEB-INF/tlds/veltag.tld" prefix="vel" %>

<jsp:useBean id="foo1" class="com.apress.pjv.ch8.Foo"/>
<jsp:useBean id="foo2" class="com.apress.pjv.ch8.Foo" scope="request"/>
<jsp:useBean id="foo3" class="com.apress.pjv.ch8.Foo" scope="session"/>
<jsp:useBean id="foo4" class="com.apress.pjv.ch8.Foo" scope="application"/>

<jsp:setProperty name="foo1" property="value" value="I am a page scope bean"/>
<jsp:setProperty name="foo2" property="value" value="I am a request scope bean"/>
<jsp:setProperty name="foo3" property="value" value="I am a session scope bean"/>
<jsp:setProperty name="foo4" property="value"
                        value="I am an application scope bean"/>

<html>
    <head>
        <title>Veltag Example</title>
    </head>
    <body>
        <vel:velocity>
            The value of foo1.getValue() is $foo1.value<br>
            The value of foo2.getValue() is $foo2.value<br>
            The value of foo3.getValue() is $foo3.value<br>
            The value of foo4.getValue() is $foo4.value<br>
            The value of servletFoo.getValue() is $servletFoo.value<br>
        </vel:velocity>
    </body>
</html>
```

When configuring the servlet in web.xml, don't forget that you need to specify the view path as an <init-param>, like so:

```
<servlet>
        <servlet-name>foo</servlet-name>
        <servlet-class>com.apress.pjv.ch8.FooServlet</servlet-class>
        <init-param>
            <param-name>viewName</param-name>
            <param-value>/veltag.jsp</param-value>
        </init-param>
    </servlet>
```

Figure 8-2 shows the output of this page.

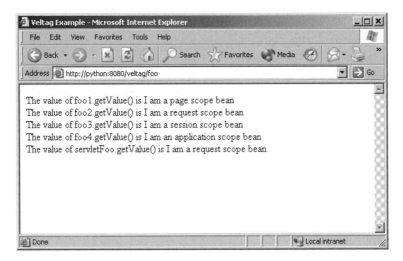

Figure 8-2. Using automatic scoping

Notice that for `$servletFoo` the value indicates that the bean stored in request scope with the name `servletFoo` has been used, not the bean stored in session scope. This is consistent with the search order I mentioned earlier, but it's no help if you want to actually get the values of both beans—for that you need to use strict scoping.

Using Strict Scoping

The previous example had no way to specify which scope to retrieve the `servletFoo` bean from, so the page displayed the first one encountered—the one stored in the request bean. Thankfully, in addition to the automatic scope-searching functionality used by default in Veltag, there's also support for strict scoping to state explicitly from which scope to retrieve a bean.

Strict scoping requires that you set the `strictaccess` attribute of the `<vel:velocity>` tag to `true` and that you use the `$scopetool` available automatically in the Velocity context to retrieve beans from the different scopes—the `veltagStrict.jsp` file highlights this (see Listing 8-3).

Listing 8-3. Using Strict Scoping

```
<%@ taglib uri="/WEB-INF/tlds/veltag.tld" prefix="vel" %>

<jsp:useBean id="foo1" class="com.apress.pjv.ch8.Foo"/>
<jsp:useBean id="foo2" class="com.apress.pjv.ch8.Foo" scope="request"/>
<jsp:useBean id="foo3" class="com.apress.pjv.ch8.Foo" scope="session"/>
<jsp:useBean id="foo4" class="com.apress.pjv.ch8.Foo" scope="application"/>

<jsp:setProperty name="foo1" property="value" value="I am a page scope bean"/>
<jsp:setProperty name="foo2" property="value" value="I am a request scope bean"/>
<jsp:setProperty name="foo3" property="value" value="I am a session scope bean"/>
<jsp:setProperty name="foo4" property="value"
                            value="I am an application scope bean"/>

<html>
    <head>
        <title>Veltag Strict Scoping Example</title>
    </head>
    <body>
        <vel:velocity strictaccess="true">
            The value of foo1.getValue() is
                    $scopetool.getPageScope("foo1").string<br>
            The value of foo2.getValue() is
                    $scopetool.getRequestScope("foo2").string<br>
            The value of foo3.getValue() is
                    $scopetool.getSessionScope("foo3").string<br>
            The value of foo4.getValue() is
                    $scopetool.getApplicationScope("foo4").string<br>
            <hr>
            The value of servletFoo.getValue() in request scope is
                    $scopetool.getRequestScope("servletFoo").string<br>
            The value of servletFoo.getValue() in session scope is
                    $scopetool.getSessionScope("servletFoo").string<br>
        </vel:velocity>
    </body>
</html>
```

Notice that each of the scopes has a corresponding getXXXScope() method
on $scopetool that's used to retrieve the bean. Using these methods I'm able to
retrieve both of the servletFoo beans—one from request scope, the other from session scope. The output from this example, shown in Figure 8-3, is as you'd expect.

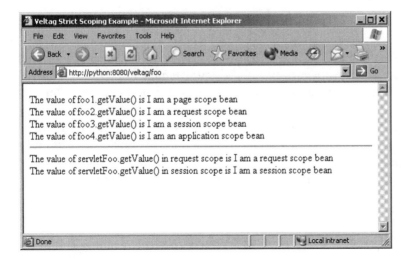

Figure 8-3. Using strict scoping

Summarizing Veltag

Veltag is still in its infancy, and as such you should consider the implications before using it in a production environment. If you're starting from a clean slate, then I advise against using Veltag at all—Velocity on its own is a much more elegant solution than using a combination of Velocity and JSP. However, if you're committed to JSP and want to start to migrate your project to Velocity, then Veltag is a good option, especially if you're using JSP pages on their own with no support from an MVC framework such as Struts or Spring. If you're already using an MVC framework, then nothing is stopping you from running Velocity and JSP side by side in the View layer.

Using Texen

Texen is a text-generation tool built on top of Ant and Velocity. Whilst Texen is similar in some respects to Anakia, it differs in the way it interacts with data. Whereas Anakia processes a set of XML input files, prepopulating the context with the XML data, Texen has no built-in mechanism for loading input data.

Texen is intended as a base class for your own Ant tasks; it takes care of the generation work, with your code populating the context with the appropriate data. That said, you can use Texen independently—although perhaps not to quite the same degree. A good example of the use of Texen is the Torque tool in the Jakarta Turbine project. Torque is an Ant task, derived from Texen, for generating Java source code.

How It Works

As I've already mentioned, Texen runs as an Ant task, so it's ideal for integrating into your build process. Texen operates on a single control template and zero or more processing templates. Texen adds a selection of useful objects, discussed in "Introducing the Texen Context Objects," to the context, which you can use from both the control and content templates. Whilst you can use the control template to generate a single file, the real power of Texen lies in using the control template to create multiple output files based on the content templates. In this case, the output from the control template can form some kind of log file for the generation process.

Introducing the Texen Ant Task

The Texen Ant task is implemented by the `org.apache.velocity.texen.ant` `.TexenTask` class, which is included as part of the standard Velocity distribution. Table 8-1 describes the properties of the `TexenTask` class, which can be set in the Ant build script.

Table 8-1. `TexenTask` *Properties*

Property	Description
contextProperties	Path to the properties file used to load data into the context. This parameter is discussed in more detail in the "Loading Additional Data into the Context" section.
controlTemplate	The name of the template resource to use as the control template. This template is resolved relative to the path specified in `templatePath` or to the classpath if `useClasspath` is set to true. This is a required parameter.
inputEncoding	The encoding to use when reading files.
outputEncoding	The encoding to use when writing files.
outputDirectory	Path to the directory where the output files should be placed. Either an absolute path or a path relative to the root folder in Ant. Required.
templatePath	Path to the directory containing the templates. Required if `useClasspath` is set to `false`.
useClasspath	Setting this to `true` will cause Texen to configure a `ClasspathResourceLoader` from which to load the templates. By default this parameter is `false`, but you must set it to `true` if you want to exclude `templatePath`.

Introducing the Texen Context Objects

TexenTask places a selection of objects in the context for you to use from your templates (see Table 8-2).

Table 8-2. TexenTask *Context Objects*

Variable Name	Description
$files	An instance of org.apache.velocity.texen.util.FileUtil, which provides useful utility methods for opening files and creating directories. Refer to the API documentation for more details.
$generator	An instance of org.apache.velocity.texen.Generator. The control object uses this object to generate output from content templates.
$now	An instance of java.util.Date representing the current date and time.
$outputDirectory	An instance of java.lang.String containing the path to the output directory.
$properties	An instance of org.apache.velocity.texen.util.PropertyUtil, which provides useful utility methods for loading property files. Refer to the API documentation for full details.
$strings	An instance of org.apache.velocity.util.StringUtils, which has a whole bunch of String manipulation methods. Refer to the API documentation for full details.

Creating Hello World with Texen

So now that you know what the task properties are and what objects are available to you in the context, it's time for an example. I'll start, as usual, with the Hello World example and then move onto something more involved. To start, you need the Ant build script (see Listing 8-4).

Listing 8-4. Using Texen

```
<project name="Pro Jakarta Velocity" basedir="." default="compile">

    <!-- properties for build -->
    <property name="dir.src" value="src" />
    <property name="dir.lib" value="lib" />
    <property name="dir.build" value="build" />

    <!-- classpath -->
    <path id="project.classpath">
        <pathelement path="${dir.build}" />
        <fileset dir="${dir.lib}" includes="*.jar" />
    </path>

    <!-- Chapter 8 specific properties/tasks -->
    <property name="texen.class"
value="org.apache.velocity.texen.ant.TexenTask"/>
    <property name="texen.output" value="texen-output"/>
    <property name="ch8.templates" value="${dir.src}/templates/ch8"/>

    <taskdef classname="${texen.class}" name="texen"
                classpathref="project.classpath" />

    <target name="texen-setup" description="Creates the Texen output directory">
        <mkdir dir="${texen.output}"/>
    </target>

    <target name="helloWorld-texen" depends="texen-setup">
        <texen controltemplate="helloWorldControl.vm"
                templatepath="${ch8.templates}/texen/"
                outputdirectory="${texen.output}"
            outputfile="helloWorld.log"
        />
    </target>
</project>
```

I won't focus too much on this because most of the issues related to defining tasks in Ant are covered in Chapter 7. Next up is the control template, in this case helloWorldControl.vm.

```
#set($name = "World")
$generator.parse("helloWorldContent.vm", "helloWorld.txt", "name", $name)
Generated helloWorld.txt in $outputDirectory on $now
```

Notice on the second line the call to $generator.parse(). This method will parse the template specified in the first argument and create the output file specified in the second argument. The fourth argument specifies a context parameter to pass to the content template, and the third parameter is the name associated with it. The content template is just a plain Velocity template with no special calls, like so:

```
Hello $name
```

Now all that remains is to run the Ant task with the ant helloWorld-texen command. The output produced from the helloWorldContent.vm template is as you'd expect:

```
Hello World
```

Also, you shouldn't get any surprises in the content generated by the helloWorldControl.vm template:

```
Generated helloWorld.txt in
/Users/robh/sandbox/pro-jakarta-velocity/texen-output
on Fri Apr 16 18:26:08 BST 2004
```

This example was very trivial; indeed, it would have been much easier to generate the output directly in the control template and ignore the generation capabilities altogether. However, as you'll see shortly, the real power of Texen comes when you want to generate a set of output files as opposed to just a single one.

Loading Additional Data into the Context

In the previous example, all the variable data was stored in the control template. To modify that data, I need to modify the template. Thankfully, a solution exists—Texen allows for a set of properties, stored in a Java properties file, to be automatically loaded into the context. To use a properties file for storing additional context data, you need to provide the path to the file in the contextProperties attribute of the <texen> tag.

When loading values from the properties file, Texen will correctly instantiate instances of Integer and Boolean for values that match. This enables you to use values loaded from the file in arithmetic expressions and evaluations. Another cool feature is the ability to load the contents of a file into the context automatically. To do this, you simply append .file.contents to the property key and specify the path to the file as the value.

Using these features, I can improve the Hello World example to allow the name to be specified in an external file and to include the contents of a disclaimer file at the bottom of the output file. I start with the Ant build target.

```
<target name="helloWorldImproved-texen" depends="texen-setup">
    <texen controltemplate="helloWorldImprovedControl.vm"
           templatepath="${ch8.templates}/texen/"
           outputdirectory="${texen.output}"
           contextproperties="${dir.src}/texen.properties"
        outputfile="helloWorldImproved.log"
    />
</target>
```

In addition to a change of target name and control template path, I've added the contextProperties attribute to point to the src/texen.properties file. The content of this file is as follows:

```
name=World
disclaimer.file.contents=src/templates/ch8/texen/disclaimer.txt
```

When specifying paths for files that you want to include in the output, you have to provide the path relative to the root of the Ant project. The control template has changed very little.

```
$generator.parse("helloWorldImprovedContent.vm", "helloWorldImproved.txt")
Generated helloWorldImproved.txt in $outputDirectory on $now
```

Notice that the name variable is no longer defined in this template, and the argument isn't included in the call to $generator.parse. The only addition to the content template is the inclusion of the $disclaimer variable.

```
Hello $name
$disclaimer
```

The output from this example now includes the name from the properties file and the disclaimer loaded from the disclaimer.txt file.

```
Hello World
--------------------------------------------------
This is a disclaimer!
```

Subclassing TexenTask

With the previous example, I pretty much exhausted the set of features available with Texen by default—yet I have still to exploit much of its power. To really get the most out of Texen, you need to subclass the Texen class and populate the context with some useful data. In this example, I'll create a simple task, subclasses from TexenTask, to generate HTML name cards from a properties file.

The properties file used will be in this format:

```
robh.name=Rob Harrop
robh.emailAddress=rob@cakesolutions.net
janm.name=Jan Machacek
janm.emailAddress=janm@cakesolutions.net
```

Each person, identified by the first part of the key, has two corresponding properties: name and emailAddress. The task will load a properties file in this format and create a Collection of Person objects. The Person class is just a simple JavaBean (see Listing 8-5).

Listing 8-5. The Person *Class*

```java
package com.apress.pjv.ch8;

public class Person {

    private String id;

    private String name;

    private String emailAddress;

    public Person(String id) {
        this.id = id;
    }

    public String getId() {
        return this.id;
    }

    public String getName() {
        return this.name;
    }

    public void setName(String name) {
        this.name = name;
    }

    public String getEmailAddress() {
        return this.emailAddress;
    }

    public void setEmailAddress(String emailAddress) {
        this.emailAddress = emailAddress;
    }
}
```

The code for the `NameCardTask` is relatively simple, but I'll explain it step by step.

```
package com.apress.pjv.ch8;

import java.io.FileInputStream;
import java.util.Collection;
import java.util.HashMap;
import java.util.Iterator;
import java.util.Map;

import org.apache.commons.collections.ExtendedProperties;
import org.apache.velocity.context.Context;
import org.apache.velocity.texen.ant.TexenTask;

public class NameCardTask extends TexenTask {

    private String peopleProperties = "people.properties";

    private static final String NAME_PROPERTY = "name";

    private static final String EMAILADDRESS_PROPERTY = "emailAddress";

    public void setPeopleProperties(String peopleProperties) {
        this.peopleProperties = peopleProperties;
    }
```

The `setPeopleProperties()` method allows for the path to the properties file to be set as an attribute of the `<namecard>` tag in Ant.

The `TexenTask` method has a protected method, `populateInitialContext(Context)`, that can be used to add additional data to the context, like so:

```
protected void populateInitialContext(Context ctx) throws Exception {
    super.populateInitialContext(ctx);

    ctx.put("people", loadPeople());
}
```

You have to remember to call `super.populateInitialContext()` to ensure that the default data and tools are available in the context.

The bulk of the processing happens in the `loadPeople()` method (see Listing 8-6).

Listing 8-6. The `loadPeople()` *Method*

```
private Collection loadPeople() throws Exception {
    ExtendedProperties props = new ExtendedProperties();
    props.load(new FileInputStream(peopleProperties));

    Map people = new HashMap();
    Iterator itr = props.getKeys();

    while (itr.hasNext()) {
        String key = (String) itr.next();

        // find the id of the person
        int index = key.indexOf('.');
        String id = key.substring(0, key.indexOf('.'));

        Person p = null;

        if (people.containsKey(id)) {
            p = (Person) people.get(id);
        } else {
            p = new Person(id);
        }

        // find which property this is
        String prop = key.substring(index + 1);

        if (NAME_PROPERTY.equals(prop)) {
            p.setName(props.getString(key));
        } else if (EMAILADDRESS_PROPERTY.equals(prop)) {
            p.setEmailAddress(props.getString(key));
        }

        people.put(id, p);
    }

    return people.values();
}
}
```

In this method, the `Collection` of `Person` objects is built from the content in the properties file and then returned to the caller so it can be added to the context. The next step is to create the control template, like so:

```
#foreach($person in $people)
    #set($fileName = $strings.concat([$person.id, ".html"]))
    $generator.parse("nameCardContent.vm", $fileName, "person", $person)
#end
```

Notice that I've used the $string.concat() method to create the filename for each output file. The concat() method requires an instance of List, so I used the Velocity list syntax to create one. The code for the content template should look familiar by now.

```
<html>
    <head>
        <title>Name Card: $person.name</title>
    </head>
    <body>
        <h1>$person.name</h1>
        E-Mail Address: <a href="mailto:$person.emailAddress">
                                    $person.emailAddress</a>
    </body>
</html>
```

All that remains it to create the build script and run it.

```
<target name="namecard" depends="texen-setup">
        <namecard controltemplate="nameCardControl.vm"
                templatepath="${ch8.templates}/texen/"
                outputdirectory="${texen.output}"
                contextproperties="${dir.src}/texen.properties"
                peopleProperties="${dir.src}/people.properties"
            outputfile="namecard.log"
        />
    </target>
```

I've omitted the code for declaring the task; you should be familiar with that by now. If you're unsure how to declare the task, then check out the build script in the code download.

Running the task will yield one file for every person defined in the properties file. The output of the file in the browser will look something like Figure 8-4.

Figure 8-4. Sample name card output

Summarizing Texen

Of the three tools discussed in this chapter, Texen is the only one currently in production status. Although Texen is useful for generating any kind of textual content, its integration with Ant, and therefore its close ties with the build process, makes it an ideal tool for code generation. Indeed, Texen is already put to great use in the Jakarta Turbine project for that very purpose. If you intend to build your own code generators for a project, then Texen is the perfect base to start from, ensuring that all your code generation tools follow the same basic model.

Using DVSL

Declarative Velocity Style Language (DVSL) is a Velocity-based alternative to XSL. You may be thinking that Anakia is a Velocity-based alternative to XSL, in that it's capable of transforming XML content into any type of textual output. However, the model used by Anakia doesn't closely match that of XSL, and although Anakia is by far simpler than XSL, it does lack some of the power. DVSL is an attempt to match the power of XSL, using a simpler, Velocity-style syntax.

Like Anakia, DVSL runs as an Ant task, but it can also be run as a command-line tool. For the examples in this section, I'll use the command line to start with and the Ant task from then on.

The following sections require some knowledge of XSL and the basic concepts behind it. If you're unfamiliar with XSL, then I recommend you pick up a good book on the subject such as *Learning XSLT* by Michael Fitzgerald (O'Reilly, 2003).

Obtaining and Building DVSL

The Jakarta Web site describes the status of the DVSL project as being "in development." Therefore, you won't find DVSL included in the standard Velocity distribution, and you won't find a distribution of DVSL itself. Instead, you must obtain the code directly from CVS, as you did with Veltag, and build it yourself. To obtain the code from CVS, simply issue the following command to log in:

```
cvs -d :pserver:anoncvs@cvs.apache.org:/home/cvspublic login
password: anoncvs
```

Now issue this command to check out the DVSL module:

```
cvs -d :pserver:anoncvs@cvs.apache.org:/home/cvspublic ➥
         checkout jakarta-velocity-dvsl
```

Once you've downloaded the code from the CVS repository, change into the jakarta-velocity-dvsl directory and build DVSL with the following command:

```
ant jar
```

This will create the JAR file in the root directory of the module. Before you can start, you'll also need to obtain the latest dom4j distribution from http://www.dom4j .org, since this is the XML API used by DVSL. Don't be worried if you get warning messages about using deprecated APIs—the code will still function correctly.

Creating Hello World with DVSL

In keeping with the rest of the examples, I'll start you off with a simple Hello World example. As with XSL, you have an input file, which is in XML format, and a style sheet, which in this case is in DVSL format. From these files you can produce a single output file that contains the input content transformed as per the rules defined in the DVSL style sheet. The input XML for this example is simple and, indeed, should look familiar.

```
<root>
    <msg>Hello World!</msg>
</root>
```

The style sheet used to transform this input into the desired output is as follows:

```
#match("root")
$node.msg
#end
```

The #match directive is synonymous with the `<xsl:template>` tag in XSL, with the argument taking an XPath expression indicating which elements to match. When an element that matches the XPath expression provided is encountered in the input, the code inside the #match directive will be executed. In this case, the expression root will match only the `<root>` tag. The $node variable holds a reference to the node matched by the expression. Notice that I'm able to access the subnode `<msg>` using just a reference to its name—under the hood this is actually an XPath expression executed on the current node to select a single node. To generate the output for this example, run the following command:

```
java -cp "lib/velocity-dvsl-0.45.jar:lib/velocity-dep-1.4.jar:lib/dom4j.jar"\
    org.apache.tools.dvsl.DVSL -STYLE src/templates/ch8/dvsl/helloWorld.dvsl \
    -IN src/xml/ch8/helloWorld.xml -OUT dvsl-output/helloWorld.txt
```

This command is intended to work correctly from the root directory of the code download—if you're experiencing trouble, it's most likely a classpath issue, so you may want to download the code for the book. If you're running Windows, you need to keep the command on a single line and replace the colons in the classpath with semicolons.

The output generated by this example is, as you'd expect, as follows:

```
Hello World!
```

As with Anakia, Texen, and Veltag, the effort required to generate that small amount of effort is relatively high; however, when you're working on large sets of input, the effort is more realistic.

Introducing Default Context Objects

By default your DVSL template has access to three objects: $context, $node, and $attrib. Used together these three objects provide a powerful mechanism to manipulate and transform XML content using familiar XSL concepts.

The $context object is an instance of org.apache.tools.dvsl.Transformer, which implements the org.apache.tools.dvsl.TranformTool interface. The $context object is used to apply the templates for additional matches and functions like the `<xsl:apply-templates>` tag. Table 8-3 lists the methods available in the $context object.

Table 8-3. Methods of the `TransformTool` *Interface*

Method	Description
`applyTemplates()`	Applies all templates defined in the style sheet to the current subtree.
`applyTemplates(DVSLNode)`	Applies all the templates to the supplied node. Only the first match is actually applied.
`applyTemplates(DVSLNode, String)`	Applies the XPath expression supplied in the second argument to the node supplied in the first. All templates are then applied to the resulting nodeset.
`applyTemplates(String)`	Applies all templates in the current subtree that match the specified XPath expression.
`copy()`	Copies the current subtree into the output stream.
`getAppValue(Object)`	Returns the value for the supplied key. You can store values here manually using `putAppValue` or retrieve values that are defined by DVSL.
`putAppValue(Object, Object)`	Stores the value supplied in the second argument under the key supplied in the first argument.

The TransformTool API looks deceptively difficult, but once you see it in action you'll see how remarkably simple it is to use. The $node object is an instance of an object that implements the `org.apache.tools.dvsl.DVSL Node` interface, with the default implementation being `org.apache.tools.dvsl.dom4j.Dom4jNodeImpl`. Table 8-4 describes the methods defined in the `DVSLNode`.

Table 8-4. Methods of the DVSLNode *Interface*

Method	Description
attrib(String)	Retrieves the value of an attribute on the current node.
children()	Returns a List of all the children of the current node.
copy()	Performs a deep copy of the current nodes subtree to the output stream.
copy(List)	Performs a deep copy of the supplied node set to the output stream.
get(String)	Gets the node specified by the supplied XPath expression. This is the method that's called when you use the shortcut syntax. For instance, the call to $node.msg in the previous example is translated to $node.get("msg").
name()	Gets the name of the current node.
selectNodes(String)	Returns a List of nodes that match the supplied XPath expression.
selectSingleNode(String)	Returns the first node that matches the supplied XPath expression.
value()	Returns the value of the current node. The behavior of this method is dependent on the type of node.
valueOf(String)	Returns the result of the specified XPath expression as an Object.

The $attrib object is an instance of java.util.HashMap and contains all the attributes of the current node, keyed by attribute name. The $attrib object provides a simpler syntax for accessing attributes than using the $node.attrib(). For instance, consider this XML fragment:

```
<root myAttrib="some value">
    <someNode/>
</root>
```

The template that matches the <root> node could choose to use either of the following methods for accessing the value of the myAttrib attribute:

```
$node.attrib("myAttrib")
$attrib.myAttrib
```

As you can see, using $attrib provides a much simpler syntax for accessing attribute values.

Using the Toolbox

If you're using the Ant task to run your DVSL transformations, you can take advantage of a Toolbox feature, similar to that available with VelocityViewServlet, to automatically add tools to the context.

 TIP *You should consider using Ant for all but the most trivial of DVSL transformations. As you saw from the previous example, the command to invoke DVSL from the command line is quite unwieldy; using Ant provides a much more structured way of invoking DVSL.*

The Toolbox allows for three different types of object to be defined externally: Strings, Integers, and Tools. Making the distinction between the String and Integer representation of externally defined numbers is important if you want to use them in arithmetic operations within you template. To place items in the Toolbox, you need to supply a Toolbox configuration file. For DVSL, the Toolbox configuration file is a simple properties file.

```
toolbox.contextname=toolbox
toolbox.tool.random=com.apress.pjv.ch6.RandomMessageTool
toolbox.string.footer=This is a footer
toolbox.integer.version=1
```

The first line of this properties file defines the name that will be used to refer to Toolbox items from within your template. The second, third, and fourth lines define different objects to place in the Toolbox. The second portion of the property key defines which type of object you're creating: tool, string, or integer. The last portion of the property key defines the name of the object you can use to refer to the object from within your template. In the previous example, I created a tool named random that's an instance of RandomMessageTool created in Chapter 6, a string named footer, and an integer named version. Accessing these objects from within your template is simple; look at the following modified version of the Hello World template:

```
#match("root")
Message from the XML: $node.msg
Random Message: $context.toolbox.random.generateMessage()
Footer set in tool box: $context.toolbox.footer
Version set in tool box: $context.toolbox.version
#end
```

As you can see, accessing objects placed in the Toolbox is simply a matter of prefixing their names with $context.toolbox. I'm sure by now you're familiar with defining additional tasks for Ant, so I'll simply show you the code required to invoke DVSL to create the output.

```
<dvsl basedir="${ch8.xml}"
            destdir="${dvsl.output}"
            includes="helloWorld.xml"
            extension=".txt"
            style="${ch8.templates}/dvsl/toolbox.dvsl"
            toolboxfile="src/dvsl.properties"
            />
```

Running this task in Ant produces the following output:

```
Message from the XML: Hello World!
Random Message: One Ring to rule them all!
Footer set in tool box: This is a footer
Version set in tool box: 1
```

The message displayed in your output is likely to be different, but you get the idea. The Toolbox provides an excellent way for linking additional functionality into DVSL without the need to create many different subclasses of DVSLTask.

Introducing the DVSL Ant Task

The DVSL Ant task, DVSLTask, has a large number of properties that you can use to control the processing behavior (see Table 8-5).

Table 8-5. DVSLTask *Properties*

Property	Description
basedir	The directory in which to search for input files. Used only in batch-processing mode and by default set to.
destdir	The directory in which to place output files. Must be specified if using batch-processing mode.
excludes	Ant pattern describing which files to exclude when in batch-processing mode.
force	Set this to true to force DVSL to always generate output, even if source files remain unchanged. The default value is false.
in	The input file. Both in and out must be set to invoke DVSL in single-file mode; otherwise, DVSL will run in batch-processing mode.
includes	Ant pattern describing which files to include when in batch-processing mode.
logFile	Name of the file to write log messages to. By default all log messages are sent to the Ant logging system.
out	The output file. See in for more details.
outputencoding	The encoding to use for output files. The default value is UTF-8.
style	The path to the style sheet file. Required.
toolboxfile	The path to the Toolbox file.
validatingparser	Set this to true to have DVSL read all input files using a validating parser. The default value is false.
velocityconfigclass	The name of a class that contains configuration properties to be passed to the underlying Velocity runtime. The JavaDoc for this property states that the class must be a subclass of java.util.Properties, but the code itself casts the class to java.util.Map. You can also specify properties for the Velocity configuration using nested <velconfig> elements such as <velconfig name="foo" value="bar"/>.

Putting It All Together

The previous sections covered the different aspects of DVSL in isolation, so now it's time to look at a more involved example. For this section, I've chosen something a little different from the typical XML-to-HTML generation. Instead, I've chosen to generate JavaBean source files from an XML representation.

The representation of the JavaBean in the XML looks like this:

```
<bean name="Person" package="com.apress.pjv.dvsl"
            desc="A class representing a person">
    <imports>
        <import>java.util.List</import>
    </imports>
    <property name="id" type="int" readonly="true"
                    desc="The person's identification number."/>
    <property name="firstName" type="String" desc="The person's first name"/>
    <property name="lastName" type="String" desc="The person's last name"/>
    <property name="children" type="List" desc="A List of the person's
children"/>
</bean>
```

The `<imports>` tag describes which imports are required in the source file. A single `<property>` tag represents each property of the bean. Setting the `readonly` attribute of the `<property>` tag to `true` will create a property with only an accessor method. The `desc` attributes will generate JavaDoc comments in the source file.

The template for this example contains three `#match` directives, starting with the one to match the `<bean>` tag.

```
#match("bean")
package $attrib.package;

$context.applyTemplates("imports/import")
/**
* $attrib.desc
*/
public class $attrib.name {

$context.applyTemplates("property")
}
#end
```

This `#match` starts by outputting the package statement using the name defined in the package attribute of the `<bean>` tag. Next the template calls

$context.applyTemplates() to apply the templates for the <import> tags defined in the XML. This will generate the import statements at the correct place in the output file. Next the skeleton of the class is created using the value of the name attribute of the <bean> tag as the class name. Notice also that the value of desc attribute is used to create a JavaDoc comment for the class. Inside the class body, the template calls $context.applyTemplates() again, this time to process the templates for the <property> tags.

The second #match directive is for the <import> tags.

```
#match("import")
import $node.value();
#end
```

This #match is quite simple, using the value of each <import> tag to create an import statement. The third and final #match directive is for the <property> tags (see Listing 8-7).

Listing 8-7. VTL for Properties

```
#match("property")
    #set($nameForMethod = $context.toolbox.beantool.initCap($attrib.name))

    /**
    * Store the value of $attrib.name property.
    */
    private $attrib.type $attrib.name;

    /**
    * Get the value of $attrib.name property.
    * $attrib.desc
    */
    public $attrib.type get${nameForMethod}() {
        return this.$attrib.name;
    }

#if(   (!$attrib.readonly))
    /**
    *Set the value of the $attrib.name property
    *$attrib.desc
    */
    public void set${nameForMethod}($attrib.type $attrib.name) {
        this.$attrib.name = $attrib.name;
    }
#end
#end
```

This #match has a substantial amount of code, but you'll find most of it familiar. The only point of note is this line:

```
#set($nameForMethod = $context.toolbox.beantool.initCap($attrib.name))
```

In the XML file, property names start with a lowercase letter, but when generating the getXXX() and setXXX() methods, I want the name to start with an uppercase letter. To facilitate this, I created the BeanTool class and added it the Toolbox. The initCap() method of the BeanTool class accepts a single String argument and returns that String with the first letter uppercased.

```java
package com.apress.pjv.ch8;

public class BeanTool {

    public String initCap(String beanName) {
        return beanName.substring(0, 1).toUpperCase() + beanName.substring(1);
    }
}
```

You add the BeanTool class to the Toolbox with the following line in the configuration file:

```
toolbox.tool.beantool=com.apress.pjv.ch8.BeanTool
```

All that remains is to run this example using the following Ant build script:

```xml
<target name="dvsl-beans" depends="dvsl-setup">
        <dvsl basedir="${ch8.xml}"
            destdir="${dvsl.output}"
            includes="beans/**.xml"
            extension=".java"
            style="${ch8.templates}/dvsl/beans.dvsl"
            toolboxfile="src/dvsl.properties"
            />
    </target>
```

Listing 8-8 shows the output generated using the XML for the Person bean shown earlier.

Listing 8-8. The Person *Class*

```
package com.apress.pjv.dvsl;

import java.util.List;

/**
* A class representing a person
*/
public class Person {

    /**
    * Store the value of id property.
    */
    private int id;

    /**
    * Get the value of id property.
    * The person's identification number.
    */
    public int getId() {
        return this.id;
    }

    /**
    * Store the value of firstName property.
    */
    private String firstName;

    /**
    * Get the value of firstName property.
    * The person's first name
    */
    public String getFirstName() {
        return this.firstName;
    }

    /**
    *Set the value of the firstName property
    *The person's first name
    */
    public void setFirstName(String firstName) {
        this.firstName = firstName;
    }
```

```java
/**
* Store the value of lastName property.
*/
private String lastName;

/**
* Get the value of lastName property.
* The person's last name
*/
public String getLastName() {
    return this.lastName;
}

/**
*Set the value of the lastName property
*The person's last name
*/
public void setLastName(String lastName) {
    this.lastName = lastName;
}

/**
* Store the value of children property.
*/
private List children;

/**
* Get the value of children property.
* A List of the person's children
*/
public List getChildren() {
    return this.children;
}

/**
*Set the value of the children property
*A List of the person's children
*/
public void setChildren(List children) {
    this.children = children;
}
}
```

That's an awful lot of repetitive code, created from a simple XML file. The real timesaver comes when you want to generate more bean code; since you already have the template in place, all that's required is a simple XML file to generate Java code.

Summarizing DVSL

I hope you can see from these examples that DVSL is a powerful tool with lots of potential. DVSL is still not an official release; the version at the time of this writing is 0.45. However, it's still suitable for use in internal projects, and you should think seriously about using it in a production environment in the future.

Summary

This chapter has covered three interesting tools that are part of the growing number of Velocity subprojects. Of the three, Texen is the most mature and is the only one suitable for use in a production application. That said, nothing is stopping you from using Veltag or DVSL in your own internal projects—certainly I've found DVSL to be a much more suitable technology than XSL for many internal XML transformation purposes.

In the next chapter I'll take you deep into the internals of the Velocity runtime, showing the implementation of the vital parts, including the parser, the introspector, and the resource loaders.

### CHAPTER 9

Going Inside
Velocity

IN THIS CHAPTER I'll depart a bit from the discussion on how to use Velocity in your applications and how you can leverage tools built on Velocity as part of your development process. Instead, I'll take advantage of the fact that Velocity is open source and discuss the internals of Velocity. So far, you've seen plenty of examples of how you use Velocity in your application, but as yet I haven't discussed what happens inside the Velocity runtime to create the output for your code. If you plan to use Velocity to build even moderately sized systems, an understanding of its inner workings will help immensely when you need to step off the beaten path or when things don't quite work as you had imagined. More specifically, in this chapter I'll discuss the following:

- A typical processing cycle

- The Velocity startup process

- The ResourceManager subsystem

- The Velocity template parser

- The Introspection implementation

Introducing a Typical Processing Cycle

Rather than simply presenting each part of the Velocity system individually, I'll discuss each part of the implementation in the context of the role it plays in the typical processing cycle of a Velocity-based application.

Within a typical application, the processing cycle of a template consists of four steps.

Initialization: The initialization step typically occurs once during any given execution of the application. During the initialization phase, the Velocity runtime will read the application configuration, load the appropriate resource loaders, configure logging and set up the parser pool. As you'll see, the initialization process is a relatively long process in comparison to the actual template processing and is best run only once each time you run your application.

Locate and load resource: After initialization, your application will undoubtedly want to acquire a reference to a Template object in order to create the desired output. Templates are located and loaded using the resource loaders configured during the initialization phase.

Parse template: Once a Template resource is loaded, the Velocity engine will parse it and create an in-memory representation of the syntax tree, called an Abstract Syntax Tree (AST). The AST is then utilized as part of the merge process.

Merge template and context: The final step in creating the output for your application is to merge the Template contents with the data stored in a Context. This process uses the AST to iterate over the VTL constructs and static content (lovingly referred to as *schmoo* in the source code comments), rendering the output for each node of the AST. This process may invoke the locate and load resource and parse template phases again in response to the #parse and #include directives.

From the perspective of your application, these four phases are represented by three distinct calls into the Velocity runtime, as shown in Listing 9-1.

Listing 9-1. Interacting with the Velocity Runtime

```
package com.apress.pjv.ch9;

import java.io.StringWriter;
import java.io.Writer;

import org.apache.velocity.Template;
import org.apache.velocity.VelocityContext;
import org.apache.velocity.app.Velocity;

public class Driver {

    public static void main(String[] args) throws Exception {

        // 1. Initialization Phase
        Velocity.init("src/velocity.properties");
```

```
    // 2. Locate and Load Phase
    // and
    // 3. Parse Phase
    Template t = Velocity.getTemplate("sample.vm");

    // create context
    VelocityContext ctx = new VelocityContext();
    ctx.put("who", "Rob");

    // create the output
    Writer writer = new StringWriter();

    // 4. Merge Phase
    t.merge(ctx, writer);

    // output
    System.out.println(writer);
  }
}
```

As you can see, the Velocity.init() method invokes the initialization phase, the Velocity.getTemplate() method invokes both the locate and load and parse phases, and finally the call to Template.merge() invokes the merge phase. If you were using VelocityEngine in your code, then the mappings of methods to phases would be the same, and as you'll see, both Velocity and VelocityEngine ultimately use the same implementation.

I'll be using this code throughout the chapter, along with the VelocityEngine-based implementation shown in Listing 9-2, as the base for all discussions.

Listing 9-2. Interacting with Velocity Using VelocityEngine

```
package com.apress.pjv.ch9;

import java.io.StringWriter;
import java.io.Writer;

import org.apache.velocity.Template;
import org.apache.velocity.VelocityContext;
import org.apache.velocity.app.VelocityEngine;

public class InstanceDriver {

    public static void main(String[] args) throws Exception {
```

```
VelocityEngine ve = new VelocityEngine();
// 1. Initialization Phase
ve.init("src/velocity.properties");

// 2. Locate and Load Phase
// and
// 3. Parse Phase
Template t = ve.getTemplate("sample.vm");

// create context
VelocityContext ctx = new VelocityContext();
ctx.put("who", "Rob");

Writer writer = new StringWriter();

// 4. Merge Phase
t.merge(ctx, writer);

// output
System.out.println(writer);
    }
}
```

For the discussions in this chapter I've configured a single `FileResourceLoader` that points to the directory holding the following template, named `sample.vm`.

```
Hello $who!
Your name has $who.length() characters in it.
```

With these four distinct phases in mind, let's now examine what happens during each phase and what impact the execution of the phase has on your applications.

Examining the Initialization Phase

The initialization phase has to execute at least once during your application in order to provide the Velocity runtime with the correct configuration details. You can use the no-arguments version of the `init()` method to initialize Velocity with the default configuration, but you must call `init()` in one form or another at least once before you attempt to process a template.

Using the Velocity-based implementation of the sample application first, let's examine what processing happens during the call to `Velocity.init()`. For the purposes of this discussion, I refer to the `Velocity.init()` method and its overloaded equivalents simply as `Velocity.init()`. More specifically, I'll use the version of init() that accepts a String argument representing the path to the configuration file, as this is the overload of init() used by the sample application.

The Velocity.init() methods simply delegate to the corresponding static method of the RuntimeSingleton object, like so:

```
public static void init( String propsFilename )
    throws Exception
{
    RuntimeSingleton.init(propsFilename);
}
```

Likewise, the RuntimeSingleton class is simply a wrapper around a static instance of the RuntimeInstance class, and all methods are delegated to the corresponding method of RuntimeInstance.

```
public class RuntimeSingleton implements RuntimeConstants
{
    private static RuntimeInstance ri = new RuntimeInstance();

    /**
    * The rest of the class goes in here...
    */
    public static void init(String configurationFile)
        throws Exception
    {
        ri.init( configurationFile );
    }
}
```

The RuntimeInstance class is where the bulk of the initialization processing occurs. The call to init(String) or init(Properties) simply loads the properties file into memory and then delegates the remainder of the processing to the init() method, as shown in Listing 9-3.

Listing 9-3. The RuntimeInstance *Class*

```
import java.io.InputStream;
import java.io.File;
import java.io.IOException;
import java.io.Reader;

import java.util.Map;
import java.util.Hashtable;
import java.util.Properties;
import java.util.Enumeration;
import java.util.HashMap;
```

```
import org.apache.velocity.Template;

import org.apache.velocity.runtime.log.LogManager;
import org.apache.velocity.runtime.log.LogSystem;
import org.apache.velocity.runtime.log.PrimordialLogSystem;
import org.apache.velocity.runtime.log.NullLogSystem;

import org.apache.velocity.runtime.parser.Parser;
import org.apache.velocity.runtime.parser.ParseException;
import org.apache.velocity.runtime.parser.node.SimpleNode;

import org.apache.velocity.runtime.directive.Directive;
import org.apache.velocity.runtime.VelocimacroFactory;

import org.apache.velocity.runtime.resource.ContentResource;
import org.apache.velocity.runtime.resource.ResourceManager;

import org.apache.velocity.util.SimplePool;
import org.apache.velocity.util.StringUtils;

import org.apache.velocity.util.introspection.Introspector;
import org.apache.velocity.util.introspection.Uberspect;
import org.apache.velocity.util.introspection.UberspectLoggable;

import org.apache.velocity.exception.ResourceNotFoundException;
import org.apache.velocity.exception.ParseErrorException;

import org.apache.commons.collections.ExtendedProperties;

public class RuntimeInstance implements RuntimeConstants, RuntimeServices
{
    private  ExtendedProperties overridingProperties = null;

    public void init(String configurationFile)
        throws Exception {
        overridingProperties = new ExtendedProperties(configurationFile);
        init();
    }
}
```

I've shown the class structure and imports here; for the sake of brevity I won't include them again for any discussions of the RuntimeInstance class. The ExtendedProperties class used in place of the standard Properties class is part of the Jakarta Commons Collections project and provides a much more flexible interface for working with property files. It's used extensively throughout Velocity and many other Jakarta projects.

The `RuntimeInstance.init()` method is the main control method of the initialization process, as shown in Listing 9-4.

Listing 9-4. The `RuntimeInstance.init()` *Method*

```
public synchronized void init()
        throws Exception
    {
        if (initialized == false)
        {
            info("*********************************************************** ");
            info("Starting Jakarta Velocity v1.4");
            info("RuntimeInstance initializing.");
            initializeProperties();
            initializeLogger();
            initializeResourceManager();
            initializeDirectives();
            initializeParserPool();

            initializeIntrospection();
            /*
             *  initialize the VM Factory. It will use the properties
             * accessible from the runtime, so keep this here at the end.
             */
            vmFactory.initVelocimacro();

            info("Velocity successfully started.");

            initialized = true;
        }
    }
```

As you can see, the init() methods perform six distinct initialization steps, each with a corresponding initializeXXX() method, and they also configure the Velocimacro (VM) factory.

As you've probably guessed, the calls to info() are calls to the logging system. Indeed, the debug(), error(), info(), and warn() methods of the RuntimeInstance class all delegate to the private log() method. I won't spend too much time on the implementation of the logging system, other than to say that although some of the calls to log() come before the call to initializeLogger(), they're still included in the log. The reason for this is that, by default, Velocity is configured to use the PrimordialLogSystem logging implementation, a configuration that's hard-coded into the Velocity implementation and thus is available before the call to initializeLogger(). PrimordialLogSystem simply stores the log message until the actual logging implementation is configured, at which point Velocity will flush the messages stored in the PrimordialLogSystem into the actual implementation.

Understanding the *initializeProperties()* Method

The initalizeProperties() method is responsible for loading the default properties for the Velocity runtime and then combining these properties with those specified by you.

```
private void initializeProperties()
{
    /*
     * Always lay down the default properties first as
     * to provide a solid base.
     */
    if (configuration.isInitialized() == false)
    {
        setDefaultProperties();
    }

    if( overridingProperties != null)
    {
        configuration.combine(overridingProperties);
    }
}
```

The configuration field is a private instance of the ExtendedProperties that, once this method has executed, will hold the final set of configuration properties. This method executes in two stages. First the default runtime properties are loaded via a call to setDefaultProperties(), and second the default properties are combined with those stored in overridingProperties, which as you'll recall was set in the call to init(String).

The default runtime properties are in a file called velocity.properties, which is stored in the Velocity JAR file under org/apache/velocity/runtime/defaults. The setDefaultProperties() method simply loads the properties in this file into the configuration object.

```
private void setDefaultProperties()
{
    try
    {
        InputStream inputStream = getClass()
            .getResourceAsStream('/' + DEFAULT_RUNTIME_PROPERTIES);
```

```
        configuration.load( inputStream );

        info ("Default Properties File: " +
            new File(DEFAULT_RUNTIME_PROPERTIES).getPath());
    }
    catch (IOException ioe)
    {
        System.err.println("Cannot get Velocity Runtime default
properties!");
    }
}
```

The absence of the default properties file, as pointed out in the comments for this method, is a serious error. In no way should that file not exist. If you encounter an error where this file doesn't exist, then it's likely that the Velocity JAR file is corrupted—you can check for the existence of the velocity.properties file in your JAR distribution by simply piping the result of a JAR dump to grep, like so:

```
jar tf lib/velocity-dep-1.4.jar | grep 'velocity.properties'
```

The ExtendedProperties.combine() method that's used to combine the default properties with the user-specified ones will overwrite any of the properties of the object on which it's called, with those that exist in the object passed in as an argument. This is the desired behavior, as it means that properties you specify will override those specified in the default configuration.

At this time no actual configuration has taken place; however, the full set of configuration properties is now available to the runtime, and the subsequent initializeXXX() methods use these configuration properties to perform their work.

Understanding the *initializeLogger()* Method

The initializeLogger() method uses the configuration properties to set up the logging implementation and then dumps the log messages stored in the preconfigured PrimordialLogSystem into the newly configured implementation (see Listing 9-5).

Listing 9-5. The RuntimeInstance.initializeLogger() *Method*

```
    private void initializeLogger() throws Exception
    {
        /*
         * Initialize the logger. We will eventually move all
         * logging into the logging manager.
         */
```

```
            if (logSystem instanceof PrimordialLogSystem )
            {
                PrimordialLogSystem pls = (PrimordialLogSystem) logSystem;
                logSystem = LogManager.createLogSystem( this );

                /*
                 * in the event of failure, lets do something to let it
                 * limp along.
                 */

                if (logSystem == null)
                {
                    logSystem = new NullLogSystem();
                }
                else
                {
                    pls.dumpLogMessages( logSystem );
                }
            }
        }
    }
```

The createLogSystem method of the LogManager class does the bulk of the work, with the current instance of RuntimeInstance being passed in as an argument. The createLogSystem() method is quite large, so I'll discuss it in pieces. Note that I've removed the code comments from the following method for the sake of brevity:

```
package org.apache.velocity.runtime.log;
import java.util.List;
import java.util.ArrayList;
import java.util.Iterator;

import org.apache.velocity.runtime.RuntimeServices;
import org.apache.velocity.runtime.RuntimeConstants;

public class LogManager
{
    public static LogSystem createLogSystem( RuntimeServices rsvc )
        throws Exception
    {
```

The first thing to notice is that the createLogSystem() method expects an argument of type RuntimeServices, but you'll recall that the current instance of RuntimeInstance is passed as an argument. RuntimeInstance implements the RuntimeServices interface, but this is a wise choice by the Velocity team because it will allow for common runtime services to be moved out of the `RuntimeInstance` class into a separate class, without having a major impact on the code.

The `createLogSystem()` method first checks to see if a `LogSystem` instance has been placed in the configuration.

```
Object o = rsvc.getProperty( RuntimeConstants.RUNTIME_LOG_LOGSYSTEM );

if (o != null && o instanceof LogSystem)
{
    ((LogSystem) o).init( rsvc );

    return (LogSystem) o;
}
```

This may be the case if the Velocity system has been configured programmatically, but obviously not if you've configured the runtime using a configuration file. This raises an important question as to why the Velocity team decided to put this check first. My view is that most applications will use a configuration file, rather than programmatic configuration, yet this check will be performed before the check to see if external configuration has been used. If startup time is important to your application, then you may want to consider using programmatic configuration to gain a little performance benefit during startup. The `RuntimeConstants` interface maintains a list of all the constants that are shared across the Velocity implementation, including the names of configuration properties.

The next check looks to see if one or more class names have been specified in the configuration for the log system. An interesting feature of `ExtendedProperties` is that the comma-separated property values are automatically stored as a `List`. The default configuration for Velocity specifies a `List` of class names for the log system, specifically `AvalonLogSystem` and `SimpleLog4JLogSystem`. If only a single class name has been specified, then this is placed inside an instance of `ArrayList`.

```
List classes = null;
Object obj = rsvc.getProperty( RuntimeConstants.RUNTIME_LOG_LOGSYSTEM_CLASS );

if ( obj instanceof List)
{
    classes = (List) obj;
}
else if ( obj instanceof String)
{
    classes = new ArrayList();
    classes.add( obj );
}
```

With the list of class names obtained, the createLogSystem() loops through them, seeing if the classes exist in the current classpath and checking to see if the classes are implementations of the LogSystem interface (see Listing 9-6).

Listing 9-6. Locating the LogSystem Implementation

```
for( Iterator ii = classes.iterator(); ii.hasNext(); )
{
    String claz = (String) ii.next();

    if (claz != null && claz.length() > 0 )
    {
        rsvc.info("Trying to use logger class " + claz );

        try
        {
            o = Class.forName( claz ).newInstance();

            if ( o instanceof LogSystem )
            {
                ((LogSystem) o).init( rsvc );

                rsvc.info("Using logger class " + claz );

                return (LogSystem) o;
            }
            else
            {
                rsvc.error("The specifid logger class " + claz +
                        " isn't a valid LogSystem");
            }
        }
        catch( NoClassDefFoundError ncdfe )
        {
            rsvc.debug("Couldn't find class " + claz
                    + " or necessary supporting classes in "
                    + "classpath. Exception : " + ncdfe);
        }
    }
}
```

If a class is found that implements LogSystem, then it will be returned immediately to the caller and thus be used as the LogSystem implementation in the current RuntimeInstance.

If the code runs past this point and no LogSystem implementation has been found, something has gone seriously wrong. Listing 9-7 shows a last-ditch attempt to use the AvalonLogSystem in case you inadvertently overrode the default configuration but didn't supply a valid implementation.

Listing 9-7. Configuring the Default LogSystem

```
LogSystem als = null;

try
{
    als = new AvalonLogSystem();

    als.init( rsvc );
}
catch( NoClassDefFoundError ncdfe )
{
    String errstr = "PANIC : Velocity cannot find any of the"
        + " specified or default logging systems in the classpath,"
        + " or the classpath doesn't contain the necessary classes"
        + " to support them."
        + " Please consult the documentation regarding logging."
        + " Exception : " + ncdfe;

    System.out.println( errstr );
    System.err.println( errstr );

    throw ncdfe;
}

rsvc.info("Using AvalonLogSystem as logger of final resort.");

return als;
    }
}
```

If Velocity manages to load the AvalonLogSystem after all, then it's returned to the caller as the LogSystem implementation and everything continues to process nicely. If, however, a LogSystem implementation is still not loaded, Velocity gives up and writes a particularly harsh error message to both standard out and standard error.

For the most part, you'll never have problems with the logging configuration, but the knowledge of how the LogSystem is loaded will come in handy in the next chapter when you create a custom implementation of LogSystem.

Understanding the initializeResourceManager() Method

The initializeResourceManager() method is responsible for loading the ResourceManager implementation and then initializing that implementation.

```
private void initializeResourceManager()
    throws Exception
{
    String rm = getString( RuntimeConstants.RESOURCE_MANAGER_CLASS );
```

The first step is to retrieve the name of the implementation class from the configuration. By default this is set to org.apache.velocity.runtime.resource.ResourceManagerImpl. Next Velocity attempts to load this class and create an instance of it, like so:

```
if ( rm != null && rm.length() > 0 )
{
    Object o = null;

    try
    {
        o = Class.forName( rm ).newInstance();
    }
    catch (ClassNotFoundException cnfe )
    {
        String err = "The specified class for Resourcemanager ("
            + rm
            + ") does not exist (or is not accessible to the current classloader.";
        error( err );
        throw new Exception( err );
    }
```

If the class can't be found, then an exception is thrown, informing you of this. If the class is found, Velocity checks to see that the instance is in fact an implementation of the ResourceManager interface.

```
if (!(o instanceof ResourceManager) )
{
    String err = "The specified class for ResourceManager ("
        + rm
        + ") does not implement org.apache.runtime.resource.ResourceManager."
        + " Velocity not initialized correctly.";

    error( err);
    throw new Exception(err);
}
```

If you specify the name of the class that isn't an implementation of
ResourceManager, then initialization will go no further and an exception is
thrown. If the instance is valid, it's stored in the private field resourceManager,
and the ResourceManager.initialize() method is called, passing in the current
RuntimeInstance as an argument.

```
        resourceManager = (ResourceManager) o;

        resourceManager.initialize( this );
    }
    else  {
        String err = "It appears that no class was specified as the"
        + " ResourceManager.  Please ensure that all configuration"
        + " information is correct.";

        error( err);
        throw new Exception( err );
    }
}
```

The final else block is invoked if you specify the appropriate configuration
property but don't specify a value.

For the most part you won't want to create a new implementation of
ResourceManager, mainly because the existing implementation works well and
there's no benefit to be gained by replacing it.

The initialize method of the ResourceManagerImpl class, which is the default
ResourceManager implementation, loads and configures the individual
ResourceLoaders as well as the ResourceCache implementation.

```
public void initialize( RuntimeServices rs )
    throws Exception
{
    rsvc = rs;

    rsvc.info("Default ResourceManager initializing. ("
                    + this.getClass() + ")");

    ResourceLoader resourceLoader;

    assembleResourceLoaderInitializers();
```

The assembleResourceLoaderInitializers() method creates a List of
ExtendedProperties, with each ExtendedProperties instance storing the configuration details for a single ResourceLoader. The implementation of this method isn't

particularly interesting, so I won't discuss it here; you can always refer to the source code yourself. The List created by assembleResourceLoaderInitializers() is stored in the private field, sourceInitializerList. One important part of the assembleResourceLoaderInitializers() method is that it will ensure that the ResourceLoader configuration contains the name given to that ResourceLoader, stored in the name property, even if you didn't set it explicitly in your configuration.

With the configuration settings for the individual ResourceLoaders available separately from the main configuration, Velocity loops through the sourceInitializerList, loads the implementation class for each ResourceLoader, loads the implementation classes, and performs the initialization of each ResourceLoader (see Listing 9-8).

Listing 9-8. Loading and Initializing the ResourceLoaders

```
for (int i = 0; i < sourceInitializerList.size(); i++)
{
    ExtendedProperties configuration =
                        (ExtendedProperties) sourceInitializerList.get(i);
    String loaderClass = configuration.getString("class");

    if ( loaderClass == null)
    {
        rsvc.error(  "Unable to find '"
          + configuration.getString(RESOURCE_LOADER_IDENTIFIER)
          + ".resource.loader.class' specification in configuration."
          + " This is a critical value.  Please adjust configuration.");
        continue;
    }

    resourceLoader = ResourceLoaderFactory.getLoader( rsvc, loaderClass);
    resourceLoader.commonInit( rsvc, configuration);
    resourceLoader.init(configuration);
    resourceLoaders.add(resourceLoader);

}
```

The ResourceLoaderFactory.getLoader() method simply attempts to load the class, throwing an exception and writing a message to log it that the class isn't found. The implementation of ResourceLoader.commonInit() and ResourceLoader.init() obviously depends on which implementation you view. Later in this section I'll discuss the implementations of these methods for the FileResourceLoader class.

The next step in this method is to check whether the resource.manager.logwhenfound configuration parameter is set.

```
        logWhenFound = rsvc.getBoolean(
RuntimeConstants.RESOURCE_MANAGER_LOGWHENFOUND, true );
```

If the configuration parameter doesn't exist, then the default value of true will be used (this is what the second argument in the call to RuntimeServices.getBoolean() means). The getBoolean() method of RuntimeInstance, which implements RuntimeServices, simply calls the corresponding method on the configuration field to retrieve the value from the configuration properties loaded during the initializeProperties() method. This level of indirection can get quite confusing at times, but in general when you see a call to the RuntimeServices interface to retrieve a configuration parameter, it's carried out using the configuration field of the RuntimeInstance class.

The next and final step of this method is to load the ResourceCache implementation, which is by default set to org.apache.velocity.runtime.resource .ResourceCacheImpl (see Listing 9-9).

Listing 9-9. Loading the ResourceCache *Implementation*

```
        String claz = rsvc.getString(
RuntimeConstants.RESOURCE_MANAGER_CACHE_CLASS );

        Object o = null;

        if ( claz != null && claz.length() > 0 )
        {
            try
            {
                o = Class.forName( claz ).newInstance();
            }
            catch (ClassNotFoundException cnfe )
            {
                String err = "The specified class for ResourceCache ("
                    + claz
                    + ") does not exist ("
                    + " or is not accessible to the current classloader).";
                rsvc.error( err );

                o = null;
            }

            if (!(o instanceof ResourceCache) )
            {
                String err = "The specified class for ResourceCache ("
                    + claz
                    + ") does not implement "
```

```
                    + " org.apache.runtime.resource.ResourceCache."
                    + " ResourceManager. "
                    + "Using default ResourceCache implementation.";

              rsvc.error( err);

              o = null;
          }
      }

      if ( o == null)
          o = new ResourceCacheImpl();

       globalCache = (ResourceCache) o;

       globalCache.initialize( rsvc );

       rsvc.info("Default ResourceManager initialization complete.");

      }
```

The code in this part of the method should look familiar by now; the main point to note is that if you attempt to override the default cache configuration with a class that doesn't exist or doesn't implement the ResourceCache interface, then no exception will be thrown. Instead the ResourceCacheImpl class will be used if no other cache implementation can be found.

Understanding the intializeDirectives() Method

The initializeDirectives() method is responsible for loading the built-in system directives and also any user-specified directives (see Listing 9-10). The Velocity parser supports Pluggable Directives (PD), but beyond some mentions in the source code, no documentation exists for this feature.

Listing 9-10. The RuntimeInstance.initializeDirectives() *Method*

```
    private void initializeDirectives() throws Exception
    {
        runtimeDirectives = new Hashtable();

        Properties directiveProperties = new Properties();

        InputStream inputStream =
            getClass().getResourceAsStream('/' + DEFAULT_RUNTIME_DIRECTIVES);
```

```
    if (inputStream == null)
        throw new Exception("Error loading directive.properties! " +
                            "Something is very wrong if these properties " +
                            "aren't being located. Either your Velocity " +
                            "distribution is incomplete or your Velocity " +
                            "jar file is corrupted!");


    directiveProperties.load(inputStream);

    Enumeration directiveClasses = directiveProperties.elements();

    while (directiveClasses.hasMoreElements())
    {
        String directiveClass = (String) directiveClasses.nextElement();
        loadDirective( directiveClass, "System" );
    }

    String[] userdirective = configuration.getStringArray("userdirective");

    for( int i = 0; i < userdirective.length; i++)
    {
        loadDirective( userdirective[i], "User");
    }


}
```

This method is fairly self-explanatory; the list of system directives is loaded from the `directives.properties` file, which is stored in the same location as the default `velocity.properties` file in the JAR file. Each entry in that file has for its value the name of the class that implements the directive behavior. Then for each directive specified in that file, the `loadDirective()` method is called. Once this process is completed, it's repeated—this time for any user directives that are specified. Chapter 10 covers the concept of user directives in much more detail.

The `loadDirective()` method loads the specified directive class and checks that it's a subclass of `Directive` (see Listing 9-11).

Listing 9-11. The `loadDirective()` *Method*

```
private void loadDirective( String directiveClass, String caption )
{
    try
    {
        Object o = Class.forName( directiveClass ).newInstance();
```

```
        if ( o instanceof Directive )
        {
            Directive directive = (Directive) o;
            runtimeDirectives.put(directive.getName(), directive);

            info("Loaded " + caption + " Directive: "
                + directiveClass);
        }
        else
        {
            error( caption + " Directive " + directiveClass
                + " is not org.apache.velocity.runtime.directive.Directive."
                + " Ignoring. " );
        }
    }
    catch (Exception e)
    {
        error("Exception Loading " + caption + " Directive: "
            + directiveClass + " : " + e);
    }
}
```

If the directive class isn't found or the class isn't a subclass of `Directive`, then an exception is thrown; otherwise, the created instance of the `Directive` is stored in the private `Hashtable` field: `runtimeDirectives`.

Understanding the *initializeParserPool()* Method

The `intializeParserPool()` method is simple: it creates an instance of `SimplePool`, setting the pool size to the number specified in the configuration or to the default of 20. The `SimplePool` instance is then populated with the appropriate number of `Parser` instances (see Listing 9-12).

Listing 9-12. The `RuntimeInstance.initializeParserPool()` *Method*

```
private void initializeParserPool()
{
    int numParsers = getInt( PARSER_POOL_SIZE, NUMBER_OF_PARSERS);

    parserPool = new SimplePool( numParsers);

    for (int i=0; i < numParsers ;i++ )
    {
```

```
    parserPool.put (createNewParser());
}

info ("Created: " + numParsers + " parsers.");
}
```

The Parser class is discussed in more detail later in the "Using the Velocity Template Parser" section. The SimplePool class is just that: a simple implementation of a pool, wrapping an Object array. I'm quite surprised that this class isn't pluggable because in a high-volume application, the implementation of the parser pool may be the cause of bottlenecks. Of course, you can always increase the pool size, but then that raises issues of memory efficiency. If you require a more advanced pooling mechanism, then nothing is stopping you from creating your own version of RuntimeInstance. However, I wouldn't recommend that unless you have the resources to test it thoroughly and integrate your changes into future releases of Velocity.

The createNewParser() method is also simple.

```
public Parser createNewParser()
{
    Parser parser = new Parser( this );
    parser.setDirectives(runtimeDirectives);
    return parser;
}
```

Here you can see that the Parser instance is created, passing in the current RuntimeInstance (as an implementation of RuntimeServices). Then the setDirectives() method is called, passing the runtimeDirectives Hashtable created by the initializeDirectives() method.

Understanding the *initializeIntrospection()* Method

The initializeIntrospection() method follows a simpler pattern to many of the other configuration methods, loading a class based on parameters set in the configuration (see Listing 9-13).

Listing 9-13. The RuntimeInstance.initializeIntrospection() *Method*

```
private void initializeIntrospection()
    throws Exception
{
    String rm = getString(RuntimeConstants.UBERSPECT_CLASSNAME);
```

```
if (rm != null && rm.length() > 0)
{
    Object o = null;

    try
    {
        o = Class.forName(rm).newInstance();
    }
    catch (ClassNotFoundException cnfe)
    {
        String err = "The specified class for Uberspect ("
            + rm
            + ") does not exist "
            + "(or is not accessible to the current classloader.";
        error(err);
        throw new Exception(err);
    }

    if (!(o instanceof Uberspect))
    {
        String err = "The specified class for Uberspect ("
            + rm
            + ") does not implement "
             + " org.apache.velocity.util.introspector.Uberspect."
            + " Velocity not initialized correctly.";

        error(err);
        throw new Exception(err);
    }

    uberSpect = (Uberspect) o;

    if (uberSpect instanceof UberspectLoggable)
    {
        ((UberspectLoggable) uberSpect).setRuntimeLogger(this);
    }

    uberSpect.init();
}
else
{

    String err = "It appears that no class was specified as the"
    + " Uberspect.  Please ensure that all configuration"
    + " information is correct.";
```

```
        error(err);
        throw new Exception(err);
    }
}
```

This method requires little explanation, other than to say that an introspection implementation must implement the Uberspect interface and may optionally implement the UberspectLoggable interface to enable logging from within the implementation directly into the Velocity logging system. The default implementation, org.apache.velocity.util.introspection.UberspectImpl, implements both interfaces. The use of introspection is discussed later in the "Understanding Introspection in Velocity" section.

Configuring Velocimacros

I won't go into vast levels of detail on the configuration of the Velocimacros, because I can see no real benefit in knowing how Velocimacros are loaded. Velocimacros are a documented extension mechanism, so you should be fully aware of their behavior. If you're interested in how Velocimacros are loaded, then you should refer to the VelocimacroFactory source file your distribution.

Introducing the FileResourceLoader Initialization Process

As you've seen, each ResourceLoader implementation is initialized during the initialization phase. Specifically, the ResourceManagerImpl class calls two initialization methods on each ResourceLoader: init() and commonInit(). The commonInit() method is actually implemented by the abstract ResourceLoader class and is used to read common configuration properties from the configuration (see Listing 9-14).

Listing 9-14. The ResourceLoader *Class*

```
package org.apache.velocity.runtime.resource.loader;

import java.io.InputStream;

import org.apache.velocity.runtime.RuntimeServices;

import org.apache.velocity.runtime.resource.Resource;

import org.apache.velocity.exception.ResourceNotFoundException;

import org.apache.commons.collections.ExtendedProperties;
```

```
public abstract class ResourceLoader
{

    protected boolean isCachingOn = false;

    protected long modificationCheckInterval = 2;

    protected String className = null;

    protected RuntimeServices rsvc = null;

    public void commonInit( RuntimeServices rs, ExtendedProperties configuration)
    {
        this.rsvc = rs;

        isCachingOn = configuration.getBoolean("cache", false);
        modificationCheckInterval =
                    configuration.getLong("modificationCheckInterval", 0);

        className = configuration.getString("class");
    }

// rest of the class...
}
```

As you can see, the common properties are considered to be cache, modificationCheckInterval, and class. The comments in the source code point out that cache and modificationCheckInterval aren't truly common across all ResourceLoaders. This is worth bearing in mind if you're building your own ResourceLoaders (discussed in the next chapter), as these "common" parameters may change.

The init method is specific to each ResourceLoader implementation. None of the built-in ResourceLoaders perform any significant initialization during the initialization phase, apart from just reading the appropriate configuration parameters from the configuration and processing these parameters as appropriate. Consider the FileResourceLoader.init() method, as shown in Listing 9-15.

Listing 9-15. The FileResourceLoader.init() *Method*

```
public void init( ExtendedProperties configuration)
{
    rsvc.info("FileResourceLoader : initialization starting.");

    paths = configuration.getVector("path");

    int sz = paths.size();
```

```
    for( int i=0; i < sz; i++)
    {
        rsvc.info("FileResourceLoader : adding path '" +
                        (String) paths.get(i) + "'");
    }

    rsvc.info("FileResourceLoader : initialization complete.");
}
```

Here the init() method simply grabs a vector containing the list of paths for the FileResourceLoader to search and stores it in the private field paths. The remainder of the code is simply logging code.

An interesting point about this code is that it shows that the configuration parameter set as file.resource.loader.path in the configuration is available inside the FileResourceLoader.init() as simply path. This is useful information for implementing a custom ResourceLoader, as in the next chapter.

Introducing VelocityEngine

So far the discussion has focused on what happens during the initialization using the Velocity class. Under the hood the VelocityEngine uses the same RuntimeInstance class, but rather than using the RuntimeSingleton class to manage a singleton instance, each VelocityEngine has its own instance of RuntimeSingleton; other than that, the process is identical.

Understanding Performance Considerations of the Initialization Phase

As you can tell from the discussion so far, the initialization phase performs a lot of processing, but can this affect the performance of your application? Maybe. It all depends on how you're interacting with Velocity. If you're using the Velocity class or a single instance of VelocityEngine in your application, then the initialization process will have little effect on the overall performance of your application. However, if you create a new instance of VelocityEngine each time you want to create some output, then the initialization process is going to run each time as well. To see the effect of this, consider the code snippet shown in Listing 9-16.

Listing 9-16. Testing Initialization Performance

```java
package com.apress.pjv.ch9;

import java.io.StringWriter;
import java.io.Writer;

import org.apache.velocity.Template;
import org.apache.velocity.VelocityContext;
import org.apache.velocity.app.VelocityEngine;

public class PerfTest {

    private static final String TEMPLATE_NAME = "sample.vm";

    public static void main(String[] args) throws Exception {
        // context for both tests
        VelocityContext ctx = new VelocityContext();
        ctx.put("who", "Rob");

        // test 1 - single instance
        VelocityEngine ve = new VelocityEngine();
        ve.init("src/velocity.properties");

        long before = System.currentTimeMillis();

        for (int x = 0; x < 250; x++) {
            Writer writer = new StringWriter();
            Template t = ve.getTemplate(TEMPLATE_NAME);
            t.merge(ctx, writer);
        }

        System.out.println("Time Taken: "
                + (System.currentTimeMillis() - before));

        // test 2 - many instances
        before = System.currentTimeMillis();

        for (int x = 0; x < 250; x++) {
            VelocityEngine ve2 = new VelocityEngine();
            ve2.init("src/velocity.properties");

            Writer writer = new StringWriter();
            Template t = ve2.getTemplate(TEMPLATE_NAME);
            t.merge(ctx, writer);
        }
```

```
        System.out.println("Time Taken: "
                + (System.currentTimeMillis() - before));
    }
}
```

This code runs two simple tests: one that generates output 250 times using a single instance of VelocityEngine and another that generates output 250 times using a new instance of VelocityEngine each time. I ran this test first of all on my machine using the FileResourceLoader with caching disabled using the following command:

```
java -cp "build:lib/velocity-dep-1.4.jar" ➥
-Xms768M -Xmx768M com.apress.pjv.ch9.PerfTest
```

This command should rule out the possibility of a heap resize affecting the results. Table 9-1 shows the results.

Table 9-1. PerfTest *Results (No Caching)*

Implementation	Time Taken (in Milliseconds)
Single instance	871
New instance each time	13153

As you can see, the implementation that creates an instance of VelocityEngine each time is more than ten times slower than the implementation that uses a shared instance. Obviously, the initalization phase is slowing the application down somewhat. Another drawback to using multiple instances of VelocityEngine is that you can't take advantage of caching. When I run the PerfTest application again, this time with caching enabled, the results are dramatically different (see Table 9-2).

Table 9-2. PerfTest *Results (Caching)*

Implementation	Time Taken (in Milliseconds)
Single instance	68
New instance each time	12745

The second test is now almost 200 times slower than the first test. Evidently using a new instance of VelocityEngine to run each generation process isn't a viable solution for applications where performance is important. The solution is to use the Velocity class or use a singleton wrapper around the VelocityEngine class, such as that discussed in Chapter 4.

Summarizing Initialization

You've now seen what goes into initializing the Velocity runtime to make it ready
for your application. You've also seen that running the initialization process multiple times within your application imposes a severe performance overhead and
should be avoided.

In the next section I'll discuss the locate and load phase and the parse
phase which, as you've seen, are invoked by a call to `Velocity.getTemplate()`.
The `getTemplate()` methods on both the Velocity and `VelocityEngine` class are
simply wrappers, calling either directly or indirectly (via `RuntimeSingleton`) to
the `getTemplate()` methods of the `RuntimeInstance` class (see Listing 9-17).

Listing 9-17. The `RuntimeInstance.getTemplate()` *Method*

```
public Template getTemplate(String name)
    throws ResourceNotFoundException, ParseErrorException, Exception
{
    return getTemplate( name, getString( INPUT_ENCODING, ENCODING_DEFAULT) );
}

public Template getTemplate(String name, String  encoding)
    throws ResourceNotFoundException, ParseErrorException, Exception
{
    return (Template) resourceManager.getResource(name,
                ResourceManager.RESOURCE_TEMPLATE, encoding);
}
```

In most cases, you'll use the `getTemplate(String)` method, passing just the
template name and relying on input encoding specified in the configuration.
Either way the loading of the actual resource is delegated to the `ResourceManager`
implementation loaded during the initialization phase. The second argument in
the call to `getResource()` is the type of resource to load—in this case a template
resource. The distinction is important when you consider the same method is
used to load static resources included in the output using the #include directive.
The default implementation of the `getResource()` method, specified in the
`ResourceManagerImpl` class, uses a simple but elegant algorithm for locating and
loading resources in the various configured `ResourceLoaders` (see Listing 9-18).

Listing 9-18. The `ResourceManagerImpl.getResource()` *Method*

```
public Resource getResource(String resourceName,
                            int resourceType, String encoding )
        throws ResourceNotFoundException, ParseErrorException, Exception
    {
        Resource resource = globalCache.get(resourceName);
```

```
    if( resource != null)
    {
        try
        {
            refreshResource( resource, encoding );
        }
        catch( ResourceNotFoundException rnfe )
        {
            globalCache.remove( resourceName );

            return getResource( resourceName, resourceType, encoding );
        }
        catch( ParseErrorException pee )
        {
            rsvc.error(
                "ResourceManager.getResource() exception: " + pee);

            throw pee;
        }
        catch( Exception eee )
        {
            rsvc.error(
                "ResourceManager.getResource() exception: " + eee);

            throw eee;
        }
    }
```

Initially the `ResourceManagerImpl` will attempt to load the resource from the cache. Remember that the cache implementation was loaded during the initialization stage. All resources are stored in the cache and keyed by their name. If the resource is retrieved from the cache, the resource manager will check for updates on the resource using the `refreshResource()` method. I'll discuss this method in more detail later in the "Understanding the refreshResource() Method" section. If a `ResourceNotFoundException` is thrown during the process, which, according to the comments in the code is a possibility and may be done on purpose, the resource is removed from the cache and the resource manager will try to retrieve the resource from fresh.

If the resource isn't in the cache, it's loaded using the `loadResource()` method. If the resource loader that's used to load the resource has caching enabled, then the resource is added to the cache to service subsequent requests (see Listing 9-19).

Listing 9-19. getResource() *(Continued)*

```
    else
    {
        try
        {
            resource = loadResource( resourceName, resourceType, encoding );

            if (resource.getResourceLoader().isCachingOn())
            {
                globalCache.put(resourceName, resource);
            }
        }
        catch( ResourceNotFoundException rnfe2 )
        {
            rsvc.error(
                "ResourceManager : unable to find resource '" + resourceName +
                    "' in any resource loader.");

            throw rnfe2;
        }
        catch( ParseErrorException pee )
        {
            rsvc.error(
                "ResourceManager.getResource() parse exception: " + pee);

            throw pee;
        }
        catch( Exception ee )
        {
            rsvc.error(
                "ResourceManager.getResource() exception new: " + ee);

            throw ee;
        }
    }

    return resource;
}
```

Any errors during this process are caught, logged, and rethrown. The
getResource() is really just a control method; the loadResource() method does
the bulk of the processing, and the key to operation of the cache is the
refreshResource() method.

Understanding the loadResource() Method

Individual resources are loaded using the loadResource() method. Whether it's a static resource or a template, it will be loaded by loadResource(), like so:

```
protected Resource loadResource(String resourceName,
                int resourceType, String encoding )
    throws ResourceNotFoundException, ParseErrorException, Exception
{
    Resource resource =
        ResourceFactory.getResource(resourceName, resourceType);

    resource.setRuntimeServices( rsvc );

    resource.setName( resourceName );
    resource.setEncoding( encoding );
```

The first job for loadResource() is to create an instance of the appropriate class to represent the resource. The ContentResource class represents static resources, and the Template class represents template resources; these both are subclasses of Resource. The resource is informed of its own name and encoding using the setName() and setEncoding() methods and is given access to the RuntimeServices instance of the resource manager.

Next each of the resource loaders configured during initialization is checked to see if it can load the resource (see Listing 9-20).

Listing 9-20. loadResource() *(Continued)*

```
long howOldItWas = 0;   // Initialize to avoid warnings

ResourceLoader resourceLoader = null;

for (int i = 0; i < resourceLoaders.size(); i++)
{
    resourceLoader = (ResourceLoader) resourceLoaders.get(i);
    resource.setResourceLoader(resourceLoader);

    try
    {
        if (resource.process())
        {
            if ( logWhenFound )
            {
                rsvc.info("ResourceManager : found " + resourceName +
                        " with loader " + resourceLoader.getClassName() );
            }
```

```
                    howOldItWas = resourceLoader.getLastModified( resource );
                    break;
                }
            }
        catch( ResourceNotFoundException rnfe )
        {
            /*
             *  that's ok - it's possible to fail in
             *  multi-loader environment
             */
        }
    }
```

If the resource is found, then it's given a reference to its resource loader, which, as you'll see, is used for caching purposes. The call to Resource.process() performs the actual loading process, returning true if the resource was loaded by the given resource loader. If process() returns false, then the process continues for the next resource loader. The process() method is covered in more detail shortly.

If the code runs to this point and the resource data is still null, then none of the resource loaders can load the resource. Thus, a ResourceNotFoundException is thrown, as follows:

```
if (resource.getData() == null)
{
    throw new ResourceNotFoundException(
        "Unable to find resource '" + resourceName + "'");
}
```

The last modified time of the resource, retrieved from the resource loader and stored in the howOldItWas variable, is stored in the Resource instance itself.

```
    resource.setLastModified( howOldItWas );

    resource.setModificationCheckInterval(
        resourceLoader.getModificationCheckInterval());

    resource.touch();

    return resource;
}
```

Also notice that the modification check interval for the resource loader is stored in the resource. The call to Resource.touch() sets the internal nextCheck field of the Resource to the current time plus the modification check interval. It's important to note that the last modified time, retrieved from the resource loader earlier, is stored in the resource with a call to setLastModified(). Only FileResourceLoader and DataSourceReader actually support this method; both ClasspathResourceLoader and JarResourceLoader return zero. This becomes relevant, as you'll see, to the operation of the refreshResource() method.

At this point, the Resource has been either retrieved from the cache or loaded using a resource loader. However, I still have to discuss the methods ResourceManagerImpl.refreshResource() and Resource.process(). To recap, refreshResource() is called when a resource is retrieved from the cache and is intended to reload resources that have been modified. But as you'll see, this behavior is dependent on the resource loader used. The process() method attempts to load the resource data and, in the case of the Template class, invokes the parser.

Using the refreshResource() Method

As I've already mentioned, the refreshResource() method is key to the caching process. The refreshResource() method itself is quite simple; indeed, most of the functionality is delegated to methods of the Resource class (see Listing 9-21).

Listing 9-21. The refreshResource() *Method*

```
protected void refreshResource( Resource resource, String encoding )
    throws ResourceNotFoundException, ParseErrorException, Exception
{
    if ( resource.requiresChecking() )
    {
        resource.touch();

        if( resource.isSourceModified() )
        {
            if (!resource.getEncoding().equals( encoding ) )
            {
                rsvc.error("Declared encoding for template '"
                            + resource.getName()
                            + "' is different on reload.  Old = '"
                            + resource.getEncoding()
                            + "'  New = '" + encoding );

                resource.setEncoding( encoding );
            }

            long howOldItWas =
                    resource.getResourceLoader().getLastModified( resource );

            resource.process();
```

```
                resource.setLastModified( howOldItWas );
        }
    }
```

The `requiresChecking()` method checks to see if the current system time is past the time stored in the `nextCheck` field (set by the `touch()` method), as follows:

```
public boolean requiresChecking()
{
    if (modificationCheckInterval <= 0 )
    {
        return false;
    }

    return ( System.currentTimeMillis() >= nextCheck );
}
```

If the resource does need checking, then the `nextCheck` counter is set again using the `touch()` method. Next, the `refreshResource()` method checks to see if the resource has been modified since it was last loaded. The `Resource.isSourceModified()` method delegates the call to the `isSourceModified()` of the resource loader that loaded. If the resource is found to have been modified, then the `Resource.process()` method is invoked again to reload the resource contents and perform any relevant processing.

It's evident that the key to the operation of this process is the implementa tion of the `isSourceModified()` method for each of the different resource loaders. Resources that have been loaded using the `JarResourceLoader` and the `ClasspathResourceLoader` will be unaware of their last modified time. This impacts the `isSourceModified()` method because it's impossible to know whether or not the resource has been modified.

The `JarResourceLoader` will always return `true` for a call to `isSourceModified()`, meaning resources are always reloaded. This isn't quite as bad as it first appears, since the JAR, once loaded, is held in memory and the reload time is relatively small. However, it does therefore make sense to disable caching for the `JarResourceLoader` because resources will never be retrieved from the cache.

The `ClasspathResourceLoader`, on the other hand, will always return `false` for a call to `isSourceModified()`, meaning that if you have caching enabled (and you should), then once the resource has been loaded, it will repeatedly be retrieved from the cache, despite any modifications to the underlying resource. In a development environment this may cause problems, because you'll have to restart the application to display any changes. In the next chapter I'll discuss how you can implement a custom resource loader that overcomes this problem.

The `FileResourceLoader` supports `isSourceModified()`, retrieving the last modified time of the original file from the underlying operating system. `DataSourceResourceLoader` also supports the `isSourceModified()` field, but it has to query the database to find the last modified time of the resource. You should bear this mind if you choose to use `DataSourceResourceLoader`, and set the modification check interval parameter suitably high so that Velocity isn't performing needless queries into the database.

Understanding the `Resource.process()` Method

As you've seen, the `Resource.process()` method is called whenever a resource is loaded or reloaded. `Resource.process()` itself is actually abstract, so it's in fact the implementation on the subclass, either `ContentResource` or `Template`, that's invoked.

The `ContentResource.process()` method is the simplest of the two implementations; it simply reads the contents of the resource via the `ResourceLoader.getResourceStream()` method (see Listing 9-22).

Listing 9-22. The `ContentResource.process()` *Method*

```
public boolean process()
    throws ResourceNotFoundException
{
    BufferedReader reader = null;

    try
    {
        StringWriter sw = new StringWriter();

        reader = new BufferedReader(
            new InputStreamReader(resourceLoader.getResourceStream(name),
                                  encoding));
```

Obviously, the implementation of `getResourceStream` is specific to the resource loader implementations. I won't discuss the implementations here because they aren't really that important. If you're interested to see how they work, then you can check out the code yourself.

The remainder of method simply reads in the resource stream and then calls `setData()`, which stores the resource contents in an `Object` field. It's evident that the actual type of the data in this case is `String`—`ContentResource` is used for static resources, and the data will simply be written to the output stream as required, with no additional processing being performed on it (see Listing 9-23).

Listing 9-23. `ContentResource.process()` *(Continued)*

```
char buf[] = new char[1024];
        int len = 0;

        while ( ( len = reader.read( buf, 0, 1024 )) != -1)
            sw.write( buf, 0, len );

        setData(sw.toString());

        return true;
    }
    catch ( ResourceNotFoundException e )
    {
        throw e;
    }
    catch ( Exception e )
    {
        rsvc.error("Cannot process content resource : " + e.toString() );
        return false;
    }
    finally
    {
        if (reader != null)
        {
            try
            {
                reader.close();
            }
            catch (Exception ignored)
            {
            }
        }
    }
}
```

Notice that if a `ResourceNotFoundException` is encountered, it's rethrown. This is a valid error and signifies that the resource wasn't found in the current resource loader. It's interesting to note that the actual locate and load of the resource happens during this method.

The `Template.process()` method is much more involved than the `ContentResource.process()` method, mainly because it not only performs the locate and load phase but also the parse phase as well. The start of the method is similar to the `ContentResource.process()` method, obtaining an `InputStream` from the resource loader (see Listing 9-24).

Listing 9-24. The `Template.process()` *Method*

```
public boolean process()
    throws ResourceNotFoundException, ParseErrorException, Exception
{
    data = null;
    InputStream is = null;
    errorCondition = null;

    try
    {
        is = resourceLoader.getResourceStream(name);
    }
    catch( ResourceNotFoundException rnfe )
    {
        /*
         *  remember and rethrow
         */

        errorCondition = rnfe;
        throw rnfe;
    }
```

Now that the InputStream is loaded, it's wrapped in a BufferedReader, which is passed to the RuntimeInstance.parse() method. RuntimeInstance.parse() grabs a Parser instance from the pool established during initialization, creating one if the pool is empty, and then invokes the parse phase (see Listing 9-25).

Listing 9-25. `Template.process()` *(Continued)*

```
if (is != null)
{

    try
    {
        BufferedReader br =
            new BufferedReader( new InputStreamReader( is, encoding ) );

        data = rsvc.parse( br, name);
        initDocument();
        return true;
    }
    catch( UnsupportedEncodingException  uce )
    {
        String msg = "Template.process : Unsupported input encoding : "
```

```
                + encoding
                + " for template " + name;


            errorCondition  = new ParseErrorException( msg );
            throw errorCondition;
        }
        catch ( ParseException pex )
        {
            /*
             *  remember the error and convert
             */


            errorCondition =  new ParseErrorException( pex.getMessage() );
            throw errorCondition;
        }
        catch( Exception e )
        {
            errorCondition = e;
            throw e;
        }
        finally
        {
            is.close();
        }
    }
    else
    {
            errorCondition =
                        new ResourceNotFoundException(
                                    "Unknown resource error for resource " + name );
            throw errorCondition;
    }
}
```

The `initDocument()` method that's invoked after the `Template` has been parsed is a kind of post–parse process, and it's explained in more detail in the next section.

At this point the resource has been loaded into memory and in the case of `Templates` has been parsed and is ready for use in the merge phase. In the next section I'll discuss what happens during the parse phase and the purpose of the `initDocument()` method.

Using the Velocity Template Parser

As you've seen, once a `Template` resource has been loaded by Velocity, the parser takes over and from the input stream creates an AST. The Velocity parser works by splitting the `Template` into tokens, which are then arranged into a tree structure based on their relationships with each other. Each node in the tree is represented in memory by a class that extends the `SimpleNode` class. For example, consider this VTL snippet:

```
$who.length()
```

Represented as an AST, this snippet would have an `ASTprocess` class as the root node. This class represents the root node of the AST for all templates. As the first child node of the `ASTprocess` node in the tree, you'd have an `ASTReference` representing the variable reference `$who`. The next node in the tree is a child node of the `ASTReference` node, representing the call to the `length()` method, and is of type `ASTMethod`.

NOTE   *The spelling of* `ASTprocess` *with a lowercase* p *isn't an error— that's the correct name of the class, although I'm not sure why!*

Don't worry if you have trouble understanding exactly the purpose of this tree—I'll discuss the structure of the tree in more detail when you look at the merge phase.

The Velocity parser is implemented using two tools: JavaCC and JJTree. JavaCC is a parser builder, written in Java, and JJTree is an extension to JavaCC that supports the creation of syntax trees. I won't actually discuss the implementation of the parser here because that topic is much too complex to discuss in full in this chapter and, indeed, even in this book. For the most part, it's enough to understand that the parsing process splits the Template into nodes, which are subsequently arranged into a tree structure to provide a logical in-memory representation of the Template. If you're interested in how the parser was created, you can find the full grammar definition for Velocity in the Velocity distribution; you can find more details on JavaCC and JJTree at `http://javacc.dev.java.net/`.

Understanding the initDocument() Method

The initDocument() method is significant because it's the first interaction with the AST outside the parser (see Listing 9-26).

Listing 9-26. The initDocument() *Method*

```
public void initDocument()
    throws Exception
{

    InternalContextAdapterImpl ica = new InternalContextAdapterImpl(  new
VelocityContext() );

    try
    {
        ica.pushCurrentTemplateName( name );

        ((SimpleNode)data).init( ica, rsvc);
    }
    finally
    {
        ica.popCurrentTemplateName();
    }
}
```

An instance of InternalContextAdapterImpl is created, wrapping an empty VelocityContext. The InternalContextAdapterImpl class is used internally within the AST, specifically the Node class methods such as init and render. The main reason for this is that internally the AST relies on many more context operations than those specified in the Context interface. If you implement a custom Context object directly using the Context interface rather than subclassing AbstractContext as does VelocityContext, then you don't have to implement the additional interfaces (InternalHousekeepingContext and InternalEventContext) required by Node. The InternalContextAdapterImpl class ensures that Node always has access to a valid Context that implements these methods. The interesting point here is that you'll almost certainly want to derive from AbstractContext so that you get an implementation of these interfaces. I can see no benefit for you to implement these interfaces manually, so instead you should rely on the implementations provided by AbstractContext.

The data field, which is set by the Parse process, contains the root node of the AST. The initDocument() calls the init() method of the root node, which in turn will call init() on its child nodes, which in turn do the same for their children, and so on. This process is important as it gives each node in the AST a chance to perform initialization. Most of the nodes in the AST use this as an opportunity to gather the information about themselves from the node and perform application-specific processing on the data. The important point to remember is that the parser simply splits the template input into the tree structure. The nodes have no meaning to the parser. The initDocument() method gives each node a chance to transform the parser supplied data, usually in the form of child nodes, into data that's useful to Velocity.

Summarizing Parsing

Parsing is one of the more low-level aspects of the Velocity system. You can do little to extend the actual parsing behavior, but understanding the basics of how the parser functions is important to understanding how Velocity itself functions. I've only touched on the subject of parsing here, but I've given you enough information to understand, from a high-level, how the parser works. I've skipped the details of how the parser works internally, mainly because it would require another book to discuss the topic fully. In the next section I'll discuss how the AST is used during the merge phase.

Introducing the Merge Phase

The merge phase is the final phase in the content creation process. During this phase, each node in the AST is processed in tree order. When a node on a particular level of the tree is processed, all its children are processed before the next node on the same level.

The merge phase starts with a call to Template.merge() (see Listing 9-27).

Listing 9-27. The merge() *Method*

```
public void merge( Context context, Writer writer)
    throws ResourceNotFoundException, ParseErrorException,
        MethodInvocationException, Exception
{
    if (errorCondition != null)
    {
        throw errorCondition;
    }

    if( data != null)
    {
        InternalContextAdapterImpl ica =
                    new InternalContextAdapterImpl( context );

        try
        {
            ica.pushCurrentTemplateName( name );
            ica.setCurrentResource( this );
```

```
                ( (SimpleNode) data ).render( ica, writer);
        }
        finally
        {
            ica.popCurrentTemplateName();
            ica.setCurrentResource( null );
        }
    }
    else
    {
        String msg = "Template.merge() failure. The document is null, " +
            "most likely due to parsing error.";

        rsvc.error(msg);
        throw new Exception(msg);
    }
}
```

This method is actually simple. The Context is wrapped in an InternalContextAdapterImpl, and the template name is pushed onto the Context stack. The data field, storing the root node of the AST, is cast to SimpleNode, and the render() method of the node is called. Each node is responsible for writing its own output to the Writer instance passed to its render() method. A vast array of different node types is available for the AST. Rather than go through the implementation of the render() method for each node type, I'll describe the different nodes in the AST of the template shown at the beginning of the chapter.

To recap, the following is the template I'll be discussing:

```
Hello $who!
Your name has $who.length() characters in it.
```

The first node in the AST, in any AST, is the ASTprocess node. The ASTprocess class itself doesn't implement render(); instead, it relies on the default implementation in the SimpleNode class.

```
public boolean render( InternalContextAdapter context, Writer writer)
    throws IOException, MethodInvocationException, ParseErrorException,
        ResourceNotFoundException
{
    int i, k = jjtGetNumChildren();

    for (i = 0; i < k; i++)
        jjtGetChild(i).render(context, writer);

    return true;
}
```

This method simply iterates over all the child nodes and calls their render()
methods. The first child of the root node in this example is an ASTText node. The
ASTText.render() method simply writes the text read in as the token to the output stream (see Listing 9-28).

Listing 9-28. ASTText.init() *and* ASTText.render()

```
public Object init( InternalContextAdapter context, Object data)
    throws Exception
{

    Token t = getFirstToken();

    String text = NodeUtils.tokenLiteral( t );

    ctext = text.toCharArray();

    return data;
}


public boolean render( InternalContextAdapter context, Writer writer)
    throws IOException
{

    writer.write(ctext);
    return true;
}
```

In Listing 9-28 you can see that in the init() method, the first token for this
node, is retrieved and the text content is converted to a character array and
stored in the ctext field. In the case of this example, the ctext char array will
hold six characters—the letters of the Hello string and the trailing space. In the
render method, the ctext array is written to the output stream.

The next node in the tree is an ASTReference node that represents the $who
reference; this is followed by another ASTText node holding the ! character that
comes after the $who reference. The init() and render() methods of the
ASTReference contain a lot of code, but they aren't really of interest. Much of the
process deals with the various ways of writing references such as silent references ($!who) and formal references (${who}), as well as with some of the nuances
of the parser in relation to references. It's enough to know that in this case the
value of the who variables stored in the context is written to the output stream.
If you're interested in how the escaping rules are implemented and how silent
references are implemented, then take a look at the ASTText code yourself.

On the second line of the template, you'll see a single ASTText node followed
by another ASTReference for the call to the $who.length() node and finally another
ASTText representing the remainder of the static text. The interesting part here is

that the ASTReference node has, as a child node, an instance of ASTMethod representing the call to the length(). This is where the introspection process comes in. You should note that at this point the structure of the AST isn't completely "tree-like"—if I were to modify the template code to read $who.toLowercase().length(), then, rather than have an ASTReference with an ASTMethod as a child (which in turn has a child ASTMethod), I'd simply have an ASTReference with two ASTMethod children.

Understanding Introspection in Velocity

I'm sure you're already familiar with the concepts of reflection and introspection. Certainly they're concepts that have existed in the Java world for a long while. Interestingly, Velocity doesn't use the introspection classes in the Java Software Development Kit (SDK); instead it uses reflection exclusively to manipulate not only method calls but also calls to JavaBean-style properties, which is where the Java introspection class become useful.

The basis of the introspection support in Velocity is the Uberspect interface and the default implementation, UberspectImpl. You're free to provide your own implementation of the Uberspect interface, but realistically you'll struggle to create an implementation better than UberspectImpl.

In relation to the ASTMethod node representing the length() call on the $who reference, the ASTMethod class calls the getMethod() method of the Uberspect implementation. In the case of UberspectImpl, the Velocity Introspector class carries out the actual reflection process, like so:

```
public VelMethod getMethod(Object obj, String methodName, Object[] args, Info i)
        throws Exception
{
    if (obj == null)
        return null;

    Method m = introspector.getMethod(obj.getClass(), methodName, args);

    return (m != null) ? new VelMethodImpl(m) : null;
}
```

As you can see, the java.lang.reflect.Method class returned by the Introspector.getMethod() method is wrapped in a VelMethodImpl class and returned to the caller. The Introspector class simply wraps the reflection operations performed by Velocity and also includes a cache for the reflection results to boost performance. This isn't the place for a full discussion of reflection, but those who are unfamiliar with reflection can get more information in the JDK documentation.

Back in the ASTMethod class, the method loaded by the introspection process is invoked by a call to VelMethodImpl.invoke(), which passes the call directly to the wrapped Method instance. From here the JDK takes over and invokes the named method that returns the result of the invocation to the caller. If there's another method call in the chain, then the result of method invocation is used as the target of the next introspection. If no other method exists in the chain, then the value returned by calling toString() on the resulting object is written to the output stream. If the result is a primitive, then the String representation of the primitive is written to the output stream.

Summarizing Merge

The merge phase is actually quite simple. A lot of code goes into the merge phase to make the simple syntax of VTL function, but the basis of the merge is to iterate over the AST, rendering each node in turn. The merge makes extensive use of reflection to support the method call and property access syntax in Velocity. A good way to understand what's happening during the merge of your templates is to look at the init() and render() methods of the different AST node types. In a typical application, the merge phase will execute more than any of the other phases, so a good understanding of what happens during this phase is key to building a high-performing and scalable application.

Summary

In this chapter you saw how the main parts of the Velocity runtime are implemented. Specifically, you looked at the four stages of processing that occur in a typical Velocity-based application, along with the key points of each stage's implementations. With this knowledge you should now have a much better understanding of what happens inside Velocity when it's creating your output.

In the next chapter, you'll see how you can extend various aspects of the Velocity system using both standard and nonstandard extension methods.

Extending Velocity

FOR THE MOST PART, the standard features of the Velocity runtime will suffice for the applications that you want to build. However, some applications may have special requirements that call for changes to the way Velocity works. Whilst you could just change the source code of the Velocity runtime and recompile it, this isn't the best solution for the future. When a new version of Velocity is released, you need to rework the source code if you want to take advantage of new features of the runtime. Thankfully, Velocity provides a variety of standard mechanisms for extending various areas of the runtime. Specifically, you can extend the runtime with the following:

- Custom event handling

- A custom `LogSystem`

- Custom `ResourceLoaders`

- Custom directives

- A custom `ResourceManager`

- A custom `ResourceCache`

- A custom `Uberspect` implementation

In this chapter, I'll cover the first four mechanisms for extension, since these are the ones you're likely to use most during the course of building Velocity-based applications. You really have no need to implement a custom `ResourceManager` unless you want to replace the `ResourceLoader` system altogether. In addition, the standard implementations of `ResourceCache` and `Uberspect` are good, so you should have no need to replace them.

Using custom event handling you can take control of some Velocity events and override the default behavior taken by Velocity when these events are encountered. As you'll see, this has some interesting uses.

A custom `LogSystem` can be useful if your application has its own logging framework and you want to redirect the Velocity log messages to that logging framework. In this chapter I'll show you how to build a simple `LogSystem` that writes all log messages to the console.

The standard ResourceLoaders included with the Velocity runtime are usually enough for any application, but one thing that bothers me is the lack of caching support in the ClasspathResourceLoader. In this chapter I'll show you how to build a custom ResourceLoader that loads resources from the classpath and fully supports caching.

In Chapter 3 you saw how to utilize Velocimacros to encapsulate presentation logic. In some cases the logic you want to encapsulate is too complex to implement effectively using VTL. In this case you can create custom directives in Java code that can be used just like a standard directive. In fact, many of the standard directives such as #foreach and #parse are created using the same mechanism as custom user directives. In this chapter I'll show you the basics of creating a custom directive and also the code for a directive I've found quite useful.

Hooking Into Velocity Events

Velocity provides three interfaces that can be implemented to catch and handle three different types of events (see Table 10-1).

Table 10-1. Event Handling Interfaces

Interface Name	Event Handling Method	Purpose
MethodExceptionEventHandler	methodException()	Using this event handler, you can intercept any Exceptions thrown by a method called by your template. You can then choose to return the Exception as it is or to return a friendlier alternative.
NullSetEventHandler	shouldLogOnNull()	This event is fired whenever a null reference is encountered in a template. You can use this to control whether a log message is written for null references. This is useful when a null reference may be valid and you don't want to fill up the log with pointless messages.
ReferenceInsertionEventHandler	referenceInsert()	This event is fired just before the value of a reference is inserted into the output stream. This allows you to override the value returned the reference and write something else to the output stream.

Implementing the event handler interfaces is quite simple; in the following sections I'll demonstrate how to use each interface and the effect it can have on processing your templates.

Building an Event Handler

You can implement each event interface in a separate class, but for the purposes of this example I'll create a single class that implements all three. The first step is to create the class, like so:

```
package com.apress.pjv.ch10;

import org.apache.velocity.app.event.EventCartridge;
import org.apache.velocity.app.event.MethodExceptionEventHandler;
import org.apache.velocity.app.event.NullSetEventHandler;
import org.apache.velocity.app.event.ReferenceInsertionEventHandler;
import org.apache.velocity.context.Context;

public class EventHandler implements ReferenceInsertionEventHandler,
        NullSetEventHandler, MethodExceptionEventHandler {

}
```

As you can see, I've created the basic class structure and declared the class as implementing the ReferenceInsertionEventHandler, NullSetEventHandler, and MethodExceptionEventHandler interfaces.

The next step is to register this class with the Velocity runtime. You can choose to have the event handler class register itself or register it in a separate class—either way, the code is same. I prefer to encapsulate the registration of the event handler in the event handler itself; that way I can ensure that the event handler is always registered, and I don't have to remember to register it every time I want to use it.

The EventCartridge class registers the event handlers. Using EventCartridge you add one or more event handlers and then attach the EventCartridge to a Context. Anytime that Context is used to generate output, the event handlers registered with the EventCartridge will be notified of the appropriate events.

In this case I use the EventHandler constructor to perform the registration.

```
public EventHandler(Context ctx) {
    EventCartridge ec = new EventCartridge();
    ec.addEventHandler(this);
    ec.attachToContext(ctx);
}
```

Each time an EventHandler class is created, it will be registered with the supplied Context automatically. All that remains is to implement the three event-handling methods.

Implementing *MethodExceptionEventHandler*

The MethodExceptionEventHandler interface declares a single method, methodException(), that accepts three parameters and has a return value of Object. The first parameter is the Class of the object that threw the exception, the second parameter is the method name, and the third is the Exception that was thrown. The Object that's returned by this method is the Object that's rendered in the output stream.

The EventHandler class implements this method and simply prefixes the Exception message with an additional message.

```
public Object methodException(Class cls, String method, Exception e)
        throws Exception {
    return "An " + e.getClass().getName() + " was thrown by the " + method
        + " method of the " + cls.getName() + " class ["
        + e.getMessage() + "]";
}
```

Of course, you can return any Object from this method; if you have a method that throws a particular Exception that you'd like to describe with a friendly message, then you can easily detect the method and Exception type and then return the message as appropriate.

Implementing *NullSetEventHandler*

NullSetEventHandler declares a single method, shouldLogOnNull(), that accepts two String parameters: one that describes the left side of the #set directive and one that describes the right side. The shouldLogOnNull() method return a boolean— true to write the log message and false to skip it.

The implementation in the EventHandler class looks like this:

```
public boolean shouldLogOnNullSet(String lhs, String rhs) {
    System.out.println("shouldLogOnNullSet");
    System.out.println("lhs:" + lhs + " rhs:" + rhs);
```

```
    if ("$validNull".equals(rhs.trim())) {
        return false;
    } else {
        return true;
    }
}
```

Here you can see that if this event handler is fired and the reference that's null is called $validNull, then no log message is written; otherwise the log message will be written. As I said earlier, this method is useful when you have references in a template that may be null, and you don't want to have messages in the log for references that can be validly null.

Implementing ReferenceInsertEventHandler

The ReferenceInsertEventHandler interface defines a single method, referenceInsert(), that accepts a String parameter for the reference name and an Object parameter that's the value that will be inserted into the output stream for that reference. Using this event handler you can override the value that's inserted into the output or add some additional information to it.

The implementation of referenceInsert() for the EventHandler class looks like this:

```
public Object referenceInsert(String reference, Object data) {
    System.out.println("referenceInsert: " + reference + " data: " + data);

    if ("$horse".equals(reference.trim())) { return "The Mighty " + data; }

    return data;
}
```

Here you can see that if the reference being inserted is for a variable named $horse, then the return data is prefixed with The Mighty.

Testing the EventHandler

As you've seen, the implementation of the event handlers is quite simple; now all that remains is to test it. To test the EventHandler class, I created a simple console application, as shown in Listing 10-1.

Listing 10-1. Testing the EventHandler *Class*

```
package com.apress.pjv.ch10;

import java.io.StringWriter;
import java.io.Writer;

import org.apache.velocity.Template;
import org.apache.velocity.VelocityContext;
import org.apache.velocity.app.Velocity;
import org.apache.velocity.context.Context;

public class EventHandlerTest {

    public static void main(String[] args) throws Exception {
        // init
        Velocity.init("src/velocity.properties");

        // get the template
        Template t = Velocity.getTemplate("eventHandler.vm");

        // create context
        Context ctx = new VelocityContext();
        ctx.put("person", "Gandalf Stormcrow");
        ctx.put("horse", "Shadowfax");
        ctx.put("rnd", new RandomExceptionGenerator());

        // create the event handler
        EventHandler hdl = new EventHandler(ctx);

        // create the output
        Writer writer = new StringWriter();
        t.merge(ctx, writer);

        // output
        System.out.println(writer);
    }
}
```

This code should look familiar now; notice that I've added three objects to Context, two Strings (one of which is mapped to the $horse variable), and a RandomExceptionGenerator. The value of the $horse variable will be modified in the output by the referenceInsert() method of the EventHandler class. The RandomExceptionGenerator class has a single method, generate(), that returns a String value and randomly throws an Exception—this should suffice for demonstrating the methodException() handler method. Also notice that an instance of EventHandler is created, passing in the Context that's used to generate the output.

The template code is quite simple.

```
#set($myNull1 = $validNull)
#set($myNull2 = $invalidNull)

$person rides $horse

$rnd.generate()
$rnd.generate()
$rnd.generate()
$rnd.generate()
```

The important points to notice here are the two #set directives that use null references and the multiple calls to the generate() method of the $rnd variable. The shouldLogOnNull() handler will be called for each of these #set directives, and one with the $invalidNull variable will result in a log message being written.

Running this example results in the following output from the template:

```
Gandalf Stormcrow rides The Mighty Shadowfax

An java.lang.Exception was thrown by the generate method of the
com.apress.pjv.ch10.RandomExceptionGenerator class [Unlucky!]
Whew! That was close
An java.lang.Exception was thrown by the generate method of the
com.apress.pjv.ch10.RandomExceptionGenerator class [Unlucky!]
Whew! That was close
```

Notice that the value of the $horse variable has been prefixed by The Mighty, which was performed by the referenceInsert() method. Also, you can see that in the cases where the RandomExceptionGenerator.generate() method threw an Exception, the methodException() method has modified the error output. If you check the log, you'll see that only a single message was logged for the null references.

Summarizing Event Handling

As you can see from the previous section, Velocity provides a selection of useful event hooks that allow you to modify the processing of a template or set of templates without the need to change the template code. Overall the ReferenceInsertEventHandler appears to be the most useful because it allows you to modify the output of a template without the need to modify the template at all. The `MethodExceptionEventHandler` is also useful for providing friendlier error messages in your output. As for the `NullSetEventHandler`, my feeling is that it's useful only if your templates will create a large amount of needless log messages without it.

Creating a Custom LogSystem

For the most part, the `LogSystem` implementations that are provided with Velocity will be sufficient for any new applications, but if you're adding Velocity to an existing application that has a custom logging framework or your new application has to work with a custom logging framework, then a custom `LogSystem` implementation will allow you to redirect Velocity log messages to your custom logger.

In the following sections I'll show you how to build a simple `LogSystem` implementation that writes all log messages to standard out. The implementation will support log-level configuration, allowing you to externally configure the maximum message level for output.

Understanding the ConsoleLogSystem Class

Creating a `LogSystem` implementation is simple; the `LogSystem` interface declares only two methods. The first method, `init()`, allows you to perform some initialization steps, and the `logVelocityMessage()` method is called each time a log message needs writing.

The `ConsoleLogSystem` class supports configurable log levels; that is, you can restrict the log messages that are written by level. The levels for log messages in Velocity start with `ERROR` as the most serious and `DEBUG` as the least serious, with `WARN` and `INFO` in between.

The `ConsoleLogSystem` class has quite a bit of code, mainly to support the configurable logging output, so I'll explain it in small pieces.

To start with, I import the required classes, create the class declaration, and declare the class fields, like so:

```
package com.apress.pjv.ch10;

import org.apache.velocity.runtime.RuntimeServices;
import org.apache.velocity.runtime.log.LogSystem;

public class ConsoleLogSystem implements LogSystem {
    private RuntimeServices rs;

    private int maxLevel = LogSystem.INFO_ID;
```

```
    private static final String[] LEVEL_NAMES =
                    new String[] { "ERROR", "WARN", "INFO",
            "DEBUG"};

    private static final int[] LEVELS = new int[] { LogSystem.ERROR_ID,
LogSystem.WARN_ID,
                LogSystem.INFO_ID, LogSystem.DEBUG_ID};
```

The maxLevel field determines whether a message should be written to the console, and by default the field is set to LogSystem.INFO_ID, which means that all messages of INFO level or higher will be written to the console. The LEVEL_NAMES array stores the names of the log levels, and the LEVELS array stores the corresponding level ID at the same index.

The init() method is called by the Velocity runtime as part of the initialization phase. This method simply stores the supplied RuntimeServices instance in the rs field and then calls the configure() method, like so:

```
public void init(RuntimeServices rs) throws Exception {
    System.out.println("ConsoleLogSystem.init() called");

    this.rs = rs;
    configure();

    System.out.println("ConsoleLogSystem.init() finished");
}
```

The configure() method looks in the Velocity configuration for a parameter called console.logsystem.max.level and uses that value to configure the maxLevel field.

```
    private void configure() {
        String maxLevelName = rs.getString("console.logsystem.max.level");

        int level = getLevelFromString(maxLevelName);

        if(level > -1) {
            System.out.println("Using log level: " + maxLevelName);
            maxLevel = level;
        }
    }
```

As you can see, the configure() method passes the level name retrieved from the configuration to the getLevelFromString() method to retrieve the corresponding level ID. If the return value is greater than -1, then it's stored in the maxLevel field.

The getLevelFromString() method simply searches the LEVEL_NAMES array for the supplied level name and then retrieves the level ID from the corresponding index in the LEVELS array. If no value is found, then getLevelFromString() returns -1.

```
private int getLevelFromString(String levelName) {
    for(int x = 0; x < LEVEL_NAMES.length; x++) {
        if(LEVEL_NAMES[x].equals(levelName)) {
            return LEVELS[x];
        }
    }
    return -1; // couldn't find the level
}
```

The logVelocityMessage() method is quite simple; it just checks to see if the supplied level argument is greater or equal to the maxLevel field, thus indicating that the level is enabled, and then writes the message to standard out.

```
public void logVelocityMessage(int level, String message) {

    if(level >= maxLevel) {
        System.out.println("[" + getLevelName(level) + "] " + message);
    }
}
```

Notice that the name of the level is retrieved with a call to getLevelName(). The getLevelName() method is similar to the getLevelFromString() method, but it works in the opposite way.

```
private String getLevelName(int level) {
    for(int x = 0; x < LEVELS.length; x++) {
        if(LEVELS[x] == level) {
            return LEVEL_NAMES[x];
        }
    }

    return "UNKNOWN";
}
```

That's all there is to the ConsoleLogSystem code; all that remains now is for the ConsoleLogSystem class to be configured as the LogSystem implementation.

Configuring the ConsoleLogSystem Class

Configuring the ConsoleLogSystem is simply a matter of adding the following lines to the velocity.properties file:

```
runtime.log.logsystem.class=com.apress.pjv.ch10.ConsoleLogSystem
console.logsystem.max.level=INFO
```

You can specify any log level you want for the console.logsystem.max.level parameters, and obviously, the name of your implementation class may be different. Try running the EventHandler example again; this time you'll see that all the log output is sent to the console window. Try changing the log level to WARN and running the application again—notice that much less log output is created.

Summarizing LogSystem

As you can see from the previous example, creating a custom LogSystem is quite simple. In most cases the LogSystem implementation will just be a bridge between Velocity and your custom logger. If you're building an application from scratch and you want to add logging support, then I recommend you use log4j and the corresponding LogSystem implementation. However, if you're working with an existing application or are building a new application that must use a custom logging component, then LogSystem is the perfect way to have Velocity log messages routed to your logger.

Creating a Custom ResourceLoader

As you've seen, ResourceLoaders are key to the Velocity runtime. By choosing the correct ResourceLoader you can obtain a noticeable performance improvement in your application. I find that the ClasspathResourceLoader is the simplest to use in terms of configuration, but it doesn't support caching fully, which can be a drawback during development and in production applications when you need to change output without restarting the system. If you want to use caching fully, then you must use FileResourceLoader; however, you then introduce the problem of file paths—overall, ClasspathResourceLoader is much simpler to use.

In the following sections, I'll show you how to build a custom ResourceLoader implementation that loads resources from the classpath in the same way as ClasspathResourceLoader but also supports caching in the same way as FileResourceLoader.

Understanding the ResourceLoader Class

Creating a custom ResourceLoader involves extending the abstract ResourceLoader class. Much of the implementation for caching is provided by the ResourceLoader class, as you saw in the previous chapter; all the ResourceLoader implementation needs to do is implement the getLastModified() and isSourceModified() methods that the ResourceLoader class uses for its caching algorithm. The purpose of these two methods should be evident: the getLastModified() method returns a long value indicating the last time a resource was modified, and the isSourceModified() method returns a boolean indicating whether a resource has been modified.

In addition to implementing getLastModified() and isSourceModified(), you must also implement init() and getResourceStream(). The init() method is called once during the initialization phase of the Velocity runtime and gives you the opportunity to perform any kind of configuration you need. The getResourceStream() method is called by the Velocity runtime when it needs to retrieve a fresh copy of the resource data and return an instance of InputStream.

Checking the Last Modified Date with URL

The key to enabling caching for the CachingClasspathResourceLoader class is to be able to retrieve the last modified date of a resource from the classpath. The standard ClasspathResourceLoader doesn't do this; instead it simply says that a resource is not modified (returns false for isSourceModified()).

Access to resources on the classpath happens through the ClassLoader, and from there you can obtain either a direct InputStream for the reference or an instance of URL that points to the resource. The standard ClasspathResourceLoader uses the InputStream method; for CachingClasspathResourceLoader I use the URL mechanism. Once an instance of URL is obtained for a particular resource, a URLConnection object can be obtained using URL.openConnection(), and from there the last modified date can be found using URLConnection.getLastModified(). The important thing to realize here is that this process is very slow compared to checking the last modified date using an instance of File. To illustrate this, I created a simple test that checks the performance of a last modified check using three different approaches: a File instance, a new URL instance each time, and a cached URL instance. Listing 10-2 shows the code for the test.

Listing 10-2. Performance Testing File *vs.* URL

```
package com.apress.pjv.ch10;

import java.io.File;
import java.net.URL;
```

```java
public class SimpleTest {

    private static final String PATH = "src/templates/ch10/customLoader.vm";
    private static final String URL = "templates/ch10/customLoader.vm";

    public static void main(String[] args) throws Exception {
        long before, after;
        int numTimes = 10000;
        ClassLoader cl = SimpleTest.class.getClassLoader();

        System.out.println("Testing File");

        before = System.currentTimeMillis();
        for (int x = 0; x < numTimes; x++) {
            File file = new File(PATH);
            long lm = file.lastModified();
        }
        after = System.currentTimeMillis();

        System.out.println("Took: " + (after - before) + " ms");

        System.out.println("Testing URL");
        before = System.currentTimeMillis();

        for (int x = 0; x < numTimes; x++) {
            URL url = cl.getResource(URL);
            long lm = url.openConnection().getLastModified();
        }
        after = System.currentTimeMillis();

        System.out.println("Took: " + (after - before) + " ms");

        System.out.println("Testing  Cached URL");

        before = System.currentTimeMillis();
        URL url = cl.getResource(URL);

        for (int x = 0; x < numTimes; x++) {
            long lm = url.openConnection().getLastModified();
        }
        after = System.currentTimeMillis();

        System.out.println("Took: " + (after - before) + " ms");
    }
}
```

As you can see, the test code is pretty basic. On my machine running this test gives the following output:

```
Testing File
Took: 128 ms
Testing URL
Took: 4631 ms
Testing  Cached URL
Took: 2060 ms
```

As you can see, checking the last modified using File is very fast; but using URL, it's quite slow. You'll get an appreciable performance gain from caching the URL instances—no doubt because the classpath needs to be searched for the resource. Interestingly, I ran this test again—this time caching the URLConnection object instead of the URL—and the time taken decreased to 362 milliseconds. However, this implies that the openConnection() does something other than simply create an object, and I don't like the idea of caching an object that represents a connection to a resource, especially in this case. The problem arises in that the class that's returned from openConnection() will differ from JVM to JVM, and it's likely they will be undocumented. Since no documentation exists on whether it's safe to keep URLConnection objects around for a long time, it's best to stick to caching the URL instance to find the balance between performance and reliability.

Understanding the CachingClasspathResourceLoader Class

Implementing the CachingClasspathResourceLoader class is remarkably simple. I started with the basic class and an empty implementation for init() (see Listing 10-3).

Listing 10-3. The CachingClasspathResourceLoader *Class*

```
package com.apress.pjv.ch10;

import java.io.IOException;
import java.io.InputStream;
import java.net.URL;
import java.util.HashMap;
import java.util.Map;

import org.apache.commons.collections.ExtendedProperties;
import org.apache.velocity.exception.ResourceNotFoundException;
import org.apache.velocity.runtime.resource.Resource;
import org.apache.velocity.runtime.resource.loader.ResourceLoader;
```

```
public class CachingClasspathResourceLoader extends ResourceLoader {

    private Map urlMap = new HashMap();

    public void init(ExtendedProperties configuration) {

    }
```

I don't need to provide an actual implementation for init() since the CachingClasspathResourceLoader class requires no configuration other than the cache and modificationCheckInterval parameters, and those are read and used by the base ResourceLoader class. You'll notice that I've added a private Map field called urlMap—this is where I'll cache the URL instances for each resource.

The next method is getResourceStream(), which simply obtains the URL for the resource and then returns an InputStream for the resource using URL.openStream().

```
    public synchronized InputStream getResourceStream(String resourceName)
            throws ResourceNotFoundException {
        try {
            URL url = getURL(resourceName);

            if (url == null) { throw new ResourceNotFoundException(
                    "Can not find resource: " + resourceName); }
            return url.openStream();
        } catch (IOException e) {
            throw new ResourceNotFoundException("Can not find resource: "
                    + resourceName + " - Reason: " + e.getMessage());
        }
    }
}
```

I'll show you the getURL() implementation shortly. Notice that if the URL instance is null, no resource could be found with the provided name, so a ResourceNotFoundException is thrown.

The next two methods are getLastModified(Resource) and isSourceModified(Resource).

```
    public long getLastModified(Resource resource) {
        try {
            URL url = getURL(resource.getName());
            long lm = url.openConnection().getLastModified();
            return lm;
        } catch (Exception e) {
            rsvc.error(e);
```

```
            return 0;
        }
    }

    public boolean isSourceModified(Resource resource) {
        long lm = getLastModified(resource);
        return (lm != resource.getLastModified());
    }
```

Both of these methods are quite simple; indeed, the main bulk of the implementation is in the getLastModified() method with the isSourceModified() method simply performing an extra check.

The getURL() method first checks the urlMap cache to see if the URL has already been found. If so, the URL is retrieved from the cache and returned to the caller. If not, then the classpath is searched for the URL instance using ClassLoader.getResource().

```
    private URL getURL(String resourceName) {
        if (urlMap.containsKey(resourceName)) { return (URL) urlMap
                .get(resourceName); }

        ClassLoader cl = this.getClass().getClassLoader();
        URL url = cl.getResource(resourceName);

        if (url != null) {
            urlMap.put(resourceName, url);
        }

        return url;
    }
```

If no URL is found for the resource, then ClassLoader.getResource() will return null, which is returned to the caller. If the URL is found, then it's added to the cache and then returned to the caller.

That concludes the implementation of the CachingClasspathResourceLoader; all that remains is to configure the resource loader and then to test it.

Configuring the CachingClasspathResourceLoader

By now I'm sure you're more than familiar with the ResourceLoader configuration, so there's no need to explain the following code:

```
resource.loader = custom

custom.resource.loader.class = com.apress.pjv.ch10.CachingClasspathResourceLoader
custom.resource.loader.cache = true
custom.resource.loader.modificationCheckInterval = 2
```

Don't forget that the `cache` and `modificationCheckInterval` parameters are used by the base `ResourceLoader` class to manage the caching, not by the `CachingClasspathResourceLoader` class.

Testing CachingClasspathResourceLoader

To test this `ResourceLoader`, I create a simple test that produces some simple output using a template loaded using the `CachingClasspathResourceLoader`, puts the thread to sleep for ten seconds, and then creates output again using the same template. The ten-second pause should give you plenty of time to modify the template contents (see Listing 10-4).

Listing 10-4. Testing the Custom `ResourceLoader`

```java
package com.apress.pjv.ch10;

import java.io.StringWriter;
import java.io.Writer;

import org.apache.velocity.Template;
import org.apache.velocity.VelocityContext;
import org.apache.velocity.app.Velocity;
import org.apache.velocity.context.Context;

public class TestCustomResourceLoader {

    public static void main(String[] args) throws Exception {
        Velocity.init("src/velocity.properties");

        VelocityContext ctx = new VelocityContext();
        ctx.put("who", "Rob");

        // create the output the first time
        Template t = getTemplate();
        write(t, ctx);

        // wait for 10 seconds
        Thread.sleep(10000);
```

```
        // get template again and write
        t = getTemplate();
        write(t, ctx);
    }

    private static Template getTemplate() throws Exception {
        return Velocity.getTemplate("templates/ch10/customLoader.vm");
    }

    private static void write(Template template, Context ctx) throws Exception {
        Writer writer = new StringWriter();
        template.merge(ctx, writer);
        System.out.println(writer.toString());
    }
}
```

Run the example; once the first set of output is written to the console, modify the template and save it again. The next block of output should reflect the changes. If you experience any problems running this, check the log file to make sure the resource is being loaded by the CachingClasspathResourceLoader, not another one.

Summarizing ResourceLoader

As you can see from the previous example, creating a custom ResourceLoader is quite simple. The ResourceLoader class provides much of the logic; all you have to do is provide implementations for getLastModified() and isSourceModified(), and the ResourceLoader class takes care of the rest.

Creating Custom Directives

In Chapter 3 you saw how to use Velocimacros to create reusable blocks of VTL for use either within a single template or across an entire application. In most cases Velocimacros are an ideal solution for increasing reusability and reducing repetition, but in some cases using custom directives is a much better solution. Custom directives are written in Java, and as such you can take advantage of the full power of the Java language. Also, for complex Velocimacros the VTL can quickly become unmanageable, so creating a directive in Java makes much more sense.

Many of the standard Velocity directives are created using the extensibility mechanism, including #parse and #foreach. You should bear in mind that creating directives is much more complex that creating Velocimacros; it involves interacting with the underlying Abstract Syntax Tree (AST) to read information about the template file.

Understanding the HelloDirective Class

All custom directives are derived from the abstract `Directive` class. The `Directive` class has three methods that must be overridden: `getName()`, `getType()` and `render()`. The `getName()` and `getType()` methods are simple to implement, requiring a single line of code each. The `render()` method is much more complicated and in general requires interaction with the AST to read information from the directive.

I'll demonstrate a simple directive that has a single argument and just writes a *Hello* message. There isn't much to the code, so I'll show it all in Listing 10-5 and then describe it afterward.

Listing 10-5. The `HelloDirective` *Class*

```
package com.apress.pjv.ch10;

import java.io.IOException;
import java.io.Writer;

import org.apache.velocity.context.InternalContextAdapter;
import org.apache.velocity.exception.MethodInvocationException;
import org.apache.velocity.exception.ParseErrorException;
import org.apache.velocity.exception.ResourceNotFoundException;
import org.apache.velocity.runtime.directive.Directive;
import org.apache.velocity.runtime.parser.Token;
import org.apache.velocity.runtime.parser.node.Node;

public class HelloDirective extends Directive {

    private static final String NAME = "hello";

    public String getName() {
        return NAME;
    }

    public int getType() {
        return LINE;
    }

    public boolean render(InternalContextAdapter context, Writer writer,
            Node node) throws IOException, ResourceNotFoundException,
            ParseErrorException, MethodInvocationException {

        if (node.jjtGetNumChildren() != 1) {
            rsvc.error("#hello error - missing first argument");
            return false;
        }
```

```
        writer.write("Hello ");
        Node child = node.jjtGetChild(0);

        writer.write(child.value(context).toString());

        Token lastToken = node.getLastToken();

        if (lastToken.image.endsWith("\n")) {
            writer.write("\n");
        }

        return true;
    }
}
```

The getName() and getType() methods are both quite simple. The name returned by getName() is the one you use for this directive in a template. The type can be either LINE or BLOCK, both of which are constants defined in the DirectiveConstants interface, which is implemented by the Directive class. A LINE-type directive is one that has no matching #end directive, such as #parse, and a BLOCK-type directive is one that has a matching #end directive, such as #foreach.

The render() method looks quite complex, but there really isn't that much to it. In a LINE-style directive all the arguments passed to the directive are child nodes of the directive node. The Node.jjtGetNumChildren() returns the number of children for a particular node. In this case, I check to see if the directive node has a single child node—that's a single argument. I write the word *Hello* to the output stream and then retrieve the first child node using the Node.jjtGetChild() method. Next, I obtain the value of the child node using the Node.value() method and write it to the output stream.

The final step for the render() method is to obtain the last Token that makes up the directive and then check to see whether the Token image (its value) ends with a line break. The image of the last Token will include the closing bracket of the directive and then, if applicable, a line break. Without this check, the line break will be missed if the custom directive is at the end of a line.

Testing HelloDirective

To see the HelloDirective in action, I created a simple demo template and driver program. Before I show you the code for the demo application, I'll show how to configure the custom directive. You can configure custom directives using the userdirective parameter in the velocity.properties file. If you have more than one custom directive, you can either add more than one userdirective parameter to the configuration or use a comma-separated list of class names.

To configure the `HelloDirective`, simply add the following line to the
`velocity.properties` file:

```
userdirective=com.apress.pjv.ch10.HelloDirective
```

The template for the demo application looks like this:

```
#hello(1)
#hello("World")
#hello($who)
Something
#hello()
#hello(1) #hello("you")
Something else
```

As you can see, it tests various uses of the `#hello` directive. Running this template through a simple driver program that adds a value for the `$who` variable to
the `Context` results in the following output:

```
Hello 1
Hello World
Hello Rob
Something
Hello 1 Hello you
Something else
```

The directive functions just as well with string and number literals for its
argument as it does with variable references. You'll also notice that it functions
correctly on its own line and on the same line as some other VTL. See what
happens if you comment out the check for a line break in the last `Token` of the
directive—the directives that are on their own lines in the template aren't on
their own lines in the output.

Understanding the ImageDirective Class

The previous directive wasn't much use; it didn't really show the power of the
custom directive functionality. In this section I'll demonstrate a much more
useful directive that highlights a few more handy features, including external
configuration support and the use of a varying number of arguments.

One of the common ways of increasing throughput in a Java-based Web
application is to host all images under a separate domain name such as `http://`
`images.mydomain.com` and serve them using a separate web server, usually Apache,
that's specifically tuned for serving static files. This reduces the load of the Java

servlet container and also allows you to take advantage of the extra performance of Apache for the static content. The problem with this solution is that you'll commonly need a different image URL for development than for production. Having to change all the URLs for all the images in an application can be time-consuming. In this section I'll show you how to build a simple #image directive that will write out an HTML image and prefix the supplied path with a domain name that can be configured globally in velocity.properties. This means you can change the URL in one place when moving from development to production.

The code for the ImageDirective class starts off in much the same way as the HelloDirective class with implementations for getName() and getType() (see Listing 10-6).

Listing 10-6. The ImageDirective *Class*

```
package com.apress.pjv.ch10;

import java.io.IOException;
import java.io.Writer;

import org.apache.velocity.context.InternalContextAdapter;
import org.apache.velocity.exception.MethodInvocationException;
import org.apache.velocity.exception.ParseErrorException;
import org.apache.velocity.exception.ResourceNotFoundException;
import org.apache.velocity.runtime.RuntimeServices;
import org.apache.velocity.runtime.directive.Directive;
import org.apache.velocity.runtime.parser.node.Node;

public class ImageDirective extends Directive {

    private static final String NAME = "image";

    private static final int ARG_PATH = 0;

    private static final int ARG_ALT = 1;

    private static final int ARG_WIDTH = 2;

    private static final int ARG_HEIGHT = 3;

    private String baseUrl = "";

    public String getName() {
        return NAME;
    }
```

```
public int getType() {
    return LINE;
}

public void init(RuntimeServices rs, InternalContextAdapter context,
        Node node) throws Exception {
    super.init(rs, context, node);

    baseUrl = rs.getString("image.directive.base", baseUrl);
}
```

You'll notice, however, that I've added four static fields, each representing the index of the child node that, for the four arguments, can be passed to the #image directive. Also, I've overridden the init() method to read in a configuration parameter for the baseUrl field, which is prefixed to the path of every image. The second argument passed to the RuntimeServices.getString() method is the default value.

The implementation of the render() method isn't particularly complex, but it does introduce some interesting concepts (see Listing 10-7).

Listing 10-7. Implementing render()

```
public boolean render(InternalContextAdapter context, Writer writer,
        Node node) throws IOException, ResourceNotFoundException,
        ParseErrorException, MethodInvocationException {

    int numChildren = node.jjtGetNumChildren();

    // must have at least two arguments
    if (numChildren < 2) {
        rsvc.error(
            "#image directive specified with invalid number of arguments");
        return false;
    }

    // write the opening tag
    writer.write("<img");

    // now write the path
    writeAttribute(writer, "src", baseUrl
            + node.jjtGetChild(ARG_PATH).value(context).toString());

    // now write the alt text
    writeAttribute(writer, "alt", node.jjtGetChild(ARG_ALT).value(context)
            .toString());
```

```
// see if the width is specified
if (ARG_WIDTH < numChildren) {
    writeAttribute(writer, "width", node.jjtGetChild(ARG_WIDTH).value(
            context).toString());
}

// see if the height is specified
if (ARG_HEIGHT < numChildren) {
    writeAttribute(writer, "height", node.jjtGetChild(ARG_HEIGHT)
            .value(context).toString());
}

// write the close
writer.write(">");
return true;
}
```

You'll notice that the first two arguments, for the path and the `alt` text, are required, and no output is created without them. For the next two parameters, `width` and `height`, the values are optional, so output for those attributes is created only if necessary. Notice that the value of the `baseUrl` field is prefixed to the image path when writing out the `<img>` tag and that no check is performed for a new line in the last `Token`. Since this directive will be used to create HTML output, the whitespace of the output stream is unimportant—it has no bearing on the rendering of the document in the browser.

The `writeAttribute()` method simply writes a normal HTML attribute with key and value into the output stream, like so:

```
private void writeAttribute(Writer writer, String attributeName,
        String value) throws IOException {
    writer.write(" ");
    writer.write(attributeName);
    writer.write("=\"");
    writer.write(value);
    writer.write("\"");
}
```

That pretty much covers the implementation of the `ImageDirective`; all that remains is to configure it and test it.

Configuring ImageDirective

Configuring ImageDirective is like configuring HelloDirective; you need to add a userdirective parameter to the velocity.properties file. However, don't forget that you also need to specify the base URL for ImageDirective. The configuration for the example looks like this:

```
userdirective= com.apress.pjv.ch10.ImageDirective
image.directive.base=http://images.mysite.com/
```

Testing ImageDirective

Testing ImageDirective is quite simple; just create a basic template like this:

```
#image("images/hello.gif" "Hello World" "100px" "200px")
```

And then run it through a simple driver program. The output generated by the previous template is as follows:

```
<img src="http://images.mysite.com/images/hello.gif" alt"Hello World"
width"100px"
height"200px">
```

As you can see, the <img> tag contains the full URL of the image, including the path loaded from the configuration file.

Summarizing Custom Directives

Creating custom directives is a good way of creating blocks of functionality that can be used across many different applications. Although creating directives is much more complex than creating Velocimacros because of the need to work directly with the AST, you'll soon find that you get used to it. I've found that a useful mechanism for working with custom directives is to create a simple demo template that contains a sample of the usage of your custom directive and then create a basic shell of the directive implementation. From here I can use my debugger to see the AST tree that's built by Velocity and get much more of an idea about what code I need to write. This is especially helpful for BLOCK-type directives where the AST is much more complicated than for LINE-type directives.

Summary

You have plenty of options for extending the Velocity runtime. For the most part, the standard tools in the Velocity distribution will be enough, but it helps to know how to extend Velocity when your application requires you to step off the beaten path. In this chapter, you saw how to hook into the Velocity event system, create a custom `LogSystem`, build your own `ResourceLoader`, and create custom directives.

In the next chapter I'll demonstrate a selection of tools that make building Velocity applications much simpler.

### CHAPTER 11

Using Velocity Development Tools

AN ADVANTAGE OF VELOCITY is that it doesn't require you to have any special tools in order to use it. However, some tools can make your life easier when developing with Velocity. In this chapter, you'll briefly look at Velocity's support for a wide range of editors and IDEs, as well as a useful utility for quickly testing a snippet for Velocity code. I won't go into great detail on any of the tools because they're all quite simple.

Introducing VeloGUI

VeloGUI is a nifty little utility that you can launch using Java WebStart. VeloGUI provides a simple GUI-based interface for prototyping templates. As you can see in Figure 11-1, the top of the screen consists of two textboxes, one that allows you to enter Java code to create the context and another that allows you to enter the VTL code to be evaluated.

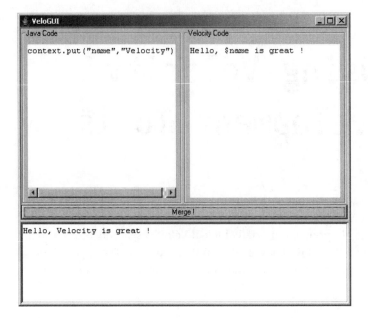

Figure 11-1. VeloGUI in action

Clicking the Merge button will create the output from the context and the VTL specified and then display it in the textbox at the bottom of the screen. This is the perfect mechanism for quickly testing a fragment of VTL code without the need to use a full driver program.

You can download the latest version from `http://www.pipoware.com/velogui/`. The Web site also contains a link to Java WebStart.

Introducing VeloEdit for Eclipse

As I've mentioned already in this book, Eclipse is my favorite Java IDE, and therefore this is the tool I use the most out of all those described in this chapter. You can install VeloEdit by pointing the Eclipse update manager to `http://veloedit .sourceforge.net/updates`.

Once installed, VeloEdit associates itself with the `.vm` and `.vsl` file extensions, meaning that this editor will be used for both Velocity templates and Anakia style sheets. VeloEdit has the basic syntax highlighting you'd expect of an Eclipse editor, as shown in Figure 11-2.

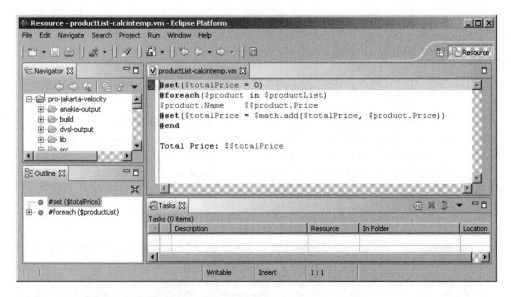

Figure 11-2. Syntax highlighting with VeloEdit

On top of this, VeloEdit includes a wide range of additional features, such as content assist and macro assist (shown in Figure 11-3), template validation and error highlighting, template outlining, and customizable external macro libraries.

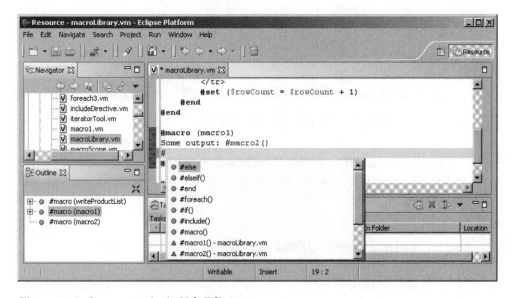

Figure 11-3. Content assist in VeloEdit

Overall, VeloEdit is a nice, polished addition to Eclipse, and it certainly makes life easier when working on large Velocity-based applications.

Using Velocity in IntelliJ IDEA

Rickard Oberg has contributed a Live Template for IntelliJ IDEA to the Velocity project, as shown in Figure 11-4. You can find the template file in the Velocity CVS repository at `http://cvs.apache.org/viewcvs/jakarta-velocity/contrib/tools/intellij`. The Live Template provides simple shortcuts for adding each of the directives to your templates, cutting down on the level of typing and reducing the chance of errors.

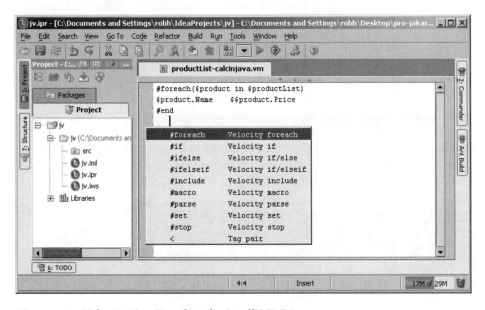

Figure 11-4. Velocity Live Template for IntelliJ IDEA

You can obtain full instructions on how to install Live Templates in the IDEA documentation at `http://www.jetbrains.com/idea/docs/help/editing/liveTemplates/defineTemplates.html`.

Using Velocity in JEdit

JEdit is a 100 percent Java-based developer text editor, as shown in Figure 11-5. You can obtain the latest version of JEdit from `http://www.jedit.org/`. You can

obtain the syntax highlighting definitions for JEdit from the Velocity CVS repository at `http://cvs.apache.org/viewcvs/jakarta-velocity/contrib/tools/jedit/`.

Figure 11-5. Syntax highlighting in VTL

Velocity support in JEdit is quite basic, but the syntax highlighting does
make it easier to spot errors in your template code.

Using Velocity in UltraEdit

UltraEdit is a Windows-based text editor, designed specifically for programmers.
It supports many syntaxes out of the box, including C/C++, HTML, Java, and Perl.
You can obtain an evaluation of the latest version of UltraEdit from `http://www`
`.ultraedit.com/`.

You can obtain UltraEdit syntax definitions from the Velocity CVS repository
at `http://cvs.apache.org/viewcvs/jakarta-velocity/contrib/tools/ultraedit/`.
Figure 11-6 shows an example of the syntax highlighting support in UltraEdit.

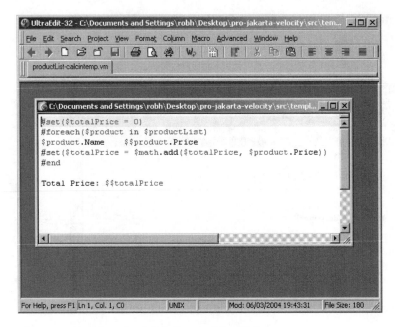

Figure 11-6. Syntax highlighting in UltraEdit

Using Velocity in TextPad

TextPad is another Windows-based text editor. You can obtain the latest version of TextPad from `http://www.textpad.com/`. You can add simple syntax highlighting using the details found at `http://www.textpad.com/add-ons/synu2z.html`.

As you can see from Figure 11-7, the Velocity support in TextPad is quite basic, but it does the job and is certainly better than just plain text editing.

Figure 11-7. Syntax highlighting in TextPad

Using Velocity in Emacs

For those of you who are using Emacs, you can obtain a Velocity minor mode for syntax highlighting from the CVS repository at `http://cvs.apache.org/viewcvs/ jakarta-velocity/contrib/tools/emacs/`.

Summary

Tool support for Velocity is already quite widespread and is becoming more so all the time. The VeloGUI tool is useful in many cases for quickly testing a fragment of VTL to ensure that it does what you require. Support is provided for a wide variety of IDEs, and even if you can't get some of the more advanced features such as code insight and template validation for your favorite IDE, chances are you'll be able to obtain support for syntax highlighting.

Velocity Reference

VELOCITY HAS A WIDE RANGE of configuration settings, directives, and resource loaders. This appendix is a reference for all aspects of Velocity configuration and usage.

Introducing the Directives

The following sections show the syntax for the standard directives included in the Velocity distribution.

#set

The #set directive assigns variables' values. These values can be a simple literal value or another variable.

Syntax

```
#set($variable=<literal value> | <variable_name>)
```

Example

```
#set($myVar = "Hello World")
```

Output

The #set directive has no output.

#if/#else/#end

The #if/#else/#end directives support conditional processing within your templates. The use of these directives is synonymous with the use of the if/else construct in Java.

Syntax

```
#if(<boolean expression> | <boolean literal> | <boolean variable reference>)
Output for true
#else
Output for false
#end
```

Example

```
#set($someVar = true)
#if($someVar)
Hello World!
#else
Goodbye Cruel World!
#end
```

Output

```
Hello World!
```

#foreach

The #foreach directive iterates over all elements in a collection or an array and performs some processing for each element.

Syntax

```
#foreach($var in $collectionOrArray)
## do something with $var
#end
```

Example

```
#foreach($num in [0..5])
$num
#end
```

Output

```
0
1
2
3
4
5
```

#include

The #include directive includes some content from another resource in the output stream. The content is added as-is with no processing by the Velocity engine.

Syntax

```
#import(<resource_name>)
```

Example

For example, the main template, template.vm, could contain the following VTL code:

```
Hello #include("world.txt")
```

And an external file resource, world.txt, could contain the following static text:

```
World
```

Output

```
Hello World
```

#parse

The #parse directive functions in a similar manner to the #include directive; however, the external resource is first parsed by the Velocity engine, and any VTL constructs are processed as if they were part of the main template.

Syntax

```
#parse(<resource_name>)
```

Example

For example, the main template, template.vm, could contain the following VTL code:

```
#set($who = "World")
Hello #parse("world.vm")
```

And an external template, world.vm, could contain the additional VTL code:

```
$who
```

Output

```
Hello World
```

Configuring Velocity

Velocity has a selection of configuration parameters that can control various aspects of the runtime. The following sections provide a quick reference to these configuration parameters.

General Configuration Options

Table A-1 shows the general configuration options.

Table A-1. General Configuration Options

Parameter Name	Description	Default Value
runtime.log	Specifies the name of the log file created by the Velocity log system. Filenames that aren't absolute are resolved relative to the current directory of your application.	velocity.log
runtime.log.logsystem.class	Specifies the class name of the LogSystem implementation. Use this if you want to use a specific LogSystem implementation.	org.apache.velocity.runtime.log.AvalonLogSystem
runtime.log.error.stacktrace	Specifies whether Velocity should output a stack trace for error-level log messages.	false
runtime.log.warn.stacktrace	Specifies whether Velocity should output a stack trace for warn-level log messages.	false
runtime.log.info.stacktrace	Specifies whether Velocity should output a stack trace for info-level log messages.	false
runtime.log.invalid.references	Specifies whether a log message should be written when an invalid reference is encountered.	true
input.encoding	Specifies the encoding to use when reading resource files.	ISO-8859-1
output.encoding	Specifies the encoding to use when creating output.	ISO-8859-1
parser.pool.size	Specifies the size of the parser pool.	20
runtime.interpolate.string.literals	Specifies whether string literals should be interpolated by the runtime.	true
runtime.introspector.uberspect	Specifies the Uberspect implementation class to use. If you choose to create your own Uberspector, then you can replace the default value of this configuration parameter.	org.apache.velocity.util.introspection.UberspectImpl

Directive Configuration

Table A-2 shows the directive configuration options.

Table A-2. Directive Configuration Options

Parameter Name	Description	Default Value
directive.foreach.counter.name	Specifies the name of the counter variable used by the #foreach directive.	velocityCount
directive.foreach.counter.initial.value	Set sthe initial value of the counter variable used by the #foreach directive.	1
directive.include.output.errormsg.start	Specifies the token to output before an error message when writing error messages to the output stream. The end token must also be specified for this to take effect.	<!-- include error :
directive.include.output.errormsg.end	Specifies the token to output after an error message.	see error log -->
directive.parse.maxdepth	Specifies the maximum parse depth when using the #parse directive. This is relevant only if you use embed templates using #parse that have #parse statements themselves.	10

ResourceManager Configuration

Table A-3 shows the ResourceManager configuration options.

Table A-3. ResourceManager Configuration Options

Parameter Name	Description	Default Value
resource.manager.logwhenfound	Specifies whether a log message should be written when a resource is located by the resource manager.	true
resource.loader	A comma-separated list of loader names. These names correspond to separate loader configurations for each name specified.	file
resource.manager.cache.class	Specifies the class implementing the resource manager cache. You can provide your own caching implementation using this parameter.	org.apache. velocity.runtime. resource. ResourceCacheImpl

ResourceLoader Configuration

An important part of configuring your Velocity system is configuring the resource loaders used by your application. The following sections are a quick reference to the configuration parameters for the different resource loaders.

For all the configuration parameters, you should replace the `<name>` variable with the name of the resource loader you want to configure.

Common Configuration

Some of the parameters are considered common to all resource loaders; Table A-4 shows these.

Table A-4. Common ResourceLoader *Configuration Options*

Parameter Name	Description	Default Value
`<name>.resource.loader.class`	The name of the class that implements the resource loader.	`org.apache.velocity.runtime.resource.loader.FileResourceLoader`
`<name>.resource.loader.cache`	Specifies whether caching is enabled for the resource loader.	`false`
`<name>.resource.loader.modificationCheckInterval`	Specifies the duration in seconds to wait before checking to see if a cached resource has been modified. Set this to 0 to prevent checks.	2

FileResourceLoader

Table A-5 shows the FileResourceLoader-specific configuration options.

Table A-5. FileResourceLoader*-Specific Configuration Options*

Parameter Name	Description	Default Value
`<name>.resource.loader.path`	The path to search for. This should be a directory or list of directories separated by commas. The template name should match a file within one of the specified directories.	`./`

JarResourceLoader

Table A-6 shows the JarResourceLoader-specific configuration options.

Table A-6. JarResourceLoader-*Specific Configuration Options*

Parameter Name	Description	Default Value
<name>.resource.loader.path	The path to the JAR file (or JAR files) that the runtime loader should search for resources in.	

ClasspathResourceLoader

The ClasspathResourceLoader has no configuration parameters other than the standard ones.

DataSourceResourceLoader

Table A-7 shows the DataSourceResourceLoader-specific configuration options.

Table A-7. DataSourceResourceLoader-*Specific Configuration Options*

Parameter Name	Description
<name>.resource.loader.resource.datasource	The JNDI name of the DataSource to use to retrieve the resources.
<name>.resource.loader.resource.table	The name of the table in which the resources are stored.
<name>.resource.loader.resource.keycolumn	The name of the column that stores the resource name.
<name>.resource.loader.resource.templatecolumn	The name of the column that stores the actual resource content.
<name>.resource.loader.resource.timestampcolumn	The name of the column that has the time stamp for the resource. This is required for caching support to function correctly.

Velocimacro Configuration

Table A-8 shows the Velocimacro configuration parameters.

Table A-8. Velocimacro Configuration Parameters

Parameter Name	Description	Default Value
velocimacro.library	Specifies the name of one or more files containing global macro definitions. If you want to use more than one global library file, then split the filenames with a comma.	VM_global_library.vm
velocimacro.permissions.allow.inline	Specifies whether macros can be defined in line in a template as opposed to in the global library.	true
velocimacro.permissions.allow.inline.to.replace.global	Specifies whether an inline macro can replace a globally defined macro with the same name.	false
velocimacro.permissions.allow.inline.local.scope	This parameter specifies whether inline macros should be scoped to the local template only. See Chapter 3 for more details on this parameter.	false
velocimacro.context.localscope	Specifies whether a reference access from within a macro can change the context.	false
velocimacro.library.autoreload	Specifies whether Velocity should check the globally defined library for changes and reload the library as appropriate. This works only when caching is disabled on the resource loader.	false

Index

Symbols

! (NOT operator), example of, 60
characters, using with comments, 43
$ (dollar symbol) and variable names,
    outputting, 50–53
% (modulo operator), purpose of, 53
\ (backslash)
    displaying, 51
    escaping quotes with, 50
<init-param>, specifying view path as,
    240
" (double quotes), embedding in strings,
    49–50
' (single quotes)
    embedding in strings, 49–50
    using, 91

A

abstraction layer
    core goal of, 105
    creating client application for, 115
    framework for, 106–107
    using, 110–115
AbstractNewsletterTemplate class, using
    with e-mail newsletter application,
    143–146
AbstractSearchTool, using with
    VelocityViewServlet, 167
AbstractVelocityContentTemplate
    in abstraction layer, 108–109
    implementing, 112
    using with e-mail newsletter applica-
    tion, 142–143, 146
ActionListener interface, implementing
    in e-mail newsletter application,
    129, 134–135
ActionMessagesTool, description of, 206
actionPerformed() method, role in
    e-mail newsletter application, 135
addActionListener() method, calling in
    e-mail newsletter application, 133
addCategoryContentsLabel() method,
    calling in e-mail newsletter
    application, 132
addCategoryContentsTextBox() method,
    calling in e-mail newsletter
    application, 132
addCategoryList() method, calling in
    e-mail newsletter application,
    130–131

addFieldLabels() method, calling in
    e-mail newsletter application, 130
addFromAddressField() method, calling
    in e-mail newsletter application,
    130
addProgressBar() method, calling in
    e-mail newsletter application, 133
AddressException, catch block for, 141
addSendButton() method, calling in
    e-mail newsletter application, 133
addSubjectField() method, calling in
    e-mail newsletter application, 130
AddToCartAction class, using with
    Velocity and Struts, 200–202
Anakia
    creating Hello World with, 216–219
    features of, 215–216
    purpose of, 6
    sample output from, 233
Anakia context data, overview of,
    225–229
Anakia projects, documenting, 229–233
<anakia> task tag, example of, 226–227
AnakiaTask tag attributes, list of,
    224–225
Ant. *See also* Texen
    downloading, 216
    installing, 9–10
    resource for, 216
    using with DVSL transformations,
    258–259
    verifying, 10
Ant build script
    for Anakia, 217–218
    downloading, 12
    for Texen, 246
Apache Ant. *See* Ant
Apache CVS server, logging into, 235
Apache Tomcat, downloading, 161
API (application programming
    interface), disadvantage of, 106, 115
applications, building with abstraction
    layer, 110
applyTemplates() methods, using with
    TransformTool interface, 256
Apress Mailer application. *See also*
    e-mail newsletter application
    interface for, 118–119
    running, 151–155
arithmetic, performing, 53

WebLink property of Category class, significance of, 124

weblogging, significance of, 6–7

WebMacro template engine, description of, 2

web.xml files
  completing for Velocity and Spring, 213
  configuring Veltag servlets in, 240
  creating for VelocityServlet, 160

$who variable, changing value of, 16

Widgetarium database. *See also* Web applications
  business tier for, 186–188
  cart classes for, 188–191
  Category class for, 178–179
  creating, 173–175
  data access layer for, 175–186
  DataAccessException class for, 181
  Hibernate config file for, 180–181

Product class for, 176–178
Product mapping for, 180
implementing ProductCatalogDAO for, 182
templates for, 191–197

writeAttribute() method, using with ImageDirective class, 336

writeTable macro, code for, 65

writeTemplateOutput() method, example of, 38

X

XML files
  using with Anakia, 227–228
  using with DVSL, 261

$xmlout variable, description of, 226

XPath queries, using with Anakia, 228

$xpath variable, description of, 226

XSL, resource for, 253